# Nature's Providence

Protective care of nature as a spiritual power

## For free societies

Independence - Intrinsic Natural Law - Sovereignty

**Kenneth E. Bartle**

aotf publishing

ISBN: 978-0-6455837-4-8 (sc)
ISBN: 978-06455837-5-5 (e)

For rights and permissions, please contact:
Kenneth E. Bartle
bartlek@me.com — http://aotf.site

## Disclaimer

This book is written and formatted in Australian English, but uses indent paragraphs for economy in keeping with most published works.

Intrinsic natural law differs markedly from all positive law, common law and everyday use of the word Law. Moreover, Lex Naturale is substantially different from Ius Naturale, although both refer to natural law as commonly understood.

Positive law dominates today's world, that in most cases, is Maritime or Admiralty Law. Within this compass, virtually every English word denoting a member of the Homo sapiens species attaches legally to some form of body politic, i.e., to a legal or judicial entity having that status and obligation. Juristic systems at large deem many words innocently used in everyday speech to have an overriding legal meaning. These include but are not limited to the terms person, a natural person (versus robot), individual, he, she, and citizen. In the Maritime or Admiralty Law system, nothing remains for any judge to address a living man or woman. The word human in legal terminology is not a man or a woman, but rather an animal or a monster. Commonly said, man, is a social animal.

Because this book disavows the subjects of legal positivism, statute laws, and the government itself, it does not infer, offer or give any legal advice whatsoever. This book has no need for the legalese of lawyers, attorneys or (legal) practitioners. Its focus is the study of Man and the orderliness of his activities, rights, respect, and responsibilities. Altogether these provide a lawful, moral, just, expansive, life-sustaining, and enjoyable objective framework for Man's free will to embrace.

All diagrams are for illustration of ideas only.

FOOTNOTE:

Some sentences, quotations, and phrases repeat my previous works for greater contextual clarity. Please keep this book close for periodic future study and pertinent cross reference. Readers will greatly benefit from reading 'Conscious Ascendance' and 'Navigate to Freedom' in that order, preferably before reading this book. All my books are available on Amazon; this information is unavailable elsewhere save for my website https://naturallawmatters.com

## Table of Contents



## Table of Diagrams

# Chapter 1

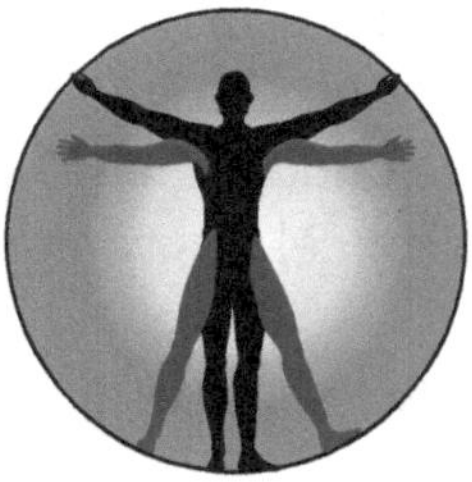

## Introduction

This book concludes the three-part series expressing a vibrant new societal future built on knowledge of the human conscious process and intrinsic natural law gifted by the Source creator.

Here, I will add a matching objective philosophy from the same source, greatly assisting humanity to embrace sovereign self-rule as our creator intended. People can now abandon the paralysing mindset of authoritarian rule that has failed abysmally over the past centuries. Considerable new learning accompanies the same degree of unlearning.

As long as any authoritarian rule exists, free passage to ever-increasing authoritarianism remains and people are slaves to the legal power of the state. Freedom means freedom from national or state power, not freedom from the landlord, one's employer or marriage partner.

How then are people to be governed? How will crime be controlled? How can we implement freedom and preserve it without people conforming to agreed behavioural standards that must be enforced? People's opinions will differ, so there must be a majority consensus with enforceable rules, surely? Doesn't that demand limited government? Doesn't world history testify unmistakably that at least a modicum of rule is essential?

No, none of those arguments testify to that outcome. History simply informs us that a 'freedom' alternative has never been discovered in the past. But that does not mean none is possible.

The simple reason why freedom is absent is because Neuroscience freely admits it does not know what consciousness is or how it works. That leaves a massive mental void filled by unending false or misleading beliefs concerning consciousness, all with the potential to lead humanity astray. Just one misconception can breed more, and so the problem magnifies through prevailing 'conscious nescience.' That term refers not to blind ignorance but to the fact we cannot be taught what is not known. In that absence, we've no means to cancel falsity and discover the truth. And that is humanity's sorry history.

This book completes twelve years of research showing exactly what consciousness is and how it works. The word 'Providence' used in this book's title refers to 'the protective care of God or nature as a spiritual power.' This comprehension beautifully answers all questions concerning how the current dystopian regime ruling the West can be replaced. Most importantly, it informs exactly what alternative will replace it, how, and why. Those answers are encrypted in the full conscious process., but none are generally known to mankind.

Consciousness is the creative operating system of our lives. It is not a 'thing.' It is not an element of physical matter. It is a psycho-epistemological 'process,' effectively the mental/spiritual equivalent of our cardiovascular and digestive systems.

Accordingly, almost everything ever written concerning consciousness is now called into question. What caught me by surprise, was learning that twenty natural laws are encrypted in our human nature and that this architecture of morality and Justness is nature's model for every human society on earth.

My 2022 books elaborate and expand the original work published in 2017. *'Conscious Ascendance'* lays out the conscious process, and *'Navigate to Freedom'* introduces natural law into protective free societies. Those books should ideally be read before this book.

The enormity of that work is profound because personal benefits fly off the charts. Better yet, the (revealed) intrinsic natural laws enshrine freedom on earth thus rendering hundreds of law libraries obsolete. Legalities die in that process as they should. The future for humanity has never looked brighter or more robust.

Free societies do not begin with political theory or a legal system. They begin with individuals protecting their freedom of mind as they go about their daily endeavours.

Philosophers do not ask, "Is the theory of evolution true?" as do biologists and physical anthropologists. They ask instead: "How do we distinguish truth from falsity? Under what conditions are we justified in claiming to know that a statement is true?" Those same questions equally apply to consciousness and its natural governing laws, from which there is no escape.

While metaphysics is the study of the fundamental nature of reality and man, and epistemology is the theory of knowledge, psycho-epistemology emerges as value communication between the conscious and subconscious mind. That study shows that **no mind can rule another**, whereby centuries of authoritarian rule is a gross violation of intrinsic natural law.

Accordingly, full consciousness with its natural governing laws offers humanity a glorious future never imagined before; a magnificent opportunity to thrive and prosper fully backed by the ethical facts of nature itself. Impossible to escape, natural law can still be refused, all consequences one's own choice.

*******

***Chapter 2*** exposes conscious ignorance and the personal and social problems that result. After exploring basic faculties and the parameters of life, consciousness shows as our mental operating system, being a value transfer process wholly given to the living of life. And that reveals how our subconscious mind works.

***Chapter 3*** explores the many aspects of life values that engender ethics and morality and our spiritual cohesion with both. Self-mastery emerges.

***Chapter 4*** examines the different branches of philosophy and their objective purpose. This leads to ***Chapter 5***, which explores rights as the fundamental necessity for societal protection, and also how our individual rights protect our consciousness from societal and governmental interference, particularly because we are born into the jurisdiction of life.

***Chapter 6*** introduces secular spirituality and full conscious power. It shows how life's jurisdiction reveals an objective philosophy from within our conscious process that in turn shows ten natural law tenets never spoken of before, save for my earlier books.

***Chapter 7*** deals with multiple aspects of ethics and morality, which gravitate to Justness and justice, culminating with Judiciary matters in free societies. Self-governance springs from this comprehension which markedly narrows our value choices pinpointing exactly how we can thrive and prosper in freedom.

***Chapter 8*** Begins with the vitality of Independence and how it is denied today. Its remedy unites with protection which then formulates a Private Declaration of Independence. This transformation leads to self-mastery, and self-governance and concludes with personal sovereignty.

***Chapter 9*** delivers the origins of rule by force that lead to natural law. Social implications emerge, leading to discussion concerning respect for law and Objective law. So we are invoked to outlaw enforced rules by which we each are our remedy to today's ills.

***Chapter 10*** describes the twenty natural laws from the philosophical perspective. That leads to ***Chapter 11*** which discusses the complexity of enforced rule, showing that natural law is superior by far.

***Chapter 12*** Discusses all to do with a (national) Declaration of Independence from all foreign government rule, and all foreign and domestic alphabet agencies. This leads to ***Chapter 13*** which (without using the formal text) describes a new Constitutional Charter of Individual Rights.

***Chapter 14*** Describes what Protectorates are, and how government may die from malnutrition despite all comforts and securities remain. It shows the equality of law and justice and the constitutional hierarchical structure necessary for free societies.

***Chapter 15*** brings forth educational revision, self-mastery and freedom within a Protectorate society as administered by the new Constitution and Charter of Individual Rights.

***Chapter 16*** looks at cooperative enterprise and sovereignty as shown by all the forgoing descriptions, offering three demonstrable historical examples. It examines how diversity promotes progress, contracts, healthcare and welfare through Protectorates, toleration censorship, public and private behaviour, corporate social responsibility, immigration and technology. It also discusses the new Constitution

***Chapter 17*** Reviews massive personal and societal benefits that seemingly no one has ever contemplated. In all, one hundred and fourteen demonstrable benefits are present across nine different categories, none witnessed in history. Multiple unforeseen benefits will grow outwards from that foundation.

***Chapter 18*** Reviews this and my last) two books concerning a summarised overview of all content. It is a standalone (4200 word) document in its own right.

Altogether this book cements consciousness to natural law, revealing an objective philosophy; this trio is inseparable. The benefits are very robust and profound, conclusively showing how life can reach heights never dreamt possible. ***The future has never looked brighter!***

# Chapter 2

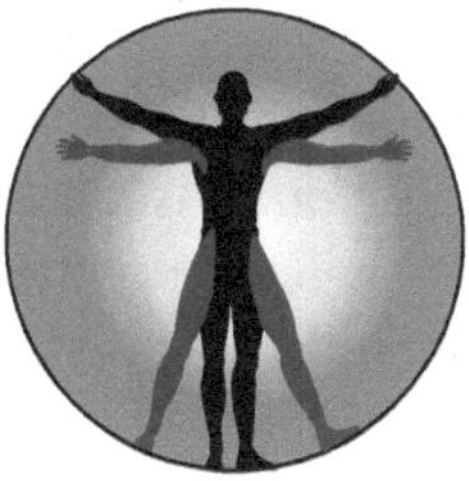

## The Conscious Enigma

Millions of people argue their nation desperately needs a new constitution, yet no such thing is possible without replacing today's apathetic mindset. To what avail is a new constitution if people remain ruled by totalitarian authority backed by force?

Unless a new constitution wipes out ignorance, it preserves the fundamental statement offered by Thomas Jefferson –

"If a nation expects to be ignorant and free, in a state of civilisation, it expects what never was and never will be."

That overthrow must happen! Jefferson's words underscore that all the laws Man has ever written deny freedom and conscious individuality, yet are inherent in every law that the Creator gifted and encrypted in our biological and psychological nature.

That principally unknown truth is the most profound but denied throughout Man's history. It has no place in the new mindset or any newly written constitution.

Simply stated, nearly every person on earth believes that government is indispensable to comfort and security. Accordingly, a legally regulated society is in Man's best interest; no alternative is possible. Thus, life in service of societal goals is Man's moral duty to self, family, friends, and the state; hence, no alternative is offered. Therefore, blind ignorance benignly disguises government control as democracy, which is willingly upheld by most citizens. All invented (so-called) laws supporting this moral inversion appear indispensable to life's comfort and security satisfaction, thus consistently repeating century after century, added to but never challenged. How long before humanity comes to its senses?

**Any society that authorises a state to rule it by force deserves all the tyranny and bloodshed that authority approves.**

That mindset must be overturned, struck out, and replaced before people can discuss new constitution topics!

Readers of parts 1. *Conscious Ascendance,* and 2. *Navigate to Freedom,* in this book series will comprehend the means to that end, hence no need for repetition. Students must come to their conclusions via their efforts, not mine.

**A mindset Change is overdue.**

Should America's revered Declaration of Independence be revived, an additional clause must ensure that Man's immutable, unalienable right to life protects the right to defend our right to life. For example–

"To secure the certain, unalienable right to life, unless all men created equal, unequivocally ensure their right to life, and their unalienable right so to do against all cancellation, violation, or usurpation, they will have neither."

Nothing will change until Man divorces from the insanity of an animalistic society ruled by tyrants with a pen in one hand and a gun in the other! Those who declare that Men are irrational animals and forcibly treat them as such are outlaws by their own (action-based) confession. They are the aggressors—the terrorists. They have forsaken morality. Their success, helped by our ignorance of their crimes, derives from the widespread acceptance of Man as a social animal. These bloody-minded, authoritarian criminals are protected at your expense and know it, but not the civil population. That mindset is long overdue criminal arrest.

**Neuroscience failings**

Neuroscience does not differentiate the conscious mind from the subconscious, whereby no two-way communication or natural orderliness and no natural laws governing that process are observably present; thus, ignorance continues without challenge. You are not ignorant; instead, you are the victim of conscious nescience, the simple fact that no one can learn what is unknown.

Without knowledge of natural laws, invented legislation is considered essential. Hence, politicians believe an 'authority' must rule humanity. Propaganda and political correctness convince the people likewise. Tragically, no one questions what moral standards might apply to (government) rule because no natural laws appear present to define morality. What began as conscious guesswork now becomes ethical and moral guesswork, with no reference to the exact nature of Man nor the mental process governing our actions.

**Conscious Neglect**

My books have explained conscious ignorance and conscious nescience. People have existed in a conscious vacuum for centuries for one of two reasons. Human sciences are stopped in their tracks by nescience because no remedy exists. Alternatively, those aware of source creators' beneficent gifts, such as elitists, bloodline propagandists, or other satanic beings, stealthily exploit conscious truth to enforce your slavery, all refusal punished. You are herded and forced to submit like animals.

This centuries-old, gaping mental chasm defies belief but is fully real. Everyone who senses financial profitability clings vice-like to the latest belief. Clickbait flourishes unchecked because no one has the cognitive means to distinguish fact from fiction. Witness the senseless 'everything is energy' notion that flatly denies reality—identity and causality collapse as a result. Identity and identification vanish, and beliefs replace knowledge. This mentally destructive feat defies comparison. Consciousness is now a mishmash of subjectivity, beliefs, illusion, energetics, vibrations, and frequencies. Belief in 'unity or mass consciousness' conceals the conscious process completely. 'Life' exits from all discussion. No mind communication is observable. Value transfer remains unseen. Our higher faculties, thus starved of fuel, demand greed for more material possessions as the only relief possible. Legality now resides unchallenged over lawfulness, and no relief is present. 'Collectivism' promotes group priority over each individual to produce socialism and communism. People scramble to learn who they are, never once comprehending this whole disaster stems from not knowing what they are.

> *"The hallmark of a mystic is the savagely stubborn refusal to accept the fact that consciousness, like any other existent, possesses identity, that it is a faculty of a specific nature, functioning through specific means. While the advance of civilisation has been eliminating one area of magic after another, the last stand of the believers in the miraculous consists of their frantic attempts to regard identity as the disqualifying element of consciousness.*
> *The implicit but un-admitted premise of the neo-mystics of modern philosophy is the notion that only an ineffable consciousness can acquire a valid knowledge of reality, that "true" knowledge has to be causeless, i.e., acquired without any means of cognition." –Leonard Peikoff.*

People who lack knowledge of consciousness and its workings know nothing of their innate natural laws. They've no intellectual weapons to combat propaganda, political correctness, or statutes ignorantly called 'law.'

Tyranny steams ahead, protected from all challenge, arrest, or elimination. Evil smashes every moral obstacle in its path. No mental means seemingly exists to crush today's mindset. So, the massive intellectual void grows progressively more prominent as many assumptions build on presumptions purportedly offering mental, emotional, or spiritual healing. And not a single one of these proselytisers describes our conscious process. The reigning common mindset never changes; all must conform to the artificial constructs of legality as though we are animals.

**Devious Control**

Are you beginning to see how easily we may be deviously and criminally mind-controlled by our ignorance of what consciousness truly is?

"Man's consciousness is his least known and most abused vital organ. Most people believe that consciousness as such is some sort of indeterminate faculty which has no nature, no specific identity and, therefore, no requirements, no needs, no rules for being properly or improperly used. The simplest example of this belief is people's willingness to lie or cheat, to fake reality on the premise that "I'm the only one who'll know" or "It's only in my mind"—without any concern for what this does to one's mind, what complex, untraceable, disastrous impairments it produces, what crippling damage may result.

The loss of control over one's consciousness is the most terrifying of human experiences: a consciousness that doubts its own efficacy is in a monstrously intolerable state. Yet men abuse, subvert and starve their consciousness in a manner they would not dream of applying to their hair, toenails or stomachs. They know that these things have a specific identity and specific requirements, and, if one wishes to preserve them, one must comb one's hair, trim one's toenails and refrain from swallowing rat poison. But one's mind? Aw, it needs nothing and can swallow anything. Or so most people believe. And they go on believing it while they toss in agony on a psychologist's couch, screaming that their mind keeps them in a state of chronic terror for no reason whatever.

*The fact [is] that man's consciousness possesses a specific nature with specific cognitive needs, that it is not infinitely malleable and cannot be twisted, like a piece of putty, to fit any private evasions or any public "conditioning." —Ayn Rand*

Conscious guesswork has existed since man put foot on earth. No political is principally concerned with true justice for Man; instead, it suffices to uphold the king, empire, monarchy, or state. Pragmatic political ideologues have capitalised counterfeit philosophies suiting their ends. Pretend justice maintains the state today, not Man. Here is the root of this plague and today's crippling mindset.

- **Plato** (c.429–c.347 bc), a Greek philosopher., argued that although likeness and equality were indeed a fact, people ought to be taught otherwise so they would accept the different benefits and burdens arising from various positions in a politically organised society.
- **Rousseau:** (1712–78), a French philosopher and writer, believed that civilisation warps the fundamental goodness of human nature and that while human freedom is a fact of nature, people should be taught to consider that it is dangerous, whereby they ought to sacrifice their individual nature to the artificial condition of citizenship. According to Rousseau, natural persons should become artificial persons, i.e., citizens —wittingly or unwittingly—willingly or by legal compulsion. Those philosophies are still taught and are the root of today's mindset!
- ***Auguste Comte*** (1798–1857), the philosopher who coined altruism, stated that 'to live for others is for all of us a constant duty, the definitive formula of human morality.' Also, we 'cannot tolerate the notion of rights, for such notion rests on individualism.' His altruistic premise stated that rights are as absurd as immoral and that 'individuals have a moral obligation to serve others and place their interests above one's own.'
- **Karl Marx** (1818–83), a German political philosopher and economist, endorsed universal socialism, asserting that only the human species can be free; no independent being can be. Individual freedom is an illusion, he claimed. Marx called those who identify themselves with Mankind as a whole to be universal individuals. These species-beings, he argued, who know themselves to be identical to the human race, are true communists, representing the superior evolution of Mankind. Moreover, they should not be dissuaded by illusions of morality and justice among those still mired in the false consciousness of their particular individuality.

- **John Dewey** (1859–1952), an American philosopher and father of pragmatism and modern liberalism, explained the collectivist notion as: 'Society in its unified and structural character is the fact of the case; the non-social individual is an abstraction arrived at by imagining what man would be if all his human qualities were taken away. Society, as a real whole, is the normal order, and the mass as an aggregate of isolated units is the fiction.' [Emphasis mine.]

That last sentence describes how today's politicians and power-seekers are empowered. Given the above rhetoric, they have little need to debunk individualism because professed experts consider no such thing to exist or that should exist. Many new-age devotees are likewise beguiled, often espousing oneness or collective consciousness. "We are all one" is the greatest oxymoron ever invented, and people swallow it like ice cream.

Jean Jacques Rousseau and every politician and university lecturer who falls for that garbage categorically dispute the facts of their nature. Nevertheless, they will happily claim a prestigious grasp of the (above-referenced) ideologies among fellow intellectuals to justify regulations in flagrant violation of the principles of natural justice. Injustice thereby incestuously feeds itself while masses gobble up more government handouts, bolstering an authoritarian nanny state upholding injustice and immorality, amply reinforced by banksters, pedophilia, human and child trafficking, and war.

Those solid truths have eluded man for millennia. While ever it is ruled wrong to rape, pillage, and plunder, so rule that rapes pillage, and plunders, is upheld as morally correct.

Inverted morality and corrupt justice appear as just, while humanity stupidly falls for both. We praise our rulers for correcting injustice, never for one-second recognising that 'rule' is criminal. We tacitly swallow all they say and vote at the polling booth to uphold injustice. They know of this and tremble in terrible fear of the day we know it, for their empire will collapse overnight. Top-down control is the seat of (today's) collectivised injustice. The state rules, while (so-called) justice upholds immoral rules.

That is today's condition exactly.

*Evil uses the authority principle to condition people to obey without questioning what, why or whom they are obeying. Destroying your identity to gain power over you is the modus operandi of evil. — Jeremy Locke.*

**Genesis**

In the book of Genesis, we read that God created plant life and animal life, and then – *"God created man in his own image; in the image of Creator God — male and female He created them."* Tragically, we do not read the differences between animal and human life, yet they are vital to understanding the fullness of human consciousness.

- Plant life is conditional. Plants remain in one place, wholly dependent on localised nutrients and the sun.
- Animal life is perceptual. They can move and adapt to nature; for example, they can change colour, grow defensive attributes, hibernate, etc.)
- Human life is volitional (free choice), both physical and spiritual. We adapt nature to ourselves. We build dams, railroads, houses, and computers because they sustain and profit our lives.

Those differences show that our operating system is vastly different from that of animals. For clear understanding, suppose we were to read in the book of Genesis–

> *"let men and women have free will to uphold their life in the manner of their choosing — a conscious mind that (two way) communicates with a subconscious mind, so men may choose their values, and receive reports through feelings and emotions, so they may alter their behaviour or change their values, and thereby thrive intellectually, emotionally, morally, and spiritually."*

Why was that never written? It is the truth of your nature, meaning all people are bountifully blessed beyond anything taught.

Suppose this new-found knowledge concerning consciousness and its governing laws was so dynamic and powerful that once enacted, our mental, spiritual, moral, financial, and political world would bear a minuscule resemblance to today's world. Having no historical precedent, the knowledge I speak of is 'spiritual consciousness,' and its comprehension is genuinely the 'great awakening.' Understanding the nature of consciousness and the spiritual process by which it joyfully propels our lives beyond limit is no longer a secret. It is within your grasp right now.

Nothing that exists can deny or refute itself. That means 'existence exists.' Those two words are the axiom, which states that there is something instead of nothing. Very briefly, the word axiom, or axiomatic, refers to the fact that one must use the existence of something to refute that it does exist. Because such denial is impossible, existence is present in everything, every circumstance or event directly or indirectly available for us to understand. Personal existence, the fact or state of our nature, is axiomatic. Unless a thing or identifiable identity exists, there is nothing to be conscious of and no consciousness.

**Metaphysics**

Metaphysics is the branch of philosophy that deals with the first principles of things, including abstract concepts such as being, knowing, identity, time, and space. Thus, metaphysics is the first branch of philosophy that properly concerns our biological integrity, cognitive (conscious) mind, subconscious mind, the nature of free will, and similar issues. Thus, 'life lives' in the same (axiomatic) manner as the statement 'existence exists.'

The philosophical branch of 'ethics concerns the use of these metaphysical faculties. Natural law, revealed by our conscious process links physicality to spirituality utilising mind communication. Physics and spirituality are thereby united.

**Biological Laws**

Health professionals have long understood the biological laws of human nature. Our systems thrive on nutritious foods and resist or repel toxins through a self-correcting immune system. Our heart and lungs interact without ceasing. Blood is oxygenated, and our heart circulates blood. Neither organ interferes with the other; both work cooperatively for a common objective, like two individuals. Our cells, tissues, organs, and systems exhibit the same functional properties. Likewise, our heart (hydraulic) and lungs (pneumatic) function as separate entities, working interactively and cooperatively to uphold our lives from start to finish without pause. Neither one can interfere with or trespass the other. Trillions of cells and our vital organs and systems do the same. Free will is in charge because our organs prosper or suffer depending on what we eat, drink, or inhale. Either we choose nutrients to maintain bodily health, or we suffer or die. Those principles are not rocket science.

Enormous complexity exists, but all are arranged in an orderly fashion so that every cell, tissue, and organ functions at optimal capacity. In truth, our bodies are a convivial society of fifty trillion individuals cooperatively working for the common cause of 'life.'

The preceding facts present some serious questions and vitally essential considerations –

- How could our cardiovascular system work without addressing its reality, self-honesty, purpose, and integrity? Failure is inevitable otherwise.

- How could any of our other systems function outside self-sustaining ethical boundaries?
- Every cell, bone, organ, system, and function within our body must abide by nature's self-sustaining and self-righting constraints.
- If not, they fail, influencing other organs or systems to compromise or cease functioning.

Accordingly, our systems show internal order, unity, interdependence, interoperability, harmony, systematisation, and sequence. Such order is an indisputable factual necessity.

**Animal vs man sensory ability**

This marked difference poses an important question. Why can many animals see, hear, smell, and feel with far greater sensibilities than we possess? Are we the superior species or not? If nature's source creator can provide superior senses for animals, birds, or fish, why are we not blessed with matching faculties?

The answer is that because animals depend entirely on the realities they perceive, sensory faculties must be more highly developed. They live or die based on the accuracy of their sensory data and their innate ability to respond instantaneously without thinking.

We do not have that ability. We live or die based on conscious inquiry and learning. Thus, our senses need only alert us that something exists, nothing more. Our (simplified) awareness necessitates learning what we are aware of and how we can profit from that knowledge.

We suffer no deprivation; in fact, we surpass animals. Fish can swim better than we can, but they cannot build swim pools. Birds can see much further and sharper, but no one can build radar systems. Our mental faculties far exceed those of animals, and that blessed ability is ours exclusively. We learn, lest we should. For the same witnessed event, an animal becomes perceptively aware, while we (each) are made consciously aware. Although perception works automatically for animals and ourselves, 'awareness' is where the similarity stops. 'Perception' instinctually guides particular responsive actions in animals, whereas the information prompts us to inquire further to learn and profit accordingly.

Are you in a universe ruled by natural laws and stable, firm, absolute, and knowable? Or are you in an incomprehensible chaos, a realm of inexplicable miracles, an unpredictable, unknowable flux, which your mind is impotent to grasp? Are the things you see around you real—or are they only an illusion? Do they exist independent of any observer—or does the observer create them? Are they the object or the subject of man's consciousness? Are they what they are—or can they be changed by a mere act of your consciousness, such as a wish?

Consciously or subconsciously, explicitly or implicitly, we each know that we need a comprehensive view of existence to choose our goals and coherently plan our future world. Prudent judgments and wise choices concerning our values are involved in every moment of our lives, choices, decisions, and actions.

The nature of your actions—and of your ambition—will be different, according to which set of answers you come to accept. —Ayn Rand

**Biological and mental Faculties**

Our task is to find those answers via epistemology, the theory of knowledge, especially concerning its methods, validity, and scope, and the distinction between justified belief and opinion. Epistemology aims to answer questions such as "What do people know?" "What does it mean to say that people know something?" "What makes justified beliefs knowledge?" and "How do people know that they know?"

This inquiry leads to ethics, the principles that govern a person's behaviour or the conduct of an activity. It is the science of moral thinking leading to the moral correctness of one's chosen conduct.

**My motivation**

My 2012 efforts to re-purpose government initially showed that statute law, common law, and natural law 'theory' were all seriously deficient, leaving human consciousness as the only possible remedy. From the beginning, I sought factual knowledge concerning consciousness, applicable to an infant without words, math, or science and to an elder with a lifetime of experience. Success far exceeded my ambitions, the icing on the cake being my discovery of natural law as a fact of human nature. The fact that 'images' are the vocabulary of our subconscious minds offers an opportunity to teach life-sustaining philosophy at primary school levels, eloquently structured to prevent conscious ignorance from ever developing. That is a monumental game changer because it stops bogus theories prescribing our thoughts and actions.

Through a subscription to the Objectivist Newsletter during the 1960's I read (in Rands's words) that –

*"Objectivity means that although reality is immutable and, in any given context, only one answer is true, the truth is not automatically available to a human consciousness and can be obtained only by a certain mental process which is required of every man who seeks*

*knowledge—that there is no substitute for this process, no escape from the responsibility for it, no shortcuts, no special revelations to privileged observers—and that there can be no such thing as a final 'authority' in matters pertaining to human knowledge."*

*"Objectivity is both a metaphysical and an epistemological concept. It pertains to the relationship of consciousness to existence. Metaphysically, it is the recognition of the fact that reality exists independent of any perceiver's consciousness. Epistemologically, it is the recognition of the fact that a perceiver's (man's) consciousness must acquire knowledge of reality by certain means (reason) in accordance with certain rules (logic). This means that although reality is immutable and, in any given context, only one answer is true, the truth is not automatically available to a human consciousness and can be obtained only by a certain mental process which is required of every man who seeks knowledge—that there is no substitute for this process, no escape from the responsibility for it, no shortcuts, no special revelations to privileged observers—and that there can be no such thing as a final "authority" in matters pertaining to human knowledge. Metaphysically, the only authority is reality; epistemologically—one's own mind. The first is the ultimate arbiter of the second." — Ayn Rand*

Our task is to find those answers via epistemology, the theory of knowledge, especially concerning its methods, validity, and scope, and the distinction between justified belief and opinion. Epistemology aims to answer questions such as "What do people know?" "What does it mean to say that people know something?" "What makes justified beliefs knowledge?" and "How do people know that they know?"

This inquiry leads to ethics, the principles that govern a person's behaviour or the conduct of an activity. It is the science of moral thinking leading to the moral correctness of one's chosen conduct.

Ignorance denies freedom absolutely, exceedingly magnified when no one knows what consciousness is or how it works. The secret to freedom, therefore, is to learn consciousness and practice it through an objective philosophy.

I asked why these patterns couldn't be translated into man's societies? I questioned whether the Creator had offered Man a law blueprint within his nature and being. If so, would it be sufficient to transcribe into his societies? Would Man need to write laws additionally? Could a society exist that would enable Man's will to run free yet prevent him from violating another's will to live as they might choose?

It became apparent that no examination of this kind would stand scrutiny unless it is factually grounded in Man's nature. So I asked myself, what is constant and consistent in Man while allowing his will to be free? What describes Man's equality with others but still allows differences from all others?

The answer was free will, jointly with natural law. For Man's will to be (forever) free, the Creator must have provided boundaries to ensure it. Thus, a governed mental process coexists with free will within each of us.

That connection hit home resoundingly. I got it! Free will content is independent of mind governance and maintenance, just as air is independent of an air conditioner's process. *It is possible to have unbridled freedom within a governing (natural law) process*! There is no conflict, nor can any be! It is perfect! We are all equal in freedom. Creator has governed Man's mental processes, not to inhibit our free will choices, but to ensure that our free will choices prevail!

That understanding caught me off guard initially, but its truth is pure beauty. Unlike anything history has shown, its implications have personal, political, and societal applications.

Then it hit me. Creators' laws and Man's laws are incompatible. The first precludes the second, but all governments have it back to front. I did not need to study common law, maritime law, positive law, or any other (nonsensical) legalities, much less senseless constitutions based thereon. No law library sufficed. I needed only to study Man.

If natural laws govern each of us, then by sensitive extrapolation, they should apply to ethics and morality respective of our social and business dealings. So, I sought to understand the essence and correspondence of natural laws within the nature of Man and his life processes. Results from that study have far exceeded my greatest expectations!

**Positive law**

Law is not what someone said or wrote, whereby all must obey. Statute law is not law; it is statute rule. Natural law addresses the orderly functioning of what already is. (Consider the law of gravity.) Not one natural law commands! All express the orderliness of that which already exists or advises rectification or remediation where it does not. Law is natural law and nothing else. How simple and beautiful is that?

- Animals adapt themselves to nature as their nature has determined. (Fangs, skin shedding, hibernation, migration, etc.)
- We adapt nature to ourselves, as free will determines. (Housing, forestry, dams, railroads, communication systems.)

In his book Real Answers to Everything, Australian biologist Jeremy Griffith discusses this difference by explaining—

*That once our nerve-based learning system became sufficiently developed for us to become conscious and able to effectively manage events, our conscious intellect was then in a position to wrest control from our gene-based learning system's instincts, that, up until then, had been controlling our lives. Basically, once our self-adjusting conscious mind emerged it was capable of taking over the management of our lives from the instinctive orientations we had acquired through the natural selection of genetic traits that adapted us to our environment. — Jeremy Griffith*

Griffith's work confirms the difference between animal and man stated previously. His book. *Is It to Be Terminal Alienation or Transformation for the Human Race* claims—

*That the rehabilitation of our environments and our social and political systems requires a rehabilitation of our psychology, not merely as individuals, but as a species – that a spiritual change must be the basis for social reform and the restoration of the earth's ecosystems. — Jeremy Griffith*

Study begins with the nature of Man, but not as an animal. Creator entirely models individual uniqueness and natural laws that we share equally and jointly within our body and mental faculties. They speak of method, system, logic, process, order, equality, and harmonious cooperation. Man cannot write this law because it already exists within you and me. Do you know why? It is so no human legislator can ever erase it. Now that is protection! Our task is to learn and implement it.

No accident of nature evidences a master plan that science and human sciences should have examined and learned from eons ago to model society on these natural laws.

**Society as Company: (Social Rules)**

What is society? The answer depends on what type of society the question refers to. Fundamentally, there are two kinds.

The phrase 'Society' as a company is generally government, but is also applicable to sporting clubs, libraries, colleges, businesses, and universities.

'Society as a Company' applies to all social systems governed by systems of invented rules. These include sporting clubs, charitable and educational institutions, corporations, and governments, which are today corporations.

Such rely on and demand that their subjects give exclusive attention to the company's societal self, especially its preservation. Rule-bound company is what the word society means. Loyalty to its members and leaders is foremost. Members, constituents, and citizens highly prize the fairness of that governance, its government. All consider themselves beneficiaries.

Society, by company, is primarily concerned with relationships between its constituent parts and its organised whole and does not always disclose purposeful existence. What members or citizens do, and how, is more fundamental to the society, its office bearers, managers, CEOs, and employees than the lives of those it serves.

Rules governing the management of these societies are not laws within their original meaning, nor a science. Instead, they are artificial orders of artificial persons whose legal systems must attach legal rights, duties, and obligations to their organisational positions.

Artificial order is an order of artificial persons; such artificial constructs are not living human beings. They are positions, roles, or functions within a particular game, social system, or society governed by a system of (invented) rules that facilitate their (respective) functioning. Think of artificial persons, for example, as white and black pieces in a game of chess, including the particular governing rules of the King, Queen, Knights, Pawns, etc. Other examples include such as Rector, Dean, Student or Faculty member in a university, or King, Government, Parliament, Minister and Citizen in a nation-state.

Such legal artifice does not attach to the actual living beings elected or appointed to occupy those positions. Indeed, this legal separation removes any misdeeds or personal liability from public accountability. It excuses and pardons those who serve those organisational roles, save for censure(s) within the company itself. E.g. Susan didn't do it, but the branch manager did. No living individual is legally accountable, only the position. Notice how an office bearer signs off every government document.

To make rules for managing government, the word person, which we all think means you and me, has been usurped and construed to have a legal meaning. Your natural (flesh and blood) nature, legally stolen from you at birth, has a body politic attached. The word 'person' now describes a fictional, LEGAL ENTITY having legal obligations within the society by company.

By usurping your born name, governments now have you believe that your legal entity is the real you. Passports, driver's licences, and ID cards are your legal ID, so you're told, but they are not your ID. Those instruments are their ID. They identify the legal entity that is the government's corporate slave. So you are recognised as that LEGAL ENTITY, a citizen by NAME, subservient to the (legal) (society by the company) government, to be ruled and regulated as a servant or enslaved person, all taught as for your benefit. Whenever you show their ID upon request, fully believing it is your ID, you agree to be their servant. So they claim 'consent of the governed.'

Little known, we are also commanded by statutes and directives and coerced by propaganda and misleading practices, including by the legal profession, into believing that natural flesh and blood living beings are natural persons. Yet, unbeknown to almost everyone, natural persons are legally deemed Legal Entities. Thus, natural persons are not legally living human beings. So it is that we all act for, and as the legal entity, our individual rights trampled as though they never existed. Natural law rejected—statute laws reign supreme—backed by deadly force.

You have no natural born rights today as a (flesh and blood) breathing individual. Nonetheless, government entirely depends on your flesh and blood body, participating as and acting in the capacity of the (fictional) legal entity, known by your citizen NAME, as though you were it.

We are fast approaching the stage of the ultimate inversion: the stage where the government is free to do anything it pleases, while the citizens may act only by permission; which is the stage of the darkest periods of human history, the stage of rule by brute force. —Ayn Rand (written 60 years ago)

Most people have no idea that we function, in positive law, as and for a counterfeit legal entity stolen from our born name without our consent. Most people live in complete ignorance of this deception. Had they given permission, they would have known. Through ignorance, they support the consent of the governed to the utter delight of those who rule us.

Common Law ostensibly overturns this misappropriation by claiming natural law as its foundation. Notwithstanding that claim, whatsoever purportedly upholds natural law but accepts rule, confesses preeminence of positive law. It follows that governments are the (legal) monopolists of terror, which they claim to despise. Although they state that their purpose is your protection, your well-being is maintained sufficient only for legal citizens, aka natural persons, to be their slave labour force. Without it, their 'society by company' would collapse.

Should it surprise that very few perceive any means to overcome legal oppression, slavery, tyranny, and unceasing war? So-called leaders know this well. They prefer that natural laws remain concealed, which probably describes why knowledge of full consciousness was occulted throughout Man's history; hence, government violence and coercion increase in quantity and severity.

We vote for its continuance out of ignorance while the government protects your legal status at all costs so that their empire survives. Censorship, propaganda, state schooling, licensing and registration, political correctness, and media control all serve their purpose. Thus structured and provisioned by your labours, governments have taken a right to use force and coercion to preserve and protect their society by company.

History repeatedly shows the foolish irrationality of majorities, proudly and loudly proclaimed today as democracy. The direction such control takes is primarily academic. Corporate political power is nothing but a state-run monopoly, using methods that enforce its perpetuity at the expense of the people enslaved to uphold it. The notion that authority is a benefactor and protector is a monstrous lie. It is impossible! No truly moral, honest individual man or woman can participate in or endorse the (initiated) coercing of others for any reason.

People cannot amend such a society to serve living beings intentionally. Hence, force protects it. Man is not his brother's keeper. We are indeed keepers in that we are not to commit acts of violence against one another. We are not keepers in that some must command others, even for their supposed benefit. Authority, backed by force, is an act of violence antithetical to all benefits it purportedly upholds.

**Symbiotic Society**

'Society-as-symbiosis, never practiced, is the radical alternative to 'Society by Company.' Symbiosis describes the interaction between two organisms living in close physical association, typically to the advantage of both.

Symbiotic Society demands the very different mindset I spoke of. Ruling society is left to wither and die by instituting a society that never will. That mindset is centuries overdue!

Participants of an organic, symbiotic society come together as equals for a mutually uncoerced benefit, or they go as they come. Freedom pertains only to single persons. The word freedom does not apply to society or any public realm. Liberty is the (proper) collective term applicable to a community. To be free means living beings, free in mind and spirit, with no exceptions, fully independent from all legal or fictional persons, citizens, or Legal Entities. Free individuals have the capacity and immutable right to act in support of their life, according to free choice, this capacity remaining until death. To destroy absolute freedom, one has to kill the individual.

**Learning the New Mindset**

When (Creator's) natural laws that govern Man's Nature correctly enable a just society, so are the means to keep it.

Save for some remote or indigenous tribes, free and convivial societies have never existed before. Notwithstanding, one free society alone would show every government that has ever existed redundant, eliminate all victimless crime, cancel all false legality and authority, and institute freedom, justness, and justice, all founded on the Nature and life of individual living men and women.

Symbiotic societies based on natural law offer a convivial order in which people interact as living beings following the natural laws of their Nature, regardless of any status, position, role, or function in any social order to which they may belong. Conviviality is objective and universal, the same at all times and places in any human population.

Before that is possible, one needs a complete understanding of natural laws' beautiful and profound simplicity within oneself. They govern your life and protect it. None command. None instruct. All uphold free will. You are the master of your life, destiny, and soul. What data or information you choose to process mentally is for your free will to decide.

First, one needs to comprehend the beautiful and profound simplicity of the conscious process and how and why life is of supreme value. No one needs to wait because you are fully equipped to learn and instrument the natural laws of your Nature today, thus beginning your mindset change, each step confirming constitutional changes in full accord with Nature's source creator consent, absent limits.

You will be a founder of the NEW constitution for your nation, and nothing will stand in your way!

Remember; criticism results from your success, not your failures.

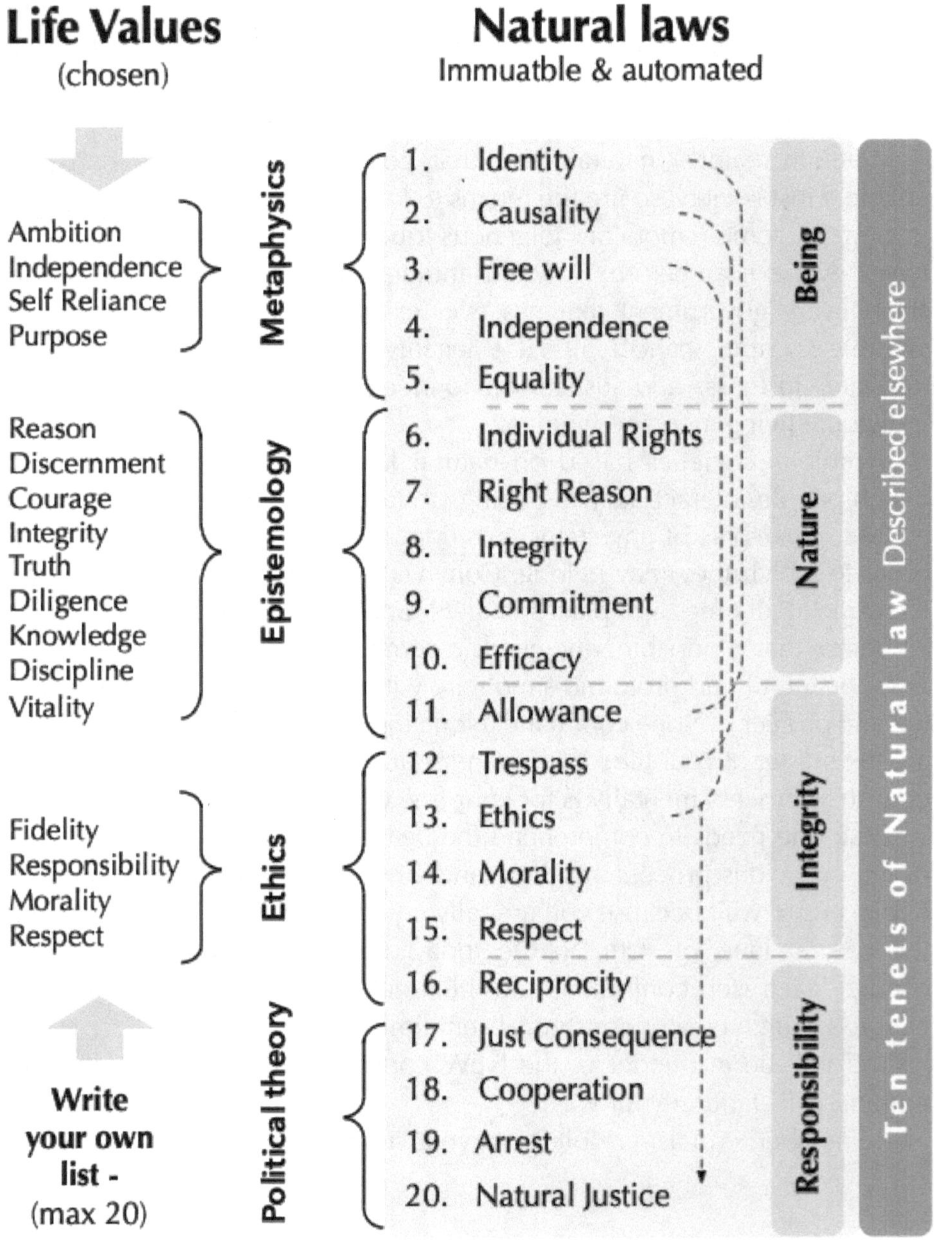
Life Values
(chosen)
Ambition
Independence
Self Reliance
Purpose
Reason
Discernment
Courage
Integrity
Truth
Diligence
Knowledge
Discipline
Vitality
Fidelity
Responsibility
Morality
Respect
Write your own list -
(max 20)
Metaphysics
Epistemology
Ethics
Political theory
Natural laws
Immuatble & automated
1. Identity
2. Causality
3. Free will
4. Independence
5. Equality
6. Individual Rights
7. Right Reason
8. Integrity
9. Commitment
10. Efficacy
11. Allowance
12. Trespass
13. Ethics
14. Morality
15. Respect
16. Reciprocity
17. Just Consequence
18. Cooperation
19. Arrest
20. Natural Justice
Being
Nature
Integrity
Responsibility
Ten tenets of Natural law Described elsewhere

# Chapter 3

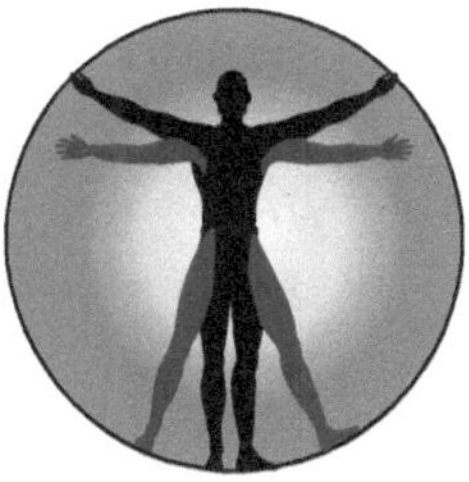

## Life Values

Discovering what consciousness is becomes necessary, and then learning how to use it to validate our conclusions. Thus, we can distinguish truth from falsehood and determine what we will accept as knowledge. Two questions are involved in our every deliberation: What do I know, and how do I know it? Success will differ according to which answers you accept and why. They belong to the 'theory of knowledge,' the science of epistemology, correctly answering those questions. No one can control their subconscious mind. That truth stops most people in their tracks despite being grossly misled. People should instead learn they can most assuredly influence what content their minds will process but can never change its functioning process.

To that end, the subject of 'values' offers a vital shortcut that has received little attention from human sciences in the past. Life is the only thing that makes the concept of value possible. The value of mental content is crucially essential, just as nutritious food is crucial to bodily health. This applies the validity of all information, beliefs, superstitions, and ideologies. Simply stated, life makes values possible and necessary for free will choices. If one chooses merely to exist, then no values are possible, no code of ethics makes sense, and when no moral actions seem necessary—disaster results.

We should, therefore, determine what values life requires and act accordingly. The subconscious mind cannot choose what you value because that would override and cancel your free will. Only our (free will) conscious mind can provide (reasoned) life-value information. Therefore, the subconscious mind must rely on what we choose to prize, particularly what spiritual value we place on our actions. I speak of courage, truth, diligence, commitment, and passion for life, no more than fifteen to eighteen life values.

When our two minds value-synchronise, harmony produces positive emotions, so we thrive to our most significant potential. Everything accords with 'natural law.'

Conversely, conflicting values produce discordance, and so we experience (so-called) negative emotions like anxiety, stress, and trauma.

The fundamental question posed by consciousness, indeed by life itself, is whether 'values' are worthy of esteem simply for their own sake or whether virtues have objective and practical import to life. Are they (metaphysical) 'destination values' that we seek to achieve, what we want to become eventually? Or are they (epistemological) 'journey values' that assist us in reaching our goals, like respect, vigilance, or integrity, for example?

**Three types of values**

My earlier books in this series explained that values fall into three categories.

- Material values. (metaphysical) House, car, recreation, vacation, and wardrobe are all a no-brainer.
- Satisfaction values (or destination values), both metaphysical and epistemological, are those we aspire to achieve for our emotional or spiritual satisfaction. Examples include happiness, joy, pleasure, contentment, peace, and fulfilment.
- Life values we find necessary to achieve our destination values.

Life values fuel our conscious (communicative) process. They inform us that we are spiritual beings. These spiritual values facilitate our material, psychological, and spiritual advancement, just like nutritious food upholds our physical health. To repeat Rand's words, "It is in this sense that man is a being of self-made soul."

Choosing life values is challenging, but two things manifestly reduce this task.

1. We can put these relatively few values and desires on autopilot.

2. We can use an 'objective philosophy' to determine our chosen values.

Most importantly, because natural laws that govern the consequences of our actions are common to all people, we are all equal in law.

Tragically, we are taught nothing about what unites our higher faculties, although identical to all others.

Focusing solely on material outcomes may overlook the spiritual value component that should be a quotient in making that choice. Take 'diligence' as one example. How could your subconscious mind function properly if it threw attentiveness and assertiveness to the wind?

Ayn Rand beautifully described three cardinal values for the glorious realisation of our lives.

> *To live, man must hold three things as the supreme and ruling values of his life: Reason—Purpose—Self-esteem. Reason, as his only tool of knowledge—Purpose, as his choice of the happiness which that tool must proceed to achieve—Self-esteem, as his inviolate certainty that his mind is competent to think and his person is worthy of happiness, which means: is worthy of living.*

Those three values are the cornerstones of an objective philosophy in life. They anchor our thoughts and validate our value judgments in support of our lives by reference to the facts of reality and our own lives. Rand explained further.

A central purpose serves to integrate all the other concerns of a man's life. It establishes the hierarchy, the relative importance, of his values, it saves him from pointless inner conflicts, it permits him to enjoy life on a wide scale and to carry that enjoyment into any area open to his mind; whereas a man without a purpose is lost in chaos. He does not know what his values are. He does not know how to judge. He cannot tell what is or is not important to him, and, therefore, he drifts helplessly at the mercy of any chance stimulus or any whim of the moment. He can enjoy nothing. He spends his life searching for some value which he will never find.

Non-material) spiritual values facilitate our material and metaphysical advancement. Accordingly, to be human is to be spiritual, even though we live in a material realm. Metaphysics comes first because physical matter is our toolbox for spiritual accomplishment and soul growth, which epistemologically explains how "man is a being of self-made soul." Metaphysics and epistemology are inextricably united.

Watching television programs gives our subconscious mind inadvertent permission to accept any or all subliminal values and ideas expressed. (The word 'program' is not accidental.) However, if we have prioritised different (overriding) values, contrary values shown in TV programs will be automatically rejected. When that value clash happens appreciably, we turn the TV off.

The subconscious image vocabulary does not distinguish between real and imagined, as psychologists have verified through laboratory experiments. Our task is to learn the difference between the (conscious) alphabetic and (subconscious) pictographic vocabularies. Word concepts are necessary to reason and choose values. Later, our subconscious mind compares (value) images to discover similarities or discrepancies, thus forming and delivering our emotional reports.

Blessings or disasters are ours to choose thereby, precisely because free will has complete autonomy. We should note that criminal mind control programs can overtly traumatise free will into submission, thus influencing or controlling our actions. Notwithstanding, coercion is not our free will agreement because it overrules our free choice.

Ayn Rand made the conscious process clear in value terms –

*Man is able to initiate and direct his mental action only in accordance with the nature (the identity) of his consciousness. His volition is limited to his cognitive processes; he has the power to identify (and to conceive of rearranging) the elements of reality, but not the power to alter them. He has the power to use his cognitive faculty as its nature requires, but not the power to alter it nor to escape the consequences of its misuse. He has the power to suspend, evade, corrupt or subvert his perception of reality, but not the power to escape the existential and psychological disasters that follow. (The use or misuse of his cognitive faculty determines a man's choice of values, which determine his emotions and his character. It is in this sense that man is a being of self-made soul.)*

Her statement is beyond equal, because in that paragraph, she most beautifully foretold what my books, describe. Her last (bracketed sentence) is of vital significance, one that her critics almost invariably ignore.

Man's consciousness is his least known and most abused vital organ. Most people believe that consciousness as such is some sort of indeterminate faculty which has no nature, no specific identity and, therefore, no requirements, no needs, no rules for being properly or improperly used. The fact [is] that man's consciousness possesses a specific nature with specific cognitive needs, that it is not infinitely malleable and cannot be twisted, like a piece of putty, to fit any private evasions or any public conditioning.

Many people believe that the subconscious mind is the 'soul.' To explain, we choose values that our subconscious mind stores in our memory database. These values, as abstractions, sum to being our soul as we have made it. If, however, we leave our values, feelings, and emotions to chance or permit others to seed their values into our subconscious mind, then we've no idea what our feelings are reporting, so people cry, *"I'm ruled by my emotions!"*

Feelings grant opportunities to update our values or alter our future behavior. It follows that feelings and emotions are Nature's gift of an automated mentoring system, of which, sadly, we know nothing! Are you beginning to see the dynamic power of full consciousness and the supremacy of a life-objective philosophy?

Only knowledge can overthrow humanity's ignorance.

- Scientists cannot study free will in test tubes or under a microscope, so they reject its spiritual value.
- Thus, everyday philosophy skirts spirituality as pure subjective theory.
- Psychologists and psychiatrists are caught in the crossfire and nod their heads approvingly.
- Social sciences bow to every resultant distortion and misconception.
- Social workers are left to sweep the streets.

The whole purpose of consciousness is to objectively sustain and uphold life, just like all our body cells and organ systems. The objectivity of life renders human consciousness a science, equal to our biology and blood flow through our veins.

Each individual's life is his ultimate value, and the role of morality is a 'check or balance' teaching us how to achieve genuine (life-sustaining) interests. Fundamentally, life is the common interest of every human being. It comprises life-sustaining values such as reason, purpose, courage, diligence, self-esteem, and virtues such as rationality, independence, pride, honesty, integrity, productivity, and justice.

It is one thing to respect the equal rights of others, but a vastly different thing to equally weigh other people's interests in one's moral decision-making. Pursuing one's happiness is morally correct, but aiding other people's happiness is one's choice, not a moral duty.

Life-values are the means for influencing or programming our subconscious mind. They amplify our physical endeavours and add valued meaning or spiritual quality to our life experience, over and above any material gain. For example, 'I will study diligently.' Here, 'knowledge' is a material gain, while 'diligence' expresses our resolve to ensure that it is pertinent, helpful, and supportive of life.

Once selected and impressed on the subconscious mind, life values fuel our emotional database in satisfaction of healthy and rewarding reports known as feelings. Such life-sustaining concepts offer a personal code of ethics that contributes to life's sustenance and ever-growing achievements in any chosen field of endeavour.

An objective philosophy tells us that the proper way to compare our values is by asking which promotes life best. By focusing on your personal life, not society, you will see how different values improve or subtract from your life overall. An objective philosophy will point you to discovering such values, aided by knowing how your conscious process will secure them.

Spirit is our connection across all boundaries and barriers. It transcends race, religion, gender, culture, nation, and education. It unites all mental understanding and ability, not to produce one unified entity or collective consciousness but to merge as our spiritual life force.

This spiritually cohesive dynamic then serves to unite independent beings. Personal and societal transformation is thereby ours to enjoy. By awakening your mind to its dynamic powers, you unleash your potential, thrive like never before, and contribute as a founder of humanity's glorious future.

That step-by-step process of inherent (self-authored value) governance maintains the orderliness of the conscious process, which upholds the bond established between one's desires, values, and actions. From etymology, that bond and orderliness is the Latin word 'ius,' which, within our conscious Nature, is 'Ius Naturale' (Latin), being 'natural law' by translation.

Those brief descriptions outline the (fundamental) sequential process of consciousness. Each step of the process must be governed, or else it fails. Therefore, there can be no substitute, no escape from responsibility for it, and no shortcuts.

The sheer beauty of it is simplicity since nine-tenths of it is fully automated. Values are a spiritual abstraction that simplifies the mechanics of our material focus to enrich both material and spiritual outcomes eventually. Develop this as an objective philosophy, and you can habitually automate it.

Values are as fundamental as your consciousness, which decides them so your subconscious mind can process them. Values are crucial to simplicity. They are the tool for abstractly expressing your desires, so they will manifest in physicality, automatically reinforced in the form of experienced emotions.

This comprehension further advances an objective philosophy founded on the facts of Nature itself. Its advised path of action is entirely conducive to its functionality. Who could ask more regarding personal and societal benefits, peace, and harmony? Observe some of its most apparent outcomes.

- Awareness holds relevant matters in abeyance while they pass through a process of inquiry, research, discovery, reason, logical determination, imagination, choice, and evaluation.
- Our automated subconscious mind utilises our chosen values; be they deliberately prioritised or (preferably not) assimilated by default from past actions or behaviour.
- Free will is in charge of the whole process, like the conductor of a symphony orchestra.
- We are obliged to author our 'values' so that our free will is not corrupted and remains free.
- Values that uphold life should harmonise with the life-sustaining values inherent in our automated subconscious mind. With our two minds on the same page, synergistic mental and spiritual power joyfully escalates.

Given sufficient thought to your objective path, you'll find little more than fifteen (primary) life values. Some will have subset values. They are the automatised spiritual elements of your Nature, your life connection to Nature's source creator, and the foundation of your creative power.

Your cognitive mind has none of these core values unless you wilfully choose to utilise them. You are free to employ life values or ignore them.

But why would anyone bother to choose values like truth, respect, and diligence if their subconscious mind already has these values built in? That would increase your mental workload, would it not? The answer is simple. By consciously choosing values that enhance your life and practicing them, no conflict exists between your two minds. There's your recipe for absolute joy. When both your minds are on the same page, glowing harmony results. If not, mental turmoil is inevitable. No other outcome is possible.

**Life values – Starter List**

Think about what values would underscore reason, purpose, and self-esteem. Our biology informs us that our primary values are health, hygiene, nutritious foods, sleep, and exercise. Our mental, emotional, and spiritual well-being likewise depends on values such as these. Write your list of about fifteen to eighteen spiritual values like those in this table.

| | | |
|---|---|---|
| Courage | Truth | Tolerance |
| Discernment | Respect | Passion |
| Honesty | Integrity | Diligence |
| Ethics | Confidence | Self esteem |
| Resolve | Logic | |
| Morality | Rationality | Knowledge |
| Productive | Reason | Independence |
| Justness | Humility | Authenticity |
| Fortitude | Patience | Understanding |

*Write your own ( 15-18)max*

*1.* **Life Value list**

Primary values will be those already used by the subconscious mind almost invariably. Several values spring to mind, like integrity, diligence, and respect. The above values are a good starter list, but choose yours, even if identical, because your happiness is at stake.

Ask what your mental powers rely on. What spiritual values or spiritual words address its priorities? That's easy. Knowledge, truth, honesty, rationality, efficiency, and independence, leap off the page!

Use a Thesaurus to look up any or all of those values, plus any that you can think of. You'll soon see that some values are subsets of another. For example, is' fairness' a subset of 'justness'? You'll also see how your chosen values fit into the different branches of philosophy, like this –

**Metaphysics**

1. Integrity – honesty, dedication –
2. Knowledge – discernment, thought –

**Epistemology**

1. Rationality – Discipline, truth, thoroughness –
2. Logic – mental confirmation

**Ethics**

1. Morality - ethics, justness –
2. Responsibility, care, caution –
3. Respect, attentiveness, courtesy –
4. Truth, honesty, vigilance –
5. Vitality – exercise, health, nutrition –
6. Ambition – Purposeful goals, heroism, leadership –
7. Self-reliance, confidence, pride, achievement, sovereignty

Mix and match your chosen values as your list takes shape. You'll soon see how little more than fifteen primary life values assume priority, and all subset values fall within your prime list. Remove any consequential values. Focus entirely on values that underscore your mental activities, just like you would choose nutritious foods for bodily well-being.

Life becomes harmonious when the same life values that already exist in your subconscious mind underwrite your cognitive process. Conflict vanishes. Everything flows smoothly. Mental efficiency improves. Emotional joy and happiness follow, and a healthy, promising, and happy life results. Such harmony produces positive emotions, so we thrive to our most tremendous potential. Ayn Rand expressed it well–

> *It is by experiencing happiness that one lives one's life, in any hour, year or the whole of it. And when one experiences the kind of pure happiness that is an end in itself—the kind that makes one think: "This is worth living for"—what one is greeting and affirming in emotional terms is the metaphysical fact that life is an end in itself.*

But the relationship of cause to effect cannot be reversed. It is only by accepting "man's life" as one's primary and by pursuing the rational values it requires that one can achieve happiness—not by taking "happiness" as some undefined, irreducible primary and then attempting to live by its guidance. If you achieve that which is the good by a rational standard of value, it will necessarily make you happy; but that which makes you happy, by some undefined emotional standard, is not necessarily the good. To take "whatever makes one happy" as a guide to action means: to be guided by nothing but one's emotional whims. Emotions are not tools of cognition; to be guided by whims—by desires whose source, nature and meaning one does not know—is to turn oneself into a blind robot, operated by unknowable demons (by one's stale evasions), a robot knocking its stagnant brains out against the walls of reality which it refuses to see.

Make life-values your most prized pathway, and your subconscious mind is overjoyed. When you've given it your blessing to succeed like never before, your intuition sharpens and leaps into top gear. Feelings testify success and blissful joy results from mind agreements.

Our whole conscious process is an utterly astonishing masterpiece of nature that no artificial intelligence can match because you live, and nothing manufactured can or ever will!

Upload your (shortlist) values to your subconscious mind as described in my book 'Conscious Ascendance,' and they will become automated. Then, you will fully understand the life value of 'efficiency,' akin to the 'Natural Law of Efficacy.'

Anxieties and stress will vanish if you consider your value list thoroughly. It will significantly assist you in learning from your feelings and emotions, as though from a mentor. Life becomes so much easier. Should adverse conditions surface, revise the relevant value or determine to act differently in the future.

Once you've mastered your mind in this manner, you'll never go back to letting erroneous beliefs and random chance play their hand.

But who teaches that today? No one does, so we are deprived of knowing how to thrive truly.

## The Conscious Process

Full consciousness is the systemic process transfering one's chosen life values between the conscious and subconscious minds, interfacing physicality and spirituality, authored by free will.

# Chapter 4

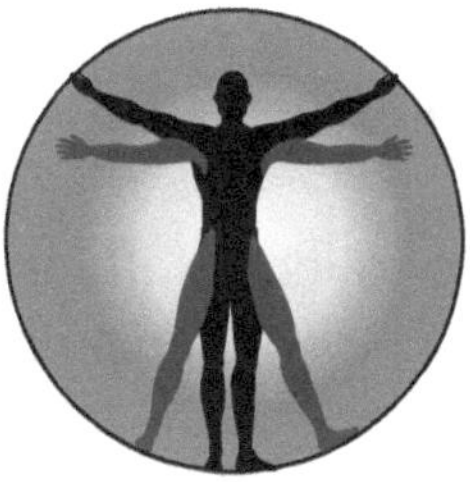

## Conscious Philosophy

Philosophy is the science that studies the fundamental aspects of the nature of existence. Its primary task is to provide a comprehensive view of life, which serves as a base frame of reference for all our mental or physical, psychological, and existential actions.

The word philosophy derives from two Greek words: philien and sophia. Philosophy means *"love of wisdom."* 'Living the examined life,' as Socrates once put it, means detaching from social personas and social scripts, thus honestly thinking for oneself, so coming to own one's thoughts and value-based conclusions, not simply being an echo of other voices.

We should adequately search for deep understanding and truth, utilising careful observation and logic, happily engaging in dialog with critical (thinking) others. Creative and critical thinking is a philosophy aimed at wisdom through full consciousness concerning one's authentic self to live well. Such practice liberates one's inner self, delivering existential release from fear, mindless tradition, propaganda, dogma, prejudice, and ignorance. Central to well-being, good, authentic, and real life offers excellent opportunities to be open, rational, fair-minded, respectful, creative, autonomous thinkers, and prudently empathic social beings.

Philosophy ought to be the guiding light of consciousness research and inquiry. Today, it is not and has not for decades, if not centuries, save for objective philosophy. Not surprisingly, today's socio-political structures are bereft of constructive thought that upholds your life and mine. Instead, people willingly reinforce the dominance of the state, dare I say, the insanity of state authority.

Leaving technology aside, why is philosophy not a science, and why is conscious comprehension arrested? Two answers loom as the most likely reason.

- First, philosophy long ago lulled us all into thinking that people could learn nothing more, so we have not examined the conscious process or researched further.
- Second, mental science has stalled as a result, and worse, ruling authoritarians know absolutely how an ignorant slave force better serves them than knowledgeable thinking, constructive, and loving people. Sociopathic rulers benefit considerably from anxiety, chaos, discord, tyranny, and wars, all demanding more control, force, and weaponised armies, even to carry the battle into space.

Three conclusions emerge.

- First, blinded by inept philosophy, we've not studied consciousness sufficiently to learn how we function metaphysically and epistemologically.
- When philosophy and psychology agree there is nothing worth studying about human consciousness, widespread ignorance and suffering follow in short order.
- Accordingly, we've not learned that natural laws governing ourselves are nature's model for free and convivial societies, thus, never imagined possible.

The solution is to study and learn what consciousness teaches and develop a cognitively coherent philosophy that upholds conscious functioning.

To live, we must act. For that, we must make choices. To make choices, we must define a code of values. We must know what we are, our nature, the nature of consciousness, our means of knowledge, and the relationship of values we choose to the outcomes that result from our actions. We need metaphysics, epistemology, and ethics, which means philosophy. We cannot escape this need. Our only alternative to not choosing the philosophy that properly guides our mind is to leave life to random chance.

Questions are fundamental, as Ayn Rand asks–

*"Are you in a universe which is ruled by natural laws and, therefore, is stable, firm, absolute — and knowable? Or are you in an*

*incomprehensible chaos, a realm of inexplicable miracles, an unpredictable, unknowable flux, which your mind is impotent to grasp? Are the things you see around you real — or are they only an illusion? Do they exist independent of any observer — or are they created by the observer? Are they the object or the subject of man's consciousness? Are they what they are — or can they be changed by a mere act of your consciousness, such as a wish?"*

At that fundamental level, correct answers will significantly depend on knowing how the conscious process works. When you do, you will understand that its governing laws make it stable, firm, absolute, and knowable, just like the universe. Immediately, the link between consciousness, natural law, and objectivism becomes certain.

**Metaphysics:** Philosophical study should adequately inform us of the nature of our universe. This philosophic branch deals with the first principles of things, including studying the fundamental nature of reality and man. It refers to the attempt to describe the nature of reality. From the Greek word' metaphysika' (literally after physics), metaphysics is the branch of philosophy investigating the nature of existence, our being, and the world of physicality. It is the foundation of philosophy, or as Aristotle called it, 'first philosophy,' i.e., the subject that deals with first causes and the principles of things. Questioning the nature of reality includes the question—if things exist, what is their objective nature?

Aristotle's concern was first the physics, and then, in sequence, what comes after physics? Hence, metaphysics is the union of physics and its derivative relationships. Many questions arise, such as the nature and makeup of the universe, whether the world is purposive or not, whether our world is eternal or created, and many other issues. Such questions represent the broad canvas approach.

As Ayn Rand described, *"Metaphysics identifies the nature of the universe as a whole."* Thus, we can learn about our world, dimensions, solid entities, facts versus illusory fragments, miracles, and natural laws. And, importantly, whether our perceptions inform us of a compressible reality or some unreal appearance that renders us helpless.

Insofar as human life is concerned, metaphysical concerns embrace biological integrity, cognitive consciousness, the subconscious mind, the nature of free will, and similar issues.

Your desires, goals, and actions will differ according to what you question and agree. As Ayn Rand spoke of in her address to the graduating class of The United States Military Academy at West Point, New York, in March 1974–

> *Since man is not omniscient or infallible, you have to discover what you can claim as knowledge and how to prove the validity of your conclusions. Does man acquire knowledge by a process of reason — or by sudden revelation from a supernatural power? Is reason a faculty that identifies and integrates the material provided by man's senses — or is it fed by innate ideas, implanted in man's mind before he was born? Is reason competent to perceive reality — or does man possess some other cognitive faculty which is superior to reason? Can man achieve certainty — or is he doomed to perpetual doubt?*

Those questions are metaphysics, and their correct answers will significantly depend on knowing what consciousness is, how it works, and what it depends on.

Natural law reveals itself through life-supporting values attached to material or physical pursuits. Metaphysics acknowledges and respects Nature's source. Our Nature confirms natural law because, without its governance, we could not function. Accordingly–

- Metaphysics now embraces natural law thoroughly. Previously considered a theory, now it is fact.
- Metaphysics also concerns the study of the ultimate cause in the Universe, while natural law governs the behavioural or actioned consequences of volitionally conscious beings.
- Natural law relies on life-supporting values communicated between the conscious and subconscious mind. Specifically, life-supporting values attach to material or physical pursuits, showing us that life-supporting values are beyond physics. (Metaphysical)

Accordingly, its study derives from physics and does not replace, usurp, or deny derivative relationships. This knowledge is essential, especially when reviewing the legal technicalities of professional metaphysical practice.

Sadly, or tragically, professional metaphysicians do not study natural law despite their examination of Nature. Because our conscious process reveals natural law and links physicality to spirituality utilising psycho-epistemology, now physics, and (life-based) spirituality are united by ethics. Another change is observable. Free choice engages life values that support and uphold natural law, logically the province of metaphysics, while life values concern ethics. It follows that natural law now fits metaphysics to perfection. Life becomes simpler.

Epistemology is the theory of knowledge, especially concerning its methods, validity, scope, and the distinction between justified knowledge versus beliefs and opinions. We each are beings of volitional consciousness. However, Nature gives us no automatic guarantee of our mental efficacy. Thus, we are capable of error, mental neglect, and psychological distortion.

Metaphysics and epistemology are ordinarily considered the theoretical foundation of philosophy, but is there more to philosophy than mere theory? If philosophy academically studies the fundamentals of knowledge, reality, and existence, and intrinsic natural laws govern our conscious process, can philosophy embrace knowledgable expertise and not be purely theoretical?

Indeed yes. People cannot disregard a philosophy dedicated to life because that is the choice to abandon it. Life makes values possible. Life makes values necessary. Full consciousness is the hardware of our mental operating system, whereby our chosen values write the software program. The (value-based) affinity that unites objective philosophy, the conscious process, and (intrinsic) natural law are inseparable.

This view of life should inform the method by which we are to deal with it, that is, the science devoted to discovering the proper techniques of acquiring and validating knowledge, which is epistemology.

**Axiology** is a sub-branch of Ethics related to worth or worthiness and commonly accepted questions concerning right or wrong. Axiology questions whether moral distinctions result from emotive feelings. Do we have (prior) mental control over our values, later resulting in feelings such that we each author our morality? Yes, emphatically so!

**Axiology** also deals with the Nature and classification of values and examining what things have value. This study spills into ethics, aesthetics, political theory, and meta-ethics. The subject can become long, tedious, and very involved, especially for those who previously concluded it is problematic. Fortunately, our entire conscious process quickly reduces it to a short list of fundamental (extrinsic) values made even simpler by an objective philosophy.

'**Psycho-epistemology**' is a branch of 'objectivist philosophy.' It is the "study of man's cognitive processes from the aspect of the interaction between the conscious mind and the automatic functions of the subconscious." Physicality interfaces at the conscious level, and our value choices interface at the (sentient) spiritual level.

During (cognitive) inquiry and discovery, we subconsciously visualize our progress and goals simultaneously, from which we select values. Our subconscious responds through memory, intuition, conscience, feelings, and perception. This two-way Value communication occurring between our two minds is called 'Psycho-epistemology.'

It beautifully explains why Nature perfectly sandwiched free will between the activation and reporting functions of the subconscious mind. That protects free will on two fronts, confirming that our conscious process is far greater than mere 'awareness.' This communicative process functions according to inherent governing laws, whereby the trio of consciousness, (intrinsic) natural law, and objective philosophy fully unite as previously explained.

Tragically, no one teaches that our subconscious mind sandwiches our free will. No one teaches how this tapestry of efficiency and protection unites all our higher faculties. So, we never learn that 'assistance' and 'protection' are woven into every aspect of our physical, mental, emotional, and spiritual life.

In sum, axiology, metaphysics, epistemology, and psycho-epistemology are powerfully interconnected. Given that these philosophy branches are grounded immutably, Human Nature, values, consciousness, and life-sustaining natural laws are the root foundation of true philosophy. Ayn Rand tells us –

> *As a human being, you have no choice about the fact that you need a philosophy. Your only choice is whether you define your philosophy by a conscious, rational, disciplined process of thought and scrupulously logical deliberation—or let your subconscious accumulate a junk heap of unwarranted conclusions, false generalisations, undefined contradictions, undigested slogans, unidentified wishes, doubts and fears, thrown together by chance, but integrated by your subconscious into a kind of mongrel philosophy and fused into a single, solid weight: self-doubt, like a ball and chain in the place where your mind's wings should have grown.*

There is the clue. Mainstream philosophy and neuroscience have not discovered that mental data must pass back and forth between our two minds, each time switching to a different vocabulary. You reinforce its inherent values by uploading (ethical) spiritual (not religious) values to your subconscious mind. Once you approve that life lives, a life-objective philosophy is your means to enact it. The two are inextricably linked, meaning both demand your active participation. Fail that task, and default values from past actions assume control precisely because you previously approved them. As a result, self-mastery vanishes without notification, and stress mounts. You've no remedy because the (value) cause is unknown.

Rand's work is mainly rejected by mainstream philosophy and even ridiculed. Nonetheless, acceptance steadily grows as its truths consistently manifest through experience. The entire conscious process tells the same story.

Ethics embraces the science of moral values, explicitly examining the rational justification for our moral judgments – what is morally right or wrong, just or unjust. In a broader sense, ethics deals with human beings and their interaction with nature and other humans, principally concerning moral choices, respect for others, responsibility, justice, and resultant freedom. Ethics expresses the science or discipline of what human behaviour ought to be, unlike sociology, which studies what human behaviour is.

Politics includes political theory and more concrete public policy issues.

Aesthetics is the philosophy of art.

From the list above, philosophy is relatively straightforward when grounded in reality, focussed on knowledge and our means of knowing. It benefits every man, woman, and child.

Tragically, that is not the state of today's (mainstream) philosophy, which sadly pursues politics, sociology, and ethics on a collective basis, as concerning a culture, state, or nation, thus ignoring our lives as individuals. Omit human consciousness and what should primarily serve you and me from philosophical consideration, and we suffer. Philosophers who disregard authentic outcomes leave philosophical, social planning devoid of raw substance, whereby our ignorance of consciousness magnifies.

The accurate method for philosophy will be deductive, meticulous, and independently verifiable. Knowledge of our conscious nature significantly enables philosophy to reach solid scientific conclusions.

People cannot understand philosophy unless they understand the past. This false belief usually results from studying historical figures who are considered philosophers. For example, Socrates, Plato, Aristotle, Augustine, Aquinas, Kant, Hume, Marx, Hegel, and Russell are all considered philosophers despite their diversified views. Commonality derives from their accepted set of problems and concerns.

By limiting philosophy to great minds from long ago and examining ancient questions and answers, philosophy effectively reduces to the study of ideas. While this approach introduces students to the great minds of the past and philosophical problems raised by thinking people of all ages, nonetheless, historical philosophy progresses only to the extent that acceptance of its self-structured embodiment permits. Critical thinking retracts to pet beliefs.

Philosophy traditionally divorces from science to pursue politics and ethics on a cultural, group, or national basis, independent of individual life. It remains that philosophical consideration of social planning is negligent until philosophy describes personal human life coherently and consistently. Philosophers refuse the most fitting outcomes and conclusions by refusing unique human science.

Before philosophy can offer a view of the world, it must first satisfy our independent nature and place in the world, critically and logically. Education should adequately support such a conclusion. The valid method, in philosophy as in science, will be inductive, meticulous, and independently verifiable. I submit that investigation and analysis of our real individual nature is the only method by which philosophy will succeed in obtaining an authentic scientific result.

In the table below, the first column defines the branches of an objective philosophy. Each is further explained in the second column, while freely chosen 'values' unite columns two and three.

| Philosophy | Rationale | Method |
|---|---|---|
| **Metaphsics** | | |
| Existence | What is there? | Reality, identity, causality |
| **Epistemology** | | |
| Knowledge | How do I know? | Senses, reason, logic, discerment |
| **Ethics** | | |
| Thought/Values | How should I think and live? | Rational self interest |
| **Morality** | | |
| Action/Respect | How should I act/treat others? | Respect, integrity, cooperation |
| **Law** | | |
| Force/Justice | Legitimate force/natural law | Restraint, justness, natural justice |
| **Aesthetics** | | |
| Art | Happiness | Romantic inspiration, sprituality |

2. Philosophy Table

**Objective consciousness in philosophic terms**

Philosophy is meaningless or counterproductive if it offers no purposeful life guidance. The conscious process intersects with objectivist philosophy at the junction of how and why we must choose between alternatives. Both speak of the same decision-making process but with one minute difference. Readers will recall that in the 'Value Transfer Wave,' cognitive thoughts are attributed to 'ethics' while subsequent actions result in 'morality. Given that the Value Transfer Wave was unknown when 'objectivism' was discovered, (cognitive) 'how and why' decision-making was not surprisingly considered morality.It's a moot point because no moral actions can transpire without the ethical choice to do so.

The worthy goal of philosophy is to show how one goes about making decisions while letting one decide whether the method can use some improvement. Conscious knowledge bolsters that objective philosophical path in several ways.

- It dramatically highlights the critical importance of concepts and principles.
- It shows how intuition is made exceedingly more trustworthy and (auto) reliable by choosing (spiritual) life values.
- It dramatises one's intellectual efficiency and efficacy through the use of imagination to place their values on autopilot, drastically reducing mental workload and cancelling much stress.
- Emotions and feelings are shown by full consciousness to definitely and accurately report the success or distress of our actions and to endorse or reprimand our morality definitively. What more could we ask of an objective philosophy than to have our 'how and why' choices adjudicated by the highest court possible, that of life itself?

Objective philosophy cannot be an academic theory that has no specific purpose. Like 'full consciousness' and natural law, it is the science of studying the fundamental aspects of the nature of existence.

The proper task of all three factions is to deliver each of us a comprehensive view of life and our living of it by offering a life-base frame of reference for all our actions, mentally, physically, psychologically, spiritually, and existentially.

'Objectivism' informs the nature of the universe with which we must deal (metaphysics), the means and method by which we can deal with it and acquire knowledge (epistemology), and the standards by which we should choose our goals and values by regard to our own life and character (ethics).

Life is yours to live! Full consciousness and natural governing laws are the means, while an objective philosophy gives guidance and purpose.

The natural law principles of ethics, morality, and natural justice are modeled smack in the core of our conscience and emotional reporting systems, exactly where they belong! Ethics and morality are fully prescribed by (intrinsic) natural law, not vice versa, as promoted by 'natural law theories.'

Ethics switches from opinionated consensus to objective science or an objective code of ethics. Once grasped that morality or immorality outwardly broadcasts to all other people, no difficulty should arise from freely choosing moral actions and bearing all consequences. The philosophical key to understanding how our two minds communicate, and share values is that the subconscious mind is one with the conscious mind, yet its functions are distinctly different.

Ayn Rand described her philosophy in essence –

> *"as the concept of man as a heroic being, with his own happiness as the moral purpose of his life, with productive achievement as his noblest activity, and reason as his only absolute." Moreover, "if you held these concepts with total consistency, as the base of your convictions, you would have a full philosophical system to guide the course of your life."*

Her summary, published in 'The Objectivist Newsletter '(Aug 1962) stated that *"Reality exists as an objective absolute—facts are facts,"* and *further that "reason, (the faculty which identifies and integrates the material provided by man's senses), is man's only means of perceiving reality, his only source of knowledge, his only guide to action, and his basic means of survival."* Additionally, *"man—every man—is an end in himself, not the means to the ends of others. He must exist for his own sake, neither sacrificing himself to others nor sacrificing others to himself. The pursuit of his own rational self-interest and of his own happiness is the highest moral purpose of his life."*

To those summaries, now add her contribution concerning the communication between our two minds (psycho-epistemology). Her work, in total, is a monumental achievement. Here's why. Suppose you add the supremacy of reason to the dominance of value communication between our two minds. In that case, you have a summary of the complete conscious process as indicated by the value transfer wave diagram (later shown).

Just as Rand began with philosophy and identified consciousness, the value transfer wave leads inexorably to an objective philosophy encrypted in our nature. The underlying (value) question behind 'objectivism' is — *"of value to whom and for what?"* Those questions necessitate consideration of the essentials, which come straight back to concepts and principles equally fundamental to full consciousness and objective philosophy.

Full consciousness is the 'objective' means of human life; its natural laws of self-governance offer complete protection of our unalienable right to life and inalienable right to the fruits of our labours. Philosophical training greatly assists our knowledge of how the conscious process works. It is necessary to gain an authentic intellectual posture and standing of what a proud and well-disciplined mastery of the mind offers.

There is no substitute for this process, no shortcuts, and no escape from the responsibility for it. Neither is there any substitute for an objective philosophy, as Ayn Rand described in her address to The Graduating Class Of The United States Military Academy at West Point, New York, in March 1974.

> *The men who are not interested in philosophy need it most urgently: they are most helplessly in its power. The men who are not interested in philosophy absorb its principles from the cultural atmosphere around them — from schools, colleges, books, magazines, newspapers, movies, television, etc. Who sets the tone of a culture? A small handful of men: the philosophers. Others follow their lead, either by conviction or by default. For some two hundred years, under the influence of Immanuel Kant, the dominant trend of philosophy has been directed to a single goal: the destruction of man's mind, of his confidence in the power of reason. Today, we are seeing the climax of that trend.*
>
> *When men abandon reason, they find not only that their emotions cannot guide them, but that they can experience no emotions save one: terror. The spread of drug addiction among young people brought up on today's intellectual fashions, demonstrates the unbearable inner state of men who are deprived of their means of cognition and who seek escape from reality — from the terror of their impotence to deal with existence. Observe these young people's dread of independence and their frantic desire to "belong," to attach themselves to some group, clique or gang. Most of them have never heard of philosophy, but they sense that they need some*

*fundamental answers to questions they dare not ask — and they hope that the tribe will tell them how to live. They are ready to be taken over by any witch doctor, guru, or dictator.*

Once recognised that the subconscious mind relies entirely on values, and specific values are vital to life. Consciousness becomes an objective science, as do ethics and morality. Both are removed from government rule and returned to each individual where they rightly belong.

Tragically, the intellectual vacuum resulting from not knowing what consciousness permits a veritable army of proponents whose offerings serve naught but obfuscation, bogus ideologies, rampant confusion, and misleading theories, all based on the notion that ethics, morality, and even consciousness itself can never be a science.

Guess what? No opposition to the catastrophic control of man's mind ever offers. It is not so much that people are innocently ignorant of consciousness, natural law, and a life-based philosophy, but that these three (nescient) problems allow an avalanche of false notions preventing us from ever learning this life-based trio even exists.

Falsity almost unanimously becomes gospel truth, and every attempt to refute it is cast out as gross ignorance because, as so often stated, – "others believe differently "– and – "what about my opinion?"

World events through 2020 – 2023 have brought the world face to face with these three problems, which, without actual address and action absent personal opinions, are humanity's inevitable downfall, even self-annihilation.

# Chapter 5

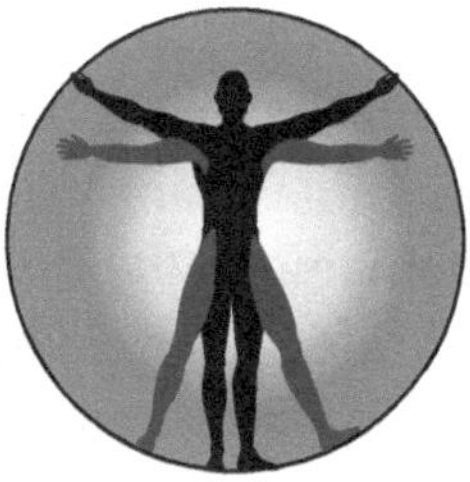

## Applied Philosophy and Rights

Little did I know some fifty-eight years ago that Ayn Rand's immense philosophical achievements would, after applying them throughout my working career, eventually point me to an expansive grasp of the human conscious process and the revelation of natural law in our human nature.

Even after publishing my book *Navigate to Freedom*, I did not initially recognise an almost identical philosophy inherent in our nature. That realisation is immense, for not only is our conscious process not understood by people today, but its mechanics echo Rand's philosophy of objectivism despite her topic being philosophy, not consciousness. Despite that being where my work began, an objective philosophy also emerged as an impressive path that singularly reinforces the other.

As a novelist, Rand found that to define her concept of an ideal man, she had to ask basic philosophical questions and resolve each answer she reached to confirm and build on her previous answers, eventually resulting in an unbeatable life-based philosophic system.

My conclusions resulted from my research, not hers. Nevertheless, my work intersects hers with pinpoint precision, and just as any area Rand touched turned to knowledge, so too did mine.

My work began with questioning how the government could be re-purposed since it had abandoned its de jure status, eventually becoming a corporate authority masked as a government. Common law did not satisfy me, and neither did natural law theory. Left no lawful or legal path, I questioned consciousness and hit a wall of widespread conscious nescience. Beginning from scratch, I had to ask hard questions and fit the answers together like jigsaw pieces; no misfits were acceptable. My research revealed an invincible life-based conscious system never explained before, and eventually, it presented an objective philosophy along with natural law.

Ayn Rand was the first philosopher to emphasise that existence underscores all knowledge; not whims or beliefs. Consciousness is unidentifiable otherwise. She named *"the primacy of existence,"* which is the beginning of the Value Transfer Wave defining the complete conscious process, without which no consciousness exists. Most importantly, it is also the faculty of learning what 'can be made to exist.' It establishes our creativity.

Consciousness is the engine of (spiritually enriched) material creativity, not psychological invention. That fundamental error over centuries specifically denotes *'the primacy of consciousness,'* which nonsensically claims consciousness precedes existence

> *If nothing exists, there can be no consciousness: a consciousness with nothing to be conscious of is a contradiction in terms. — Ayn Rand*

That explains how the contents of one's consciousness are changeable at will but not the process. To mistake content for the procedure is easy but disastrous!

Rand's unified, hierarchically ordered system arrests that ambiguity and thus confirms the inherent sequential structure of the conscious process. Both uphold the nature of principles and values, highlighting their crucial role in man's nature, thus in human life, freedom, and society.

With this new appraisal and knowledge, here are five breakthroughs representing the major turning points in consciousness and natural law that reveal an objective philosophy together.

**1. The Engine of integration**

Perception is the subconscious process delivering conscious awareness as its end product, hence the first part of two-way communication.

The 'engine of integration' subsumes vast sums of data, condensing them into manageable data packages for (free will) conscious processing, concurring with Objectivism. Rand observed that (word) concepts derive from marked similarities and differences. Moreover, this (conceptual) *"similarity is the relationship between two or more existents which possess the same characteristic(s), but in different measure or degree."*

Consequently, the metaphysical basis of concepts lies in facts of reality, such that similar concretes differ only in their measurements. (Small and large books are all 'books.' Red and blue cars are all 'cars.' )

Rand's algebraic explanation is nothing short of astounding. Here's why. The 'motor of integration' used by the (subconscious) perceptive process is nearly identical to (word) concepts (and principles) used by the conscious mind as perceptual abstracts. Data is condensed to the smallest size for both without compromising any fundamentals. In other words, our two minds use the same language of abstracts, despite one mind using a word vocabulary and the other using an image vocabulary. (A picture paints a thousand words.) The following subconscious revelation vastly enlarges Rand's algebraic perspective.

Specifically, our subconscious ability is shown to us by the 'law of allowance' that enables infants to progress without cognitive ability by using the engine of integration that powers the faculty of perception. Data bypasses the cognitive mind during infancy and early childhood, causing an apparent deficit. But no, subconscious perceptive imagery motivates subconsciously driven action. That ability, the 'law of allowance,' teaches that imagery is our subconscious vocabulary. In turn, it affirms the duality of voluntary and involuntary actions the subconscious mind performs, fully endorsing its role of affirmatively upholding and sustaining life.

**Integration Diagram**

As shown in the diagram, the engine of integration powering perception also powers five other faculties, further integrating all six higher (subconscious) faculties.

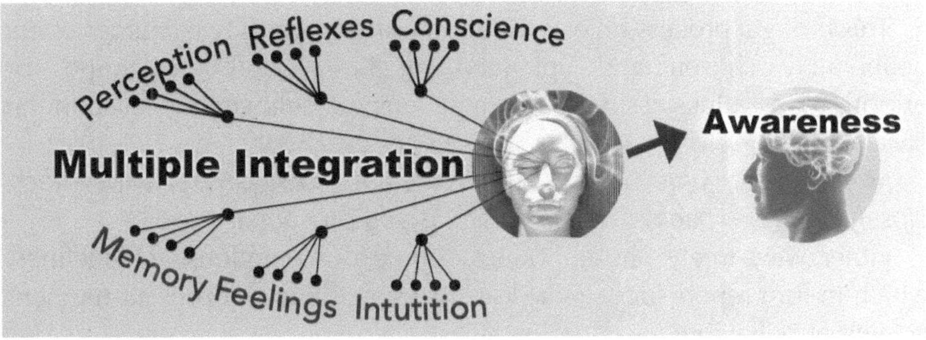


3. Six integrations - all integrated

Thus, all six subconscious faculties mirror 'word concepts' (algebraic) power, confirming that both minds are abstractly and truthfully powered for efficiency and efficacy, regardless of chosen mental content. Such ability founds the 'natural law of efficacy.'

**2. The role of life values.**

Life is the supreme value, and all other values are subsets of life. Enormous cognitive complexity vaporises once we understand that nutritious food sustains our bodies and that life values are equivalent to our mental operating system.

> *Man cannot survive, as animals do, by the guidance of mere percepts. A sensation of hunger will tell him that he needs food, (if he has learned to identify it as 'hunger'), but it will not tell him how to obtain his food and it will not tell him what food is good for him or poisonous. He cannot provide for his simplest physical needs without a process of thought. —Ayn Rand*

The full conscious process shows that during the nurturing phrase infants are indeed guided by percepts, this being the natural law of allowance. However as Rand concludes, the process of thought builds increased reliance on cognitive faculties for which there is no substitute.

> *Thinking requires a state of full, focused awareness. The act of focusing one's consciousness is volitional. Man can focus his mind to a full, active, purposefully directed awareness of reality-or he can un focus it and let himself drift in a semiconscious daze, merely reacting to any chance stimulus of the immediate moment, at the mercy of his undirected sensory-perceptual mechanism and of any random, associational connections it might happen to make." —Ayn Rand 1*

This thought process relies on life values from one of two sources. If not deliberately chosen and uploaded to the subconscious mind for prioritisation, values assimilate from actions we deliberately chose in the past.

*[Refer to the Value Transfer Wave diagram - next page. Please study closely and refer back to this diagram as you proceed.]*

Either way, freely chosen values source our emotions and feelings, which in turn report success or distress respectful of our present-moment activity or behaviour.

There is no escape because free will is the chosen process arising from awareness involving the senses, logic, values, and concepts. Rational people intentionally implant their life values into their subconscious minds.

Resultant feelings allow them to quickly correct their values or

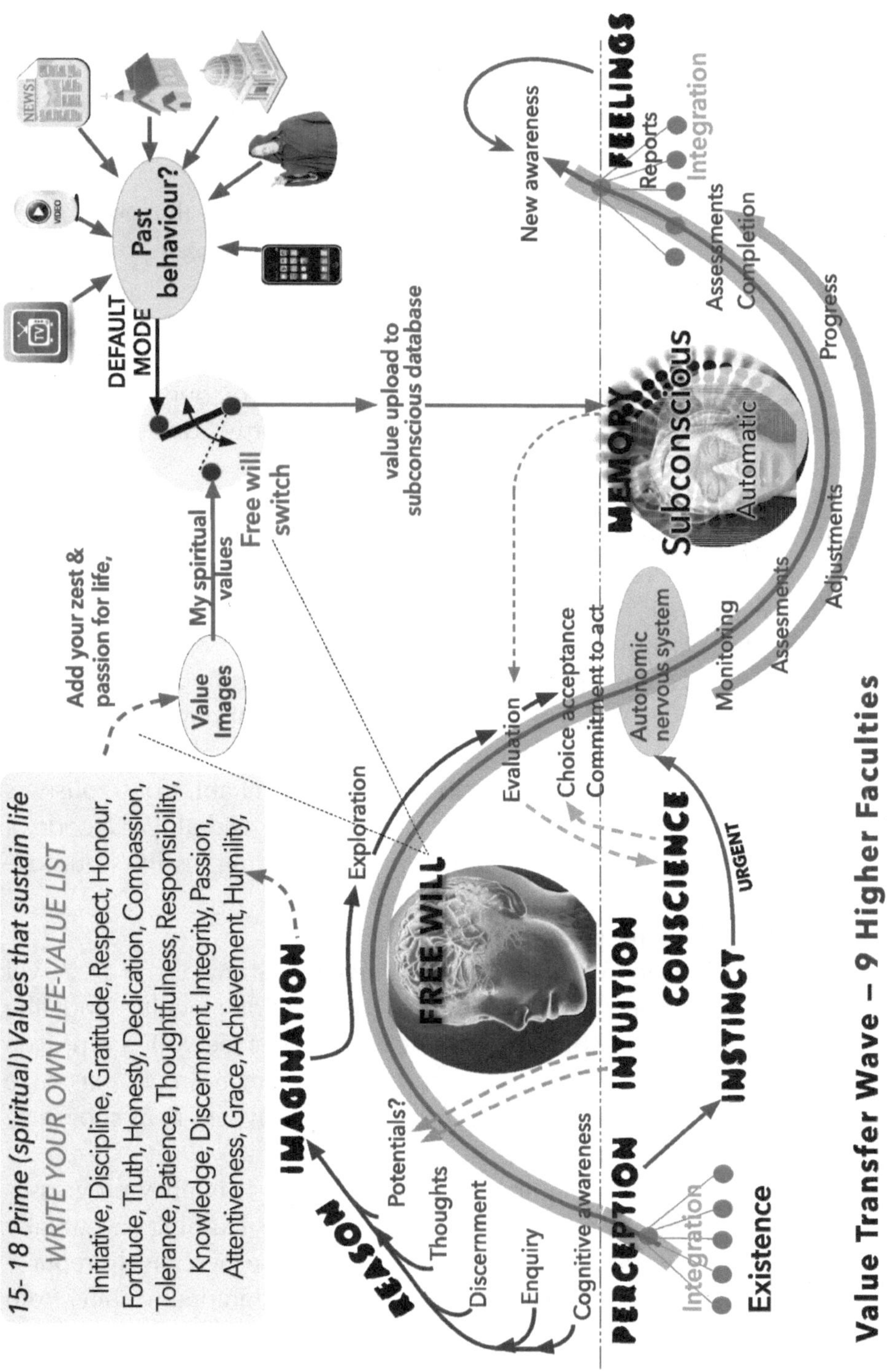


4. Value Transfer Wave – the full conscious Process (Loop also)

behaviour. Emotions are not enemies; instead, they reinforce the (valued) means of enjoying life, our Creator's gift of an automated mentoring system. Feelings guide remedy for sure, but once one understands that feelings are outcomes, correction comes by changing the source values in one's mind or the source behaviour. As Ayn Rand said–

An emotion that clashes with your reason, an emotion that you cannot explain or control, is only the carcass of that stale thinking which you forbade your mind to revise.

That means emotions are our 'automated mentoring system,' which, although reliant on free will for learning from that place, remains a fact never described before. As the mental equivalent of our autoimmune system, values can only prompt free will corrections. Corrective instructions violate free will.

Our ethical or unethical thought values manifest through our actions as morality or immorality. Our conscience faculty approves or disapproves of them before their enactment, while feelings approve or disapprove of them following their enactment. Thus, three value checks are included in the completed wave pass, as shown by the diagram.

Our emotions are the products of the premises held by our minds.

Given that (chosen) life values are the spiritual (not physical) driver of the subconscious mind, we are spiritual beings living a spiritual life, albeit in a physical realm on which consciousness is also reliant. Consciousness jointly interfaces spiritually and physically, therefore. Morality is a code of values guiding man's choices and actions, determining his life's purpose and course.

**4. Ethics and objective philosophy.**

The Value Transfer Wave diagram (3) clearly shows how free will sandwiches between the subconscious perception faculty and the 'actioning' functionality of the subconscious mind. Free will is a proven fact of existence, whence all philosophical debate regarding its existence is void. No one can deny free will, but people can bypass it, as shown by the law of allowance for infants.

Later, a significant mental transformation occurs as infancy progresses through childhood into adolescence. Cognitive learning eventually replaces infant nurturing, so our cognitive choices progressively replace subconsciously motivated actions. Thus, motivation gradually shifts from the subconscious mind to the conscious mind as directed by free choice.

## 5. Adolescent mind switch

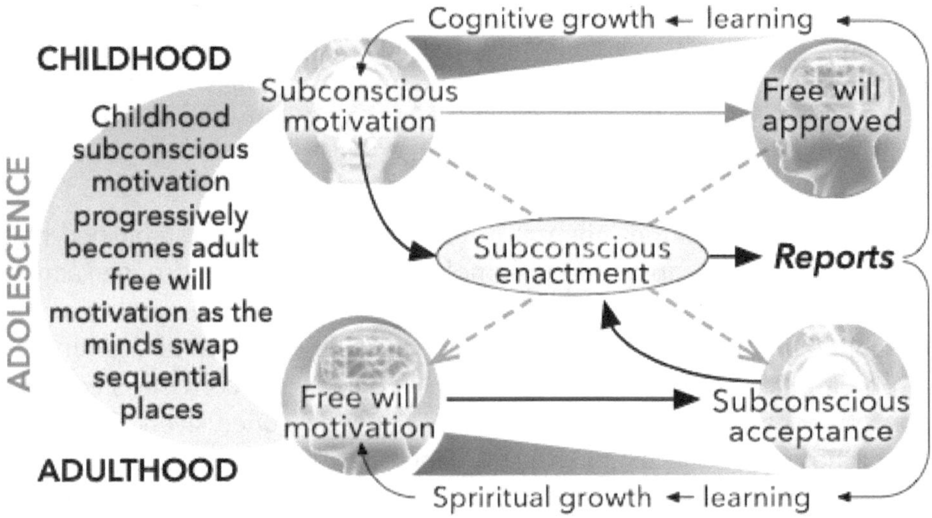


If one's values are not consciously chosen, uploaded, and thereby prioritised, the subconscious mind has no alternative but to adopt values from past (chosen) actions. It cannot work in a mental vacuum any more than an empty stomach can process food. By default, therefore, past values do not automatically and unknowingly apply to present-moment actions; thus, feelings have no known basis. With no correction possible, people's emotions rule their minds. That state of animality arises from conscious nescience; its only remedy is an objective life philosophy utilising the full conscious process as nature intends.

I've previously mentioned how animals can see, hear, and smell much better than we can, yet we are not disadvantaged. Instead, our awareness prompts us to exercise reason, logic, and imagination. Should we not do so, two disastrous circumstances result. First, people must depend on technology as their saving grace. Second, technologists seek to fill the supposed gap left by sensory inadequacy. As a result, scientists over-engineer our apparent sensory abilities. By equating consciousness with physicality, a non-existent problem results; for example, *"everything is energy whereby reality is an illusion."* Not only is 'reality' dismissed, but so too is consciousness, both prime requisites upon which life entirely depends.

Catastrophic results are crystal clear. All former problems appear resolved, but they are not. So what is hidden? No one sees the relationship of free will to the law of causality, whereby the law of identity remains hidden. The axioms of identity and existence vanish, making life nigh impossible since no reference base or hallmark seemingly exists.

Correct those errors, and consciousness, natural law, and philosophical integrity are found true; theories no more!

**5. Inherent natural protection.**

Natural law is found inherent in human nature; once established that consciousness is a (psycho-epistemology) value transfer process across two different vocabularies within natural law guidance authored by (reasoned) free will, Add that the same natural laws differently administer our biology, and it is clear that an objective philosophy correctly steers our enactment of the whole process. Personal benefits conclusively result.

Further, the same personal governance transposes to societal natural law with no revisions or amendments necessary. All forms of positive law are canceled, and all fraudulent legal entities retire to history. This radical overthrow calls for revised education within all the human sciences and concerns all matters of law and government.

I owe a debt of gratitude for Rand's remarkable thoughts and her contribution to humanity, and I am most sincerely grateful for having been able to practice her philosophy over many years. Her knowledge and my experience greatly assisted my comprehension of the conscious process, but both must mesh together without discrepancy. As the big picture filled, the more its authenticity had to be established without question. Before long, multiple correlations began emerging between Rand's work and mine, thus reinforcing all facts, principles, and methodology. So comprehensive were these matches and interlocks that all ambiguity and falsity vanished.

Observational science and deductive reasoning proved invaluable. From watching countless videos showing how infants learn to crawl, I saw how they teach us the subconscious mind is programmed by imagery, without words, science, or math, and how our values author our feelings. Learning the free will sandwich proved a monumental leap forward. The engine of integration likewise opened many doors of inquiry, much fueled by Rand's algebraic explanations of concepts. Both paths are remarkable in a world that knows nothing about consciousness and how it works, nor anything about an objective philosophy.

**Human Rights**

The term' human rights' is collective, meaning people have a right to what they need. Tragically, this false conclusion coercively demands that others must satisfy those needs. For example, the United Nations Declaration of Human Rights (UDHR) lists the 'right' to free education, which implies that other people are obliged to pay for it. Thus, people conclusively believe that rights are obligations imposed on others and that governmental enforcement and coercive damage created by compulsion are unavoidable.

The free society solution is 'Individual Rights,' meaning that all people have the right to seek education but never demand it from others. That denies authoritarian force. Accordingly, there is no right to welfare in free societies. People may freely support others, but no duty or obligation exists. Poor or disabled people do not suffer any worse than in a welfare culture. Indeed, welfare funded by 'taxes' almost inevitably discourages work, making society poorer and encouraging greater dependency on welfare handouts. The whole concept of 'welfare benefits' funded by theft is a fraud. Philanthropic bodies in wealthy free societies are far better supported, plus their need dramatically diminishes.

Unlike most philosophers, Ayn Rand hailed, *"a social system is based on the recognition of individual rights, including property rights, in which all property is privately owned."* Capitalism is a moral system, not a financial system.

Individual rights support that definition. When one observes that our bodies are a free society of some fifty trillion individual cells, tissues, bones, organs, and organ systems living in a cooperative society authored by free will absent all authority, what better model exists for some eight billion people? None. Once grasped that free will cannot overrule the subconscious mind because it is fully automated, which itself cannot overrule free will or the conscious process disintegrates, the 'law of no trespass' is shown axiomatically irrefutable.

The fact that *'no mind can rule another'* morally informs that no right to authoritatively rule can exist, thus abolishing all government as we know it. Moreover, ethics and morality are removed from government and placed within all individuals where they rightfully belong.

Rights are moral principles that define and sanction our freedom of action in a social context.

Frank van Dun makes this principle very clear.

*A natural right in the strict sense is that which is naturally under a person's control, his body with its faculties of movement, feeling, thought, and speech. By extension, a natural right is what a person brings under his control without violating any other person's natural rights.*

Ayn Rand adds...
*A right is a moral principle defining and sanctioning a man's freedom of action in a social context. —Ayn Rand 4*

Observe the profound accuracy of those statements. No ambiguity exists. The fundamental (natural) right is our right to life, specifically to uphold and sustain it.

Neither quotation says a natural right is one's action. Both tell that a 'right' is freedom of action. Nothing declares one has a natural right to a thing or some outcome, e.g., education, welfare, or health care. You have the natural right to seek an education or health care but no right to demand that someone provide it. Thus, natural rights are your freedom of action in a social context using self-governance that respects another's rights.

Since we each live as individuals, our rights to life can only be 'individual rights,' existent properties of our independent selves. Because there is no collective lung, heart, brain, or digestive system to sustain, there is no communal life to be maintained by collective 'human rights.' No act, decree, or legislation of Man can alter that fact. It follows that the source of individual rights is not divine law or congressional law but the Law of Identity. Nature impels each man and woman to sustain their life through their effort. If not so chosen, they perish unless another person steps in to fulfil that function.

Because we each live independently from others, then 'rights' are 'individual rights' and none other.

Intrinsic natural law seeks integrity, morality, and justice, not compliance, hence it cannot be an alternative system to Positive Law statutes that enforce compliance. As mentioned, so-called 'Human Rights' are not rights at all. Study the works of John Locke, William Blackstone, and Thomas Jefferson, and you'll come to an inevitable conclusion. If we each have an immutable right to live, do we not also have an incontestable right to the fruits of our labours? Unequivocally yes! Accordingly, we each have the right to live, plus rights to the product of our efforts.

Our right to life, and our right to life-sustaining efforts, is now unmistakable. It should now be a self-evident fact that our right to life is inherent in the meaning of life and is not separately granted or bestowed. That means our right to life is inseparable from our nature. Every abrogation or refusal of these facts represents death in some form.

The subject of 'rights' is not usually considered a matter of consciousness but a political matter. However, if conscious thought drives our actions, our 'right to action' is intimately related to human consciousness. Consider what should be five self-evident truths.

1. **Right to life:** Every person is born equal into the jurisdiction of life, having a similar (unalienable) right to live free from all incursion and trespass.

2. **Right to Property**: For the same reason, everyone has an equal (inalienable) right to the fruits of their labours to uphold and sustain their lives.

3. **Rights Protected**: To protect other people's rights is to guarantee one's own.

4. **Rightful justice:** Any trespass of another's rights automatically relinquishes one's right to life, such manifest action being one's agreement to remediate all harm or loss respectively, and in that measure. Criminals confess their crimes by their actions and thus convict themselves. That is how natural justice works.

5. **All such rights** are inherent within the born nature of every man, woman, and child, whereby all who dispute those facts dispute their own nature, thereby rendering all their claims or protests invalid and void from pronouncement. That statement is the secret by which authoritarian rule cancels itself.

In the simplest form, there is your freedom and your means to a free society! (Rights are discussed in my book, '*Navigate to Freedom.*')

'Natural rights,' as spoken of by Jefferson, include the right to life, which requires that each individual be free to work and acquire property to 'pursue happiness.' In political terms, we also possess the natural right to defend our life, liberty, and property from invasive attacks.

Individual rights stand above all others because only individuals can be responsible or irresponsible, moral or immoral. Groups have no collective morality, neither a country, a town, a race, a tribe, a club, or a company, just as no collective heart, liver, or mind exists. Only individual members can be moral or immoral. Naturally business leaders should build an ethical culture in their organisations. But moral responsibility manifests through actions taken by individuals, not groups.

Initially, it was the government's purpose to use its defensive power of force to repel all assaults on our freedoms. Should it overstep that boundary, it becomes the greatest tyrant. With a virtual monopoly of force, its potentialities for evil are far greater than that of any other institution.

Two fundamental lessons are present for our consideration. First, no man has any authority to rule over other men; no emperor, king, monarch, or government is a superior moral agent having rights over the people, regardless of their purported consent. Even majority consent cannot be universal since majority consent must overrule minority dissent, whence gang warfare is nigh impossible to prevent.

Second, today's problem is that (falsely believed contractual) consent is given only to the institution of government, never to the separate legislations it enacts. Thus, despite our (falsely believed) 'consent to be governed,' our right of dissent is denied. People are captive, and their rights and freedoms are restricted. The corrective lesson is crystal clear. Individual rights stand above all others because only individuals can be responsible or irresponsible, moral or immoral. Groups have no collective morality, neither a country, a town, a race, a tribe, a club, or a company, just as no collective heart, liver, or consciousness exists. Only individual members can be moral or immoral. Of course business leaders should build an ethical culture in their organisations. But moral responsibility manifests through actions taken by individuals, not groups.

Initially, it was the government's purpose to use its defensive power of force to repel all assaults on our rights and freedoms. Should it overstep that boundary, it becomes the greatest tyrant. With a virtual monopoly of force, its potentialities for evil are far greater than that of any other institution.

Two fundamental lessons are present for our consideration.

1. First, no man has any authority to rule over other men, no emperor, king, monarch, or government is a superior moral agent having rights over the people, regardless of their purported consent. Even majority consent cannot be universal since majority consent must overrule minority dissent, whence gang warfare is nigh impossible to prevent.
2. Second, today's problem is that (falsely believed contractual) consent is given only to the institution of government, never to the separate legislations it enacts. Thus, despite our (falsely believed) consent to be governed, our right of dissent is denied. The corrective lesson is crystal clear. People can abolish governments, but never rights.

Throwing off the government is not only an option; we have now reached a point in history where it is our positive moral duty. Fortunately, we have before us the charter of a new nation and the rationalisation of rebellion. Jefferson himself launched the political principle that when the instrument of government fails, or worse, nothing forbids, we can only better our circumstances by destroying that instrument of failure. Amending tyrannical rule will not escape it.

Question: Is government necessary if the only thing required is to preserve the people's right to life, freedom, and pursuit of happiness? My answer is a resounding no! There is no better quest than to abolish what punishes us, accept our unalienable rights and freedom, and protect both in perpetuity. Today's need is not for more government but instead for protection from unlawful governance.

We have all the means necessary to orchestrate a free society, doubly blessed because all actions by trespassers and outlaws self confess their crimes against humanity. Thus, all need for government is canceled, provided that our free will and rights are never trespassed.

Governments steal people's private property, although they protect it from common theft. Conversely, the inalienable right to our property protects individuals from coercion and theft by all criminals, including governments.

Property ownership in free societies is not a granted privilege open only to a few; everyone has the same rights to benefit, thrive, and prosper. Property allows us to make our own choices, formulate our plans, pursue our desires and ambitions, and express our views, free from the arbitrary will of others. Justness results if people obtain their property legitimately and without coercion. No (additional) justice is called for. Peaceful cooperation with others allows mutual advantage without disputes, intimidation, or violence.

Property ownership is fundamental to upholding and sustaining our lives and critical to everyone in free societies. They can use it, enjoy it, loan it, rent it, trade it, give it away, bequeath it, and even destroy it. But your right to property means none can be taken or stolen from you or even used without your consent. No freedom is possible without your right to private property. Nor can justice exist since your right to live depends on your right to the property you cultivate or produce. Without the right to the fruits of their labor as their possession, people are easily enslaved by others, robbed, denied life, and made victims of criminal injustice without protection.

We cannot own our lives as many people claim. One cannot

(separately) own the life that they already are. Life is what you are. That is the natural law of Identity. It remains that every man, woman, and child has the unalienable right to life and the inalienable right to sustain it. The difference between 'owning one's life' versus possessing the 'unalienable right to life' is profound. The first is a claim of 'right' made by oneself. The second is the 'Law of Identity,' life being the heart and soul of a life-based philosophy.

The solution, therefore, is to categorically uphold that life is what you are; hence, we each have an inherent and immutable right to its continuance. All dispute with that position is self-extinguished by those who relinquish their life by legally denying yours.

Just as the right to life is the right to act, we have the right to sustain our lives through our actions. Governments cannot axe our rights and freedoms, but we can axe them.

Just as the right to life is the right to act, we have the right to sustain our lives through our actions.

> *The right to life is the source of all rights—and the right to property is their only implementation. Without property rights, no other rights are possible. Since man has to sustain his life by his own effort, the man who has no right to the product of his effort has no means to sustain his life. The man who produces while others dispose of his product, is a slave.*
>
> *Bear in mind that the right to property is a right to action, like all the others: it is not the right to an object, but to the action and the consequences of producing or earning that object. It is not a guarantee that a man will earn any property, but only a guarantee that he will own it if he earns it. It is the right to gain, to keep, to use and to dispose of material. —Ayn Rand*

Our right to act in support of our lives is immutable. The right to the product of our efforts is in our efforts and bound within the products and services we perform. Because Unalienable and Inalienable Rights are not adequately defined, I have chosen to make that distinction and represent them.

- An unalienable right is our right to action, our unfettered right to live and sustain our life within the rights of all others. Our immutable right to live and maintain our lives is drawn about us by the 'equal' rights of all others.
- All trespass, violation, and aggression of our right to life are outlawed. 'Unalienable' means Unable to be removed by any means. Unable to

be sold, given away, or bequeathed.

- An inalienable right is our right to the product of our action(s), the right of entitlement (or belonging) to that which our efforts produce, including improvements (and cultivations) made to the land. Accordingly, no one has a right to confiscate, usurp, plunder, defile, or steal any individual's inalienable right to their property. 'Inalienable' means inherent in the product or within the product.

Frank van Dun offers further clarification. [5]

*It is advisable, then, to keep in mind that while some things simply are my natural rights, it does not follow that I simply have the natural right to do something or other.*

*There is an easier and more elegant formulation of this fact. Leave the etymology of 'rights' aside and substitute the word 'property' whenever you mean 'that which is controlled by a person'. Likewise, substitute 'natural property' whenever you mean 'that which is by nature under the control of a person'. Then a person's right to do something is simply his lawful use of his property. His natural right to do something is simply his lawful use of his natural property, or else, in a wider sense, his use of his property in a manner that is consistent with natural law.*

Do you see what van Dun has just clarified? Let me repeat. Natural property is, by nature, under the control of an individual man or woman. All the organs of your body, including your two minds, are your 'natural property' because they are under the control of your nature. Accordingly...

- People who own, grow, or manufacture products may gift, sell, trade, or bequeath them.
- Heart, lungs, organs, or minds are not transferable while controlled by a man, woman, or child because those organs and faculties are their 'natural property.' 'Life' cannot be transferred because it can never be detached from what it is.

There lies the clear-cut difference. Bodily constituents are our 'property' under our control. But because 'life' is what we are, it cannot simultaneously be a separate entity we own. Life is not an associative attachment, extension, product, or separately distinguished 'property' of our being. It is our being. The instant we concede that life can be 'owned,' even by ourselves, we confess that life is a property available to all who might take, steal, sell, enslave, claim ownership, or trade it.

One cannot refute or deny one's life without using it. Thus, life is the conditional foundation stone on which an objective philosophy rests. Life lives. That is its identity. Life ownership cannot separately exist. Property ownership can and does. A protected society must protect all individual rights to life and property.

I submit that those descriptions and reasons are the most proper and lawful descriptions of individual rights ever offered. None belong to inert fictional legal entities because a dead fiction cannot take any action.

Does that explain why the Universal Declaration of Human Rights (UDHR) document states that' human rights' are to be ruled by the United Nations (Article 29.3) – in contravention of its (Article 1) statement that *"all human beings are born free and equal in dignity and rights"*?

Do you notice how that document begins with the word 'free' (individual) in Article One, then swaps it for the phrase 'liberty' (collective) in Article twenty-nine, and trusts that no one will notice the profound difference between freedom versus slavery, notwithstanding some permissions thrown in for comfort's sake?

Do you now see why states rule that 'equitable title' be separate from the 'legal title'? Do you see that when claiming to own our own lives, we concede that ownership is up for grabs? Do you now see how unalienable rights immutably uphold your right to life, whereby 'life ownership' is entirely irrelevant?

Does that concealed theft of your life as property – that very covert form of mind control – help explain why the Thomas Jefferson Memorial in Washington DC has the word INALIENABLE engraved in twelve-inch high letters, despite that Jefferson used the word 'Unalienable'?

The more we strive to develop our consciousness, the more unalienable and inalienable rights are categorically denied authoritative misappropriation by anyone or any group (government) for any purpose.

Now, observe what that means in practice.

- Your rights are guaranteed when your actions preserve other people's right to life.
- Actions that violate others' rights forfeit your own and freely confess so doing.
- Your free choices and values are the deciding factor.

Notably, a life-objective philosophy drives ethical and moral consciousness – likewise, a non-objective philosophy wreaks havoc on our conscious ability.

Virtually everyone credits the American Declaration of Independence as the most definitive expose of 'Rights' ever written.

History has exposed that upholding our right to life and, by analogy, the vital need to protect our right to life are two distinctly separate issues. That fact was not self-evident in 1776, or I would not be discussing 'Rights' protection now. Admittedly, Jefferson offered that "whenever any form of government becomes destructive of these ends, it is the right of the people to alter or to abolish it." Sadly, that remedy allows the horse to bolt before the gate closes.

In retrospect, we should have fully protected our declared right to claim our right to life! If America's revered 'Declaration of Independence' is ever to be retrieved, an additional clause must specifically protect our right to life. For example–

"To secure the certain, unalienable right to life, unless all men created equal, unequivocally ensure their right to life, and their unalienable right so to do against all cancellation, violation, or usurpation, they will have neither."

To repeat, only by endorsing other people's right to their life can we ensure our own right to life. Freedom, respect and individual rights are inseparable. The evidence is incontrovertible as witnessed by full consciousness. Neither of our two minds can violate the process of the other, whereby each respects the other. Nature obliges that we respect our own life, and the lives of all others.

Let's not 'beat about the bush,' as the saying goes. Ayn Rand called her philosophy 'Objectivism' but informally called it *"a philosophy for living on earth."* You will find an explicit presentation of it in her books, particularly in her novel *Atlas Shrugged*.

Full consciousness, the process no one had ever previously explained, fills the same role. It is "consciousness for living on earth," described in my book Conscious Ascendance and its derivative, Navigate to Freedom.

The conscious process reveals specific governing laws that uphold and support mindful functioning. None rule. None order. All are advisory in that they explicitly direct the conscious process so that it properly fulfills our desires so that we live according to what we most value. Because these laws govern the consequences of our actions, our free will is fully protected. In sum, this beneficial gift from Nature's source creator is our invitation to live in the form of *"natural laws for living on earth."*

So, how do we resist? How do we reclaim ourselves? We do not! Why not? Because to plead deliverance from evil is to admit its criminal authenticity. It isn't valid now, and it never was. Evil holds no power but what we grant it. So stop! Tyrants have no legitimacy precisely because they had to abandon their born Nature to command yours authoritatively!

- They walked out on life – voluntarily. **You didn't.**
- You've not spat in the face of your creation. **They have.**
- They voluntarily relinquished their born Nature; **you didn't.**

Call them out, and they must defend their (supposed) right to disagree with your position. They cannot because the more they support the insanity of invented 'straw men,' 'citizens, and 'persons,' the more they express their ignorance of life itself – which confirms their incompetence to hold any public office!

We do not need to exit the government's legal jurisdiction. Criminals confess crimes by their harmful actions, whereby they convict themselves. That is how natural justice works. And that means no indemnity can apply to a legal' office.' The individual man or woman who (from that office) actioned any trespass or crime against society is fully responsible, mitigating circumstances accepted.

Although a legally instituted office dictates legally necessitated actions, each action is the product of a single living man or woman's choice to act criminally. No legal protection or indemnity is possible, therefore. (See The Nuremberg Trials for evidence.)

To protect other people's rights is to guarantee one's own. Jurisprudence instructs that any trespass of another's rights automatically relinquishes one's right to life, manifestly being one's agreement to remediate all (victim) harm or loss, respectively, in that measure. Criminals confess crimes by their actions, whereby they convict themselves. That is how natural justice works.

What better could we ask than that value, purpose, and morality be spiritually determined by our 'free will' concordant with the same rights in all others? All just actions testify to morality. Police officials must arrest any immorality or aggression arising so natural justice is administered.

Consciousness now unites with life value selection, determining how those values will be used. Now add that natural laws reinforce the consciousness process and the objective philosophy required of both, and all three incontrovertibly unite as one.

# Chapter 6

## Philosophy from Within

Implanting some superior master over one's life through deed or belief is to scorn one's life and pay a hefty price. For Christians and other monotheistic religions, God is the Creator and ruler of the universe and the source of all moral authority, the supreme being. In certain other faiths, our 'source creator' is a superhuman being or spirit, worshipped as having power over nature or human fortunes, a deity. Various names are ascribed, such as Jehovah, Elohim, Alpha and Omega, Lord, and more, while Jews say "Adonai" ('Lord'). Again, what matters is that creation exists as fact. But is it superior to our nature? Think seriously about that. Why would a 'creator' intentionally create inferior beings?

In the 1776 American Declaration of Independence, Thomas Jefferson referred to the *Laws of Nature and Nature's God*. Still, few people recognise that nothing further exists in the Declaration that might reference Christianity or does so. The term 'Nature's God' was used by deists of the time. Deism, or 'the religion of nature,' was a form of rational theology that emerged among 'freethinking' Europeans in the 17th and 18th centuries. Deists insisted that religious truth should be subject to the authority of human reason rather than divine revelation.

I have sparingly used the word God and the term 'nature's god' in my three previous books and the word Creator in the same way that Jefferson used those terms. That means 'Nature's god' is the Life that Lives, being one's nature exactly! One's reverence for life and creation is to live it.

Do you see the connection? Jefferson referred to the Laws of Nature and the power of human reason rather than divine revelation, thus canceling all connotations of superior authority. Jefferson engaged science and materiality to manage his views on religion, rejecting the superstitions and mysticisms of Christianity. The Jefferson Bible even edited the gospels to remove the miracles and mysticism of Jesus, retaining what Jefferson deemed the correct moral philosophy of Jesus. People must comprehend that the power of human reason is never dominance over others.

Thomas Jefferson's letter to John Adams on January 24, 1814 states in part–

*The whole history of these books [the Gospels] is so defective and doubtful that it seems vain to attempt minute enquiry into it: and such tricks have been played with their text, and with the texts of other books relating to them, that we have a right, from that cause, to entertain much doubt what parts of them are genuine. In the New Testament there is internal evidence that parts of it have proceeded from an extraordinary man; and that other parts are of the fabric of very inferior minds. It is as easy to separate those parts, as to pick out diamonds from dunghills.*

From Jeffersons 'Notes on Virginia' 1782 we read...

*Millions of innocent men, women and children, since the introduction of Christianity, have been burnt, tortured, fined and imprisoned; yet we have not advanced one inch towards uniformity.*

In Jefferson's letter to Francis Hopkinson, March 13, 1789 we read...

*I never submitted the whole system of my opinions to the creed of any party of men whatever in religion, in philosophy, in politics, or in anything else where I was capable of thinking for myself. Such an addiction is the last degradation of a free and moral agent.*

Jefferson aimed squarely at laissez-faire liberalism in the name of individual freedom. His view was that any form of government control, not only of religion but of individual mercantilism, consisted of tyranny. The fact that he thought our civil rights should have *"no dependence on our religious opinions, any more than our opinions in physics or geometry"* points exactly to an objective philosophy pertinent to how our conscious process works in 'value' terms.

As a sub-branch of philosophy, axiology relates to worth or worthiness. The first aspect concerns ethics and morality, commonly accepted as questions concerning right or wrong. Ethics is generally the science or discipline of what human behaviour ought to be, unlike sociology which studies what human behaviour is.

People say morality is not verifiable in a scientific way but that we can discuss actions and agree on some means of objective evaluation in terms of reason. Do some moral distinctions result from 'emotive feelings'? Alternatively, do we have mental control over our feelings such that we are authors of our own morality? The whole conscious process answers those questions since it revolves around life values being its tools of excellence and completion.

As a branch of metaphysics, 'spiritual metaphysics' refers to studying metaphysical concepts, events, and emotions connected to a person's spirit. It is a particular philosophy that purportedly explains how people relate to the world through belief in one or more significant spirits or forces.

People typically meditate to supposedly learn about spiritual metaphysics and who they are, which poses a vital question. At what point does metaphysics fade out, and ethics begin? For example, if matters relating to or affecting our human spirit or soul differ from material or physical things, from material values or pursuits, are those spiritual values unrelated to ethical thought and moral behaviour? That question becomes more difficult if 'spiritual metaphysics' also concerns other beings, such as angels or gods, and whatever connection a person's spirit has with those beings. Do they even exist? Pursued even further, is spiritual metaphysics an investigation into individuals' connections with everything? Or is metaphysics a "science" that asks about the meaning of life and what determines or affects spiritual wellness? If so, then what is spirituality?

Further complications arise; many people seek a connection to the energy of the world or universe. These people accept that everything that comes into existence is related to something bigger than themselves. They seek a relationship with this larger spiritual concept, believing they will grow, develop, and understand themselves far better while accepting some humility from being just one individual in a vast network of creatures, things, and events.

If spiritual metaphysics studies metaphysical concepts, events, and emotions connected to a person's spirit, how are concepts, events, intuition, conscience, and feelings related to spirit? Human consciousness is the answer and is far more significant than mere awareness. Spiritual metaphysics cannot be an actual science if it omits the subject of life while using it simultaneously. Suppose spiritual metaphysics is motivated by a desire for personal growth and fulfilment as part of one's physical or emotional wellness journey. In that case, people must fully utilise consciousness.

Moreover, if spiritual metaphysics references the study of human nature and experience from a spiritual, non-physical standpoint, including the true nature of human existence as a union of mind, body, and spirit in one interconnected reality, then 'mind' is fully inclusive. If everything in the physical world has its basis in the spiritual world, so does human consciousness. What, then, is non-religious or secular spirituality? Does it lead people away from biblical truth, as many suggest? Or does it lead to the reality of our nature?

If metaphysics is the philosophical exploration of the ultimate nature of life, consciousness, and reality, then stop and comprehensively deal with those issues.

What is consciousness? With no answer, there can be no clear definition of spiritual metaphysics. Since its philosophy is not associated with any specific church, religion, or belief system, it can only be compatible with new-age thinking absent conscious knowledge. Such a pantheistic worldview closely aligns with the common belief that *"all is one,"* which oxymoron crushes 'individualism' automatically denying our independent conscious nature on which life depends.

Despite *"all is one"* nonsense, spiritual metaphysicians hold there is no fundamental disconnection between individual aspects of our nature and that the ultimate reality is one uniform human experience — body, mind, and spirit. It remains that if all things visible and invisible are part of one collective truth whereby "energies" can shape and manipulate one's reality to bring healing, inner peace, self-discovery, and growth, none of these metaphysicians explains our means of success. Accordingly,' spiritual metaphysics' is a pop culture combination of philosophical, scientific, and religious concepts, purportedly allowing theologians, new-agers, and scholars to describe how the spiritual and physical realms purportedly meet. The problem is that no one explains the mental or emotional process that allows that to happen. 'Spiritual metaphysics' remains a highly dubious combination of philosophical, scientific, and religious assumptions deriving from presumptions.

Central to this debate is the idea that spirituality is experiential while metaphysics is philosophical. That being so, spiritual metaphysics suggests that our reality is not physical but 'spiritual.' That term conveys positive connotations in that, as a human being, your life has meaning or sacredness. It suggests you have some depth, vitality, and purpose.

That realisation is worthy of serious enquiry. It means you're not unquestioningly accepting a faith passed down from your parents, and neither are you buying or rejecting the possibility of a higher power. The burning questions are: Is there such a thing, and if so, what? What value does it bring to life, and how can it be used to advantage? And that raises more questions. Is reality singularly physical, singularly spiritual, or the unification of both? Does material reality enhance spirituality or vice versa? Is spirituality a faith, a metaphysical reality, or an ethical construct that invokes moral behaviour?

In contrast to 'Spiritual metaphysics,' secular spirituality is considered one's adherence to a spiritual philosophy without necessary adherence to a religion. More particularly, it emphasises the inner peace of the individual rather than a relationship with the divine. Secular spirituality thus recognises the link between technology and spirituality, much as the subconscious mind unites physicality with values that advance our lives, physically, mentally and emotionally, instead of viewing technology as competing with such spiritual values or virtues.

The Dutch term ietsism is becoming more widely used in Europe, as opposed to the phrase *'spiritual but not religious'* (SBNR), which prevails in Western societies. Ietsism denotes an unspecified belief in an undetermined transcendent reality. The term is born of the belief that *'there must be something undefined beyond the mundane, which can be known or can be proven,'* while not accepting or subscribing to long and well-established beliefs relating to a Deity offered by any particular religion. *"The name 'iets' derives from answering 'no' to the question - 'Do you believe in (the conventional 'Christian') God?' while insisting "but there must be something."*

That conclusion begs us to look more closely at nature itself. My book *'Conscious Ascendance'* imparts the idea that individuals can foster a connection to the spiritual force within nature, resulting in an open experience of joyous wonder. Here, spirituality is a broader reality, a purposeful (secular) search for a deeper dimension to one's life – an objective search for meaning and purpose. That came home to me very vividly when writing that book as a demonstrable spiritual experience rooted in the feeling of awe concerning nature, most notably the conscious process. On the one hand, it is very complex, quickly dispelled by its intricate working simplicity, depth, power, majesty, and the joyous beauty of its creation as one's spiritual buddy.

Life was no longer a mystery to me. Its oft-spoken-of sacredness had become the power of being a conscious and creative practitioner of life, fully recognising that one's (steering) free will ability orchestrated a much larger (fully automated) realm devoted to upholding one's life choices and desires.

This realisation was far greater than all the beautiful manifestations of nature I had witnessed as a landscape photographer. I awakened to much more than white beaches bordering turquoise waters and sunrises that paint the ocean red, much more even than meditation or deep reflection to maintain vital mental wellbeing. I sensed a far greater power, born of values that I chose, and that their exercise was a spiritual activity within the conscious process instilled by nature. That being true, a specific life force of nature exists, its inherent power ideally regarded with great respect and reverence for its identity and fidelity, but never as a separate accompaniment or spiritual attachment.

Vicki Grieves began using research to analyse and interpret the contemporary development of Australian original (Indigenous) groups, whose spirituality, although diverse, seems to uphold the sacredness of nature. Australian (First Nations) people soon learn that all elements of nature, whether plants, animals, or insects, should be treated with the same respect as humans. Grieves believes that Original Australian's deep spiritual connection to nature builds a robust community belief system that has the potential to unite all living beings. This "*spirituality stems from a philosophy that establishes the wholistic notion of the interconnectedness of the elements of the earth and the universe, animate and inanimate.*" In one study, these people describe spirituality as a (felt) connection to their people's past and present community and a connectedness with land and nature. From this spiritual essence, they attained knowledge, inner strength, and a better understanding of their cultural roots' contributing to feelings of acceptance, balance, focus, and an overall sense of profound wellbeing.

However, the question of treating plants, animals, or insects with the same respect as humans is more than philosophical. To repeat–

- **Plant life is conditional.**
- **Animal life is perceptual.**
- **Human life is volitional.**

All three groups live most surely, but they markedly differ insofar as their means of living, whereby human spirituality cannot possibly apply to all three life forms. Plants and animals respond to their (unchangeable) environment according to their nature, even adapting their nature to those circumstances. Man changes his environment according to his material desires, augmented by higher (spiritual) desires for mental, emotional, and spiritual betterment. Thus, four more aspects arise for consideration., But first, here is the Value Transfer Wave in its correct loop form,

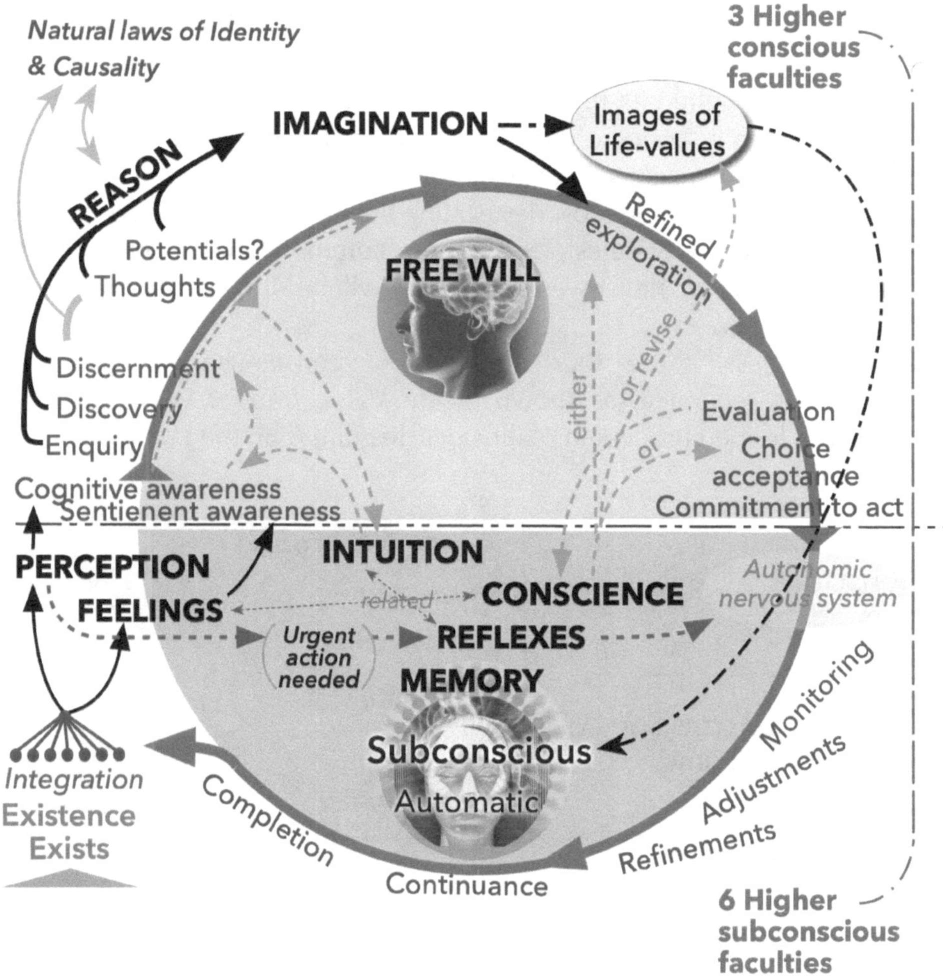


6. Value Transfer Loop The conscious process

Suppose we accept that the word 'spiritual' means relating to or affecting the human spirit or soul instead of material or physical things. In that case, the spirit is the power of raw consciousness, independent from particular objects of attention. Spirit is pure and unadulterated. Our first encounter with this power is through intelligence; the intellectual ability to recognise self-evident truths, usually called IQ ('intelligence quotient').

Later in the conscious process, we experience an emotional intelligence, or an 'emotional quotient,' often called EQ; such feelings complement our IQ.

Between these two quotients lie our (spiritual) life values, representing a Spiritual intelligence, or 'Spiritual quotient' which I'll refer to as SQ. 'Natural law' encrypted in our nature is the missing factor or quotient, which may be called (LQ). It is vital yet never spoken of because 'law' is always externally conceived and authoritatively applied to our lives by others. No one considers 'Law' a factual quotient inherent in our nature.

That, I venture, is the most devastating lie in history. Law is natural law and nothing else! Statutes, legislations, common law, mandates, and orders are NOT law, never were, and never will be! Today, 'Law' is a stolen or plagiarised concept.

Nevertheless, those four quotients of consciousness interact in harmonious sequence, as shown by the Value Transfer Wave diagram, which is a looped process in reality, per diagram 6 on the previous page.

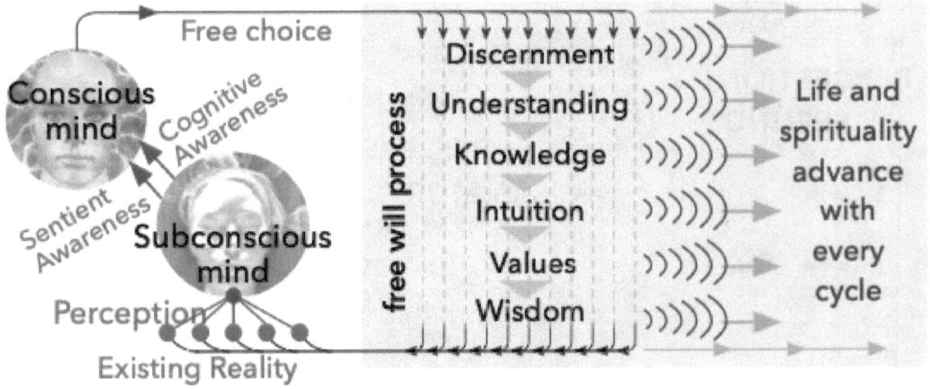


7. Consciousness is a repeating (looped) process

The driving force of this completeness is not a selected target of wisdom, compassion, integrity, joy, love, creativity, peace, and such. Instead, our chosen life values uphold and propel the whole conscious process toward those targets, most especially because those moral values fuel emotional and spiritual success.

Thus, spiritual intelligence (SQ) is not merely believing in one's soul but fully engaging with it; hence, we each are its makers creatively. Life does not happen to us resulting from some applied externality; it derives from all four (IQ,EQ,LQ,SQ) quotients interacting within us.

Diagram 7 shows how these link through pared (subconscious higher faculties. Connections are unmistakable as *Conscious Ascendance* showed.

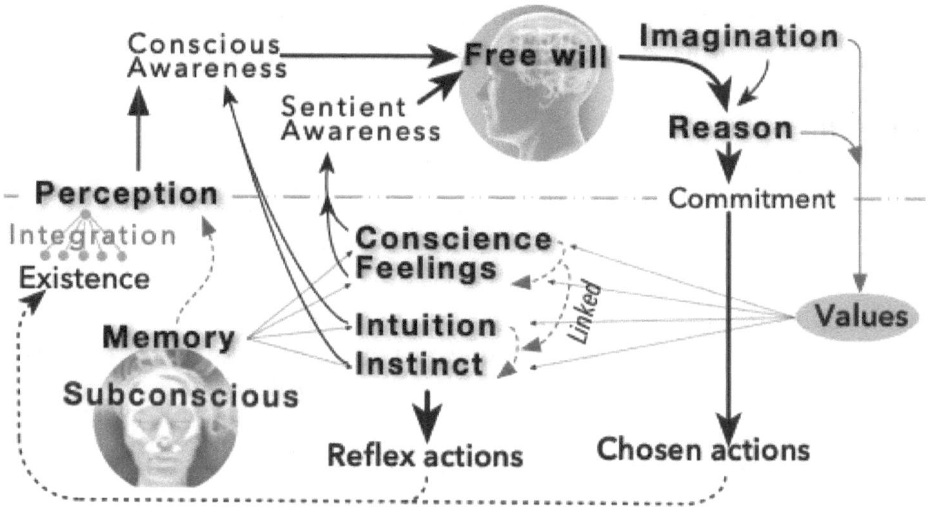


8. Faculty Relationships

Mere belief in one's soul does nothing to transform the ego. Absent spiritual intelligence, religious belief is an exercise of the mind that merely consoles the ego without altering it. Do not be misled by the word' ego.' Despite being polar opposites, egoism and egotism result from our chosen values and actions.

**Egoism** is legitimate (self-earned) self-esteem that arises from exercising the four quotients. It is the hallmark of sovereignty.

**Egotism** is the opposite, namely inflated self-aggrandisement, or 'ego.' Thus, the ego does not magically transform, as many people believe. Instead, spiritual transformation replaces one's inflated self-aggrandized egotism with egoism deriving from the elevation of one's soul.

Do not expect to find the egoism/egotism difference in a dictionary. Life values, which truthfully are spiritual intelligence directing our journey through life, are not generally known. Fortunately, the days of id and superego consign themselves to history.

Objectivist ethics holds that man's life is the standard of value—and his own life is his ethical purpose. Not surprisingly, our whole conscious process tells the same story exactly. Since the ultimate value is life itself, it is the hallmark standard by which we choose our specific values and purposes.

Observe the word 'value' and notice that in all the (above) discussions about spiritual metaphysics,' value' was never mentioned. Thus, all that is proper to the life of a rational being is the good, and that which negates, opposes, or destroys it is the evil. So now the conversation shifts from Spiritual Metaphysics to Value Ethics.

**Value Ethics**

That shift is vitally essential because the conscious process is not spirituality per se but 'value-based ethics' that uphold and sustain spirituality. Values may be material, as in a new house, swimming pool, clothes, vacation, or a surfboard. These values assist in sustaining our lives, but so do values like truth, respect, and diligence, none of which can be purchased. Life values bring healing, inner peace, self-discovery, and growth. They speak of having a life with meaning or sacredness, depth, vitality, and purpose. In that non-materialistic sense, they are spiritual values but more accurately described as 'life values.'

> *Consciously or subconsciously, explicitly or implicitly, man knows that he needs a comprehensive view of existence to integrate his values, to choose his goals, to plan his future, to maintain the unity and coherence of his life—and that his metaphysical value-judgments are involved in every moment of his life, in his every choice, decision and action. — Ayn Rand*

Observe what has happened. The need to uphold our lives by choosing and using values is not to write a philosophy for life. Instead, nature informs us that an objective philosophy is already grounded in life. It is not ethics or morality for enforcement or a spiritual code delivered as rigid doctrine. The natural law that expresses a value-based objective philosophy is nature's invitation for every man, woman, and child to live, choose, thrive, and prosper consistently.

Mainstream classical or early modern philosophy is mainly responsible for shaping philosophy as commonly believed, yet its practitioners cannot tell us what consciousness is or how it works. If we can invent assumptions and presumptions that deny valid means of testing them, how on earth can mainstream philosophy be taken seriously? It cannot.

At least that was the case until Rand revealed her 'Objectivism' philosophy in the mid nineteen-hundreds. Everything turned face up with knowledge pointing to the whole conscious process.

Later, my work revealed consciousness as never described in history. It shows natural law inherent in human nature, reversing the false notion of inherent morality theorizing natural law. Natural law theory no longer exists. The reverse is true. Natural law functions with freely chosen values, thus revealing an objective (nature-based) philosophy. Not surprisingly, this aligns completely with Rand's objective philosophy to dually reinforce their veracity.

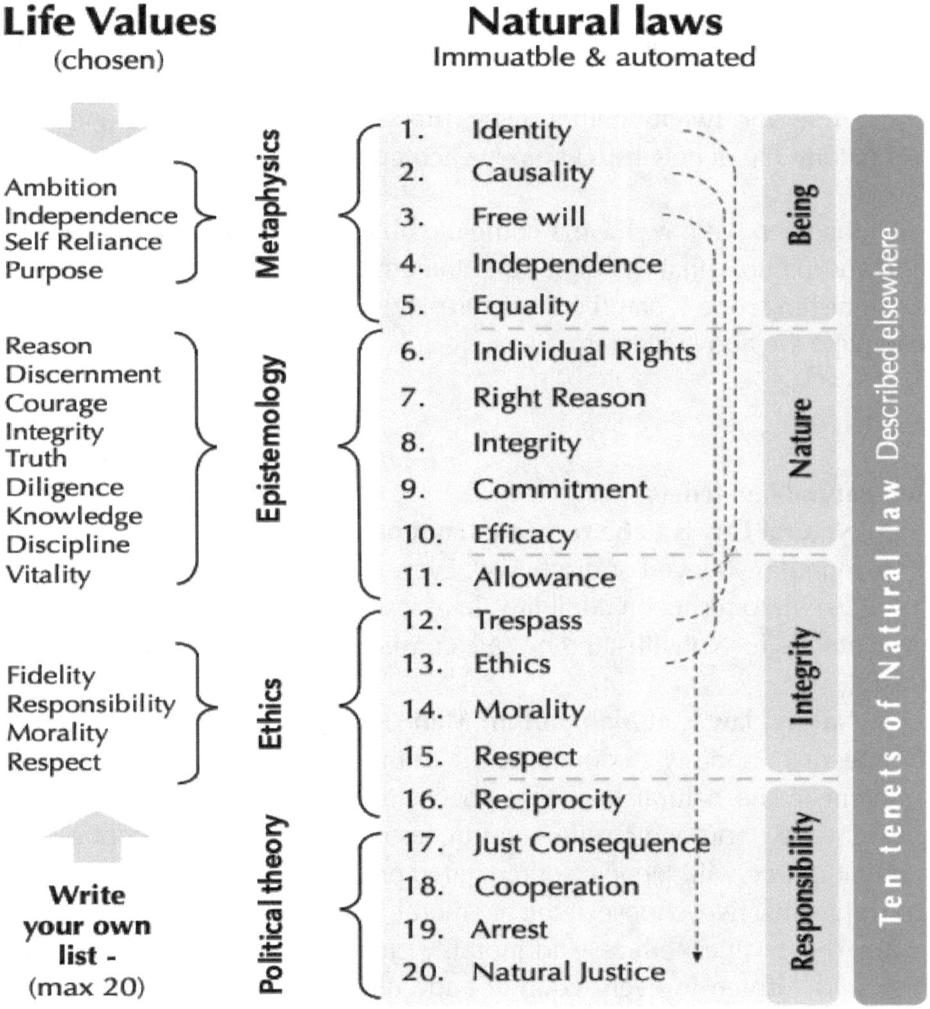


9 Philosophical - intrinsic natural law parity

This match-up is unprecedented, the reason being that not only does natural law and a matching (spiritually based) objective philosophy spring from within. Consciousness marries life values so closely that life-sustaining. A few minor discrepancies are not worth debating.

Seventeen life values on the left side of diagram 9 are like those examined elsewhere in this book. The diagram shows how they interface the different branches of an objective philosophy, all interfacing with the source creator's (twenty) natural laws and their groupings. Notice that some values are also natural laws. They reinforce that all values and laws, and their groupings, synchronise to form an inherent objective philosophy founded in the conscious process and its natural laws.

Although spoken of in my previous books, nothing past has shown this correlation so clearly, including the counterparts described in the chapter concerning the Twenty natural laws. They lock in place to reference the ten natural law tenets listed below, each applicable to all twenty natural laws.

Altogether, we now have a complete objective philosophy founded in human nature that cannot be (axiomatically) dismissed without relinquishing one's nature. Here are the ten natural law tenets that complete the above diagram.

**Ten natural law tenets**

**1. Natural Law is to be respected, not obeyed**

It cannot be obeyed or disobeyed. Every living man, woman, and child has free will to respect natural law, treat it with hostility or contempt, and even refuse it. Notwithstanding, all consequences that occur are one's own.

**2. Natural law is of Man, not for Man**

Integrity, honesty, commitment, truth, and self-preservation are inherent in the natural laws that govern all our faculties, systems, and processes, without which life would cease. Nature does not control the content of free will. Hence, source gifted emotional faculties that prompt and urge that we choose (ethical, moral, and spiritual) life-supporting goals. Thus, values, ethics, and morality emanate from within individual men and women in every country and culture, each according to their personal choice, corresponding with the right of all others to choose.

**3. Natural law is objective, not subjective**

Natural law does not refuse subjective opinion, but such is fundamentally irrelevant if it offers no spiritually life-sustaining purpose.

Therefore, actions that respect natural law uphold life objectively and serve justice. Acts that do not are unlawful and unjust, mitigating circumstances admitted.

**4. Natural law is immutable**

Natural law is inviolate. No human or any construct of Man can erase it without confessing by such action the unlawfulness of so-doing.

**5. Natural law upholds independent human life**

As an aggregation of independent living beings, we are all equal by species while wholly unique in expression, thus independent. No (common) lung, organ, brain, stomach, mind, or consciousness exists. The individuality of human life cannot fuse into one unified entity or collective that has no life of itself.

**6. Natural law grants no authority**

Natural law permits no individual to command another. It grants no permission or authority to trespass upon another's life. (This is testified by neither of our two minds being able to overrule the other.)

**7. Natural law refuses all authority**

Natural Law denies all orders and all authority save its own, whether from a partner, neighbour, pulpit, parliament, congress or any other.

**8. Natural law admits no trespass**

Whosoever knowingly initiates the use of physical or coercive force, or fraud against others, negates and paralyses the victim's means of survival. By such actions, perpetrators self-abdicate from the free will right to choose. Outlaws are not free. Natural law refuses initiated force in all its forms. Hence, one's right to exercise force to arrest such assaults is morally justifiable. Murder and self-defence are opposites.

**9. Natural law seeks integrity**

Natural and positive laws apply to different things so that no alternative rules can apply to both. Natural orderliness that governs our being is complete and without lack, entirely given to maintaining our life with immutable, undivided, wholesome integrity. Natural law obliges that we act in spiritual accordance with the same integrity of purpose that upholds our physical life. Spiritual integrity is vital to sustaining and enhancing inestimable joys that result from living a life of moral integrity!

**10. Natural law supports our life and is respectful of all others**

Integrity, lawfulness, and justice are the foundation and culmination of natural law, the full expression and manifestation of body, mind, and soul, respectful of life. When our actions outwardly manifest honesty and integrity found within, the orderliness and morality of our societal structures will correspond. Not one thing more is needed but to arrest violence. Nothing less will suffice.

Observe what has happened. The need to uphold our lives by choosing and using values is not man writing life-based philosophy. Instead, nature informs us that such a philosophy is factually grounded in life already. It is not ethics or morality for enforcement nor a spiritual code delivered as rigid doctrine. It is nature's invitation for every man, woman, and child to live, choose, thrive, and prosper by utilising all four quotients on auto-pilot. Do that and you will never (look) think back!

## Objective Philosophy

Objectivity is the concept of truth independent from individual subjectivity (bias caused by one's perception, emotions, beliefs, or imagination). An Objective Philosophy of life consists of philosophical constructs and directives that engage truthful life sustenance and maintenace without bias caused by the mind of a sentient being

# Chapter 7

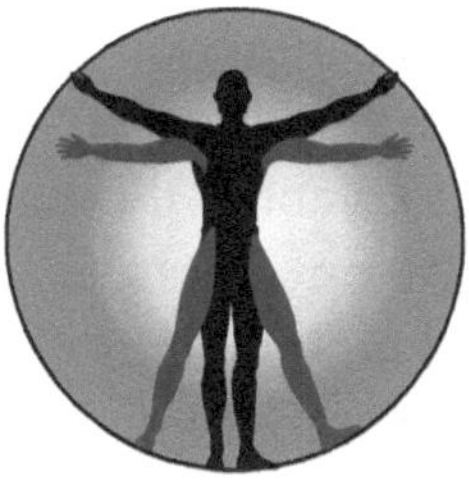

## Ethics And Morality

The topics or disciplines of ethics and morality have long swapped places, with justice ignored like a feather in the wind. It is high time this insanity ceased! No one in any rational debate can dispute respect for one another. The order or law of the human world is precisely that condition by which people enter into logical discussion. Each takes the other seriously and respectfully, and their commitments just by talking to one another. That orderliness is precisely what the (Latin) word 'ius' conveys.

If we take ourselves seriously, the conclusion we are obligated to respect each other is inescapable. Each individual has a right to the respect of others as long as they respect us. Respect thus forms a bond.

These are not idle musings. We each are real living beings from which are derived the fundamental obligations respectful of facts concerning the human world. We can only derive the natural rights of all and what respectful obligations those rights invoke by distinguishing our separateness and distinctiveness.

Concerning the more basic dynamic natural rights, our genetically given capacity for independent action, speech, and thought determines a human mode of existence precisely because humans must think, speak, and act. No one can rationally deny natural rights. To do so confesses disrespect and denial of another's right to life.

Natural rights can only be denied by conscious refusal, even to legislate and enforce refusal. Freedom is contrary. It imparts and necessitates thinking, which implies judging and making choices, accepting an idea, opinion, plan, or valuation, or rejecting it for another while remaining conscious of the rejected alternatives. Every action shadow testifies our refusal of what could have resulted.

Accordingly, human beings can and must inevitably choose; choice is a necessary condition of man. Choosing not to choose is a choice nonetheless. It is impossible to wander through life and not make choices without becoming dependent on others by (one's) wilful choice, such immorality a burden imposed on humanity.

> *Being human implies the right to think, speak, judge, make choices and act. To deny these rights to any human person is to deny his very being. But such a denial logically entails that the denier renounces his own rights and makes himself an outlaw. —Frank van Dun.*

That last sentence is invaluable but one that very few people comprehend. It suggests a science or code of ethics devoted to how men and women should think of life values and life itself, respectively, of self and others. Its premises are straightforward.

- **Life:** Nothing is more pertinent to every man, woman, or child on earth than life itself. Life is the base reference for all that concerns it. Life differentiates ethics from its lack and morality from immorality.
- **Virtues** are attitudes, values, or developed character traits that enable us to act in life-supporting ways that foster and master our potential. These uphold our spiritual essence.
- **Respect** is the voluntary endorsement of the vital need to support one's life by lawfully exercising one's faculties. The same applies to not hindering or harming the lives of others.

As mentioned, the conscious process interfaces physicality and spirituality, whereby we each live a spiritual life, albeit in a material world. Physicality is merely a toolbox for exercising our spiritual life and nature. We are creators, and we need to learn that.

Ethics is effectively the technology of philosophy, specifically as it applies to every aspect of man's life: his character, his actions, his values, and his relationship to all of existence. Ayn Rand poses more vital questions–

> *Before you come to ethics, you must answer the questions posed by metaphysics and epistemology: Is man a rational being, able to deal with reality — or is he a helplessly blind misfit, a chip buffeted by the universal flux? Are achievement and enjoyment possible to man on earth — or is he doomed to failure and disaster? Depending on*

*the answers, you can proceed to consider the questions posed by ethics: What is good or evil for man – and why?*

You cannot know what you should do until you know the nature of the universe you deal with, the nature of your means of cognition — and your own nature.

Rand also offers that *"ethics defines a code of values to guide man's choices and actions — that determine the course of his life. "* Who decides those values? How are they chosen? And that begs my question. Do you think that knowing how consciousness works would greatly assist in you making those choices, most especially if consciousness has governing laws?

*"Should man's primary concern be a quest for joy — or an escape from suffering? Should man hold self-fulfilment — or self-destruction — as the goal of his life? Should man pursue his values — or should he place the interests of others above his own? Should man seek happiness — or self-sacrifice?"*

Answers to those questions define an ethical code of values to guide one's choices and actions. Conscious knowledge will greatly assist in finding answers that will power your life with supreme confidence. Hence, the link between consciousness, natural law, and objective philosophy is specific.

The cognitive infant bypass (described in my *Conscious Ascendance* book) gifted by Nature's source creator for our benefit is the '*Natural law of Allowance*.' It obliges that we recognise and accept others' rights and ability to progress at their pace, according to their choices and skills, materially, ethically, morally, and spiritually. It also chastises our failure to do so. Nothing surpasses its spiritual invocation, personally and societally.

'Service corporations,' aka 'governments,' hold a knife to the throat of humanity to prolong the 'legal life' of the state, and we, like sheep, vote to sharpen it. Until we abolish artificial law, our right to life remains denied. We are fraudulently enslaved to fake legalities while their criminal enforcement of that condition hails as morally lawful. Conscious nescience is the (root) culprit once again.

When people grasp that 'values' drive full consciousness, they learn how 'spirit' interacts with itself in an objectified, life-enriching form, as Nature's source creator intended. That comprehension allows the knife at our throat to be driven through any evil that holds it, and without mercy! Therefore, ethics, morality, individual rights, and natural justice are essential learnings.

'Belief' is a grossly misunderstood concept. Properly understood, beliefs are mental propositions or proposals held in abeyance while they pass through examination, i.e., from possibilities, through probabilities, to specific knowledge, perhaps including falsity.

Beliefs are neither true nor false. No evidence offers, or people would call them, knowledge, not beliefs.

Such postulates should, therefore, pass through a process of investigation and inquiry. The belief then becomes knowledge or vanishes. It has served its purpose, much like a shopping trolly where the checkout confirms one's values. 'Truth' is what you take home because of the value it provides.

Very few people use the word 'knowledge' today because it allows them to say what they consider truthful while avoiding any charge of certainty. Certitude is not intolerance of another's beliefs, yet it is expected we apologise for certainty, to avoid offending someone's feelings.

Your teachers, the mystics of both schools, have reversed causality in their consciousness, then strive to reverse it in existence. They take their emotions as a cause, and their mind as a passive effect. They make their emotions their tool for perceiving reality. They hold their desires as an irreducible primary, as a fact superseding all facts. An honest man does not desire until he has identified the object of his desire. He says: *"It is, therefore I want it."* Others say: *"I want it, therefore it is."*

> *They want to cheat the axiom of existence and consciousness. They want their consciousness to be an instrument not of perceiving but of creating existence, and existence to be not the object but the subject of their consciousness—they want to be that God they created in their image and likeness, who creates a universe out of a void by means of an arbitrary whim. But reality is not to be cheated. What they achieve is the opposite of their desire. They want an omnipotent power over existence; instead, they lose the power of their consciousness. By refusing to know, they condemn themselves to the horror of a perpetual unknown. —Ayn Rand*

Actions affecting ourselves are primarily ethical (or unethical) since no one else is involved. Actions and behaviours that affect others are moral principally (or immoral). Aristotle reached similar conclusions. Ethics and morality are long separated, therefore.

Observably, as shown by the Value Transfer Wave diagram, the point at which we commit to action is where our ethical thoughts and considerations cease being private. (Those distinctions allow ethical and moral education to be formulated and taught across all curricula, from preparatory school onwards.)

Ethics deals with the means of determining a moral course of action. Our behaviour now affects others, thus demonstrating our morality. Our intentions and values transfer from our private domain of thought into society, open to public scrutiny. Since we are the author of our actions, we originate our morality or its lack and are fully accountable for both. Observably, ethics and morality are now stripped from the claws of vultures and restored to men and women where they rightfully and responsibly belong.

Initially, I thought writing a code of ethics based on my findings might be necessary if they lived up to my expectations. My greatest delight was comprehending that nature had already determined ethics to be a science and written it within human nature. Our individual task is to discover, understand, and live it. Nothing more is needed.

We each are a living, breathing, walking advertisement of our ethics and morality, not only as a visible image, but our ethical standing is emotionally (not energetically) transmitted by ourselves and received by others.

Morality is the enacted expression of one's ethical principles. Immorality, in contrast, manifests a lack or refusal of ethical considerations, a lack of moral discipline, or a lack of justness.

This comprehension suggests a science, or code of morality, describing how men and women should act and behave based on ethical principles respective of self and the lives of all others. Its premises are equally straightforward.

- **Precedence:** Morality is the (enacted) product of our ethical (or unethical) choices and intentions. Ethics harms no one but ourselves, while immorality harms others.
- **Virtues:** Virtues, attitudes, values, and developed character traits that foster and master our material and spiritual potential are the source of our enacted morality.
- **Respect:** Considered respect for others manifests an enacted morality entirely conducive to 'individual rights,' without which rights, morality, and respect vanish.
- **Justness:** Justness is the sum of just actions, a testament to our morality. Justness unto ourselves must manifest as justness unto others, or it is a

lie.

Such a code of morality would be independent of human opinion, rule, and authoritarian interpretation. Howls of protest would undoubtedly follow, for example, *"How on earth will immoral behaviour be arrested if we each are our moral governor?"*

The answer lies in the Natural Law of Just Consequence. Every instigator of an immoral action publicly confesses guilt through their action(s). One's immoral or unjust actions self-confess one's guilt and liability for remediation. Once guilt is proven, natural justice steps in to remediate established harm.

If this science, or code of morality, describes just actions and behavior, the makings of a life-based philosophy embedded in our human nature are sure. Tragically, these facts remain completely unrecognised due to ignorance of the conscious process.

Now consider the often repeated saying that *'service to others comes before service to self.'* Does it? We may choose to assist others, but that is not our moral duty. Your freely chosen, value-based ethics are a primary service to yourself. However, since ethical thoughts eventually manifest as moral actions, what first serves you ultimately becomes your service to others. You've morally shown what is possible and upheld other people's choice to emulate your achievements. 'Life values' are your ethics. From this understanding, *'self-service comes before service to others.'*

Many standard beliefs regarding morality are inverted thereby. Morality is not a social mandate. It is not 'collective.' We are accountable for our morality or lack thereof because we each are its author.

This discussion shows that free will, ethics, morality, and justice are all-encompassing. Our right to live is exclusively independent and immutable. Our life is what we are. Our singularity, beautiful uniqueness, and the natural order of our life ordain boundaries separating us from others. Each one's rights, words, deeds, works, and property are separate from another's and other things. Nothing could be simpler or more in tune with nature herself.

Today's *"rule of law"* purports to uphold (legal) respect for other 'persons,' but our conscious process relies on self-chosen values, not enforced rules or statutes. No system of rules can countermand. The principle purpose of morality is to instill respect for the moral order of individuals, not command / rule a collectivised society.

In fact, the confusion of law and morality is the critics' own. First, they subsume both the concept of law and the concept of a moral order under the concept of a system of rules, thereby obliterating in one go the logical distinctions between the lawful, the legal and the moral. Then they try to explicate the difference between 'law' and 'morality' in terms of some logically irrelevant characteristic such as the manner of enforcement of rules. Thus, they arrive at the conclusion, say, that while 'law' is an officially or legally recognised, applied and enforced system of rules, 'morality' is a system of rules without official or legal recognition, application or enforcement. That conclusion will not do.

> *It implies that a morality can become law overnight merely by being embraced and imposed by the powers that be—and that hardly is a solid basis for insisting on the difference between law and morality. On top of that, the critics also confuse 'natural law' and 'un-enforced morality', ending up with the proposition that natural law theories fail to distinguish between law (officially enforced rules of conduct) and morality (rules of conduct without official backing).— Frank van Dun.* [2]

Morality is the enactment of self-mastery that honours and ensures freedom for others. To that extent, it ensures our own freedom.

- **Ethics** are our (value-based) benchmark.
- **Justness and morality** are our social benchmark, the sum of just actions and testament of our morality.

So now we have an answer to the question — how can uniform moral uprightness be achieved if each chooses their own? As a collective, we cannot, as history has long proven, but as individuals, we each can. Everything in our nature and its governing laws urge that we should. We may consider the resultant implications by ascribing ethics to the thought process and morality to behaviour.

- **Ethics and morality** are removed from the (collective)' political domain' and placed squarely in the individual's 'private domain.'
- **Morality** demands our unalienable right to life and inalienable right to our property be fully protected from violation and usurpation. Such protection arbitrates just restoration when needed. Without individual rights, morality is unprotected.
- **Convivial society** results from moral actions in aggregate.
- **Independence**, one from another, enters with respect for each other.
- **Co-operation** amongst equals, or one's likes, results in mutual benefits.
- **Those who prize ethics and morality** as spiritual progenitors of life

relish these steering virtues because others learn to respect and unceasing justness from their joint dealings. Moral actions are the flip side of natural justice.

Do you see how a life-based philosophy develops from ethics and morality deriving from natural law inherent in the conscious process?

If so, be wary because there is a hidden trap. Traditional or commonly accepted ethical theory holds that the 'universe' has an in-built moral dimension considered as God's will and that it determines right from wrong. Considered far more profound and fundamental than private feelings, majority opinion, party dictates, or some despot's will, this moral law is believed to be a crucial facet of the nature of things, whereby it is binding on all men and women. And there lies a tremendous problem.

No one questions why beliefs, absent facts, should be binding! Throw in that every one of us is fallible purportedly, and it soon becomes apparent that a moral law that idealistically floats over our heads like a summer cloud is utterly worthless. It permits others to dictate ethics and morality, which, when authoritatively ruled, robs everyone of free will.

As already hinted, this widely held belief in inherent morality is the foundation of '*natural law theory,*' said to be the father of natural law. Yet, none of its theorists recognise that having a biased mind from birth entirely denies free will and morality.

Alternately, if we solicit the counsel of the most ethically advanced men and women, we find solid unanimity. All tell us that the right and the good can only be advanced by reason, by persuasion, by our free choice, and also by example. In other words, moral freedom can only result from conscious knowledge employing a philosophy of life embracing our respect for other people's right to do likewise. In short, personal liberty and a free society must be founded on consciousness, natural law, and objective philosophy, all authored by free will.

Natural law *theory* is thereby defunct, entirely replaced by intrinsic natural law as fact. It sustains and bolsters life, promoting morality and freeing us to accept or reject it, whereby free will is forbidden denial.

Of course, people may howl in protest. *"How on earth will immoral behaviour be arrested if we each morally govern ourselves?"* That's easy because everyone who commits an immoral action self-confesses guilt through their action(s). Once their trespass is proven, natural justice (lawfully) steps in, and the question vanishes. No judge must rule against them because they have already ruled against themselves.

Thus, with governmental prescriptions gone, a new definition of morality and its subset qualities becomes almost self-evident.

> ***Morality is the conscious will to live according to one's nature, never depriving others of the same opportunity.***

Briefly stated, 'actions and behaviour publicly testify our pre-conceived moral stature and confessed moral accountability.'

Morality does not prescribe natural law and never can it. Therefore, we are constrained to deal with the consequences of our actions, just as we are obligated to learn from our feelings.

That is how nature upholds our values, ethics, actions, and morality while preserving our free will. That inbuilt protection is what no authoritarian ruler will admit because their evil empire would collapse within hours!

For authoritarian tyrants and people like Rousseau, freedom is a danger to authoritarian rule by which they command our slave existence.

**Individuated morality**

Wrong behaviour must be legally prevented from occurring. Our legal system, senselessly built on that false premise, is now the source of gross injustice. Innocent people are punished for victimless crimes as though morally justifiable; all premised on the forbiddance of one's right to life, which is utterly immoral and unjust.

Fortunately, nature's 'Natural Law of No Trespass' is not open to debate or such idiotic consensus agreement. It is an immutable scientific fact of self that has existed since the advent of man not open to erasure. It is as though we are told by nature's source, *"I've perfected societal governing within your very self, precisely so that you may translate its Natural Laws into your societies."*

What is so beautiful is that spiritually-based ethics are none less than spiritual life values we put on autopilot. Do that, and our ethics are fundamentally automated, which subsequently puts our morality on autopilot as nature intends we should.

Observe how profound all of the above achievements are.

- False beliefs concerning ethics and morality overturn.
- All 'collectivised' jurisdictional claims over ethics and morality are invalidated.
- Authoritarian government abandons itself, permitting our self-governance under natural law.
- Present natural law theories, holding that morality determines natural

law, are inverted. Natural law now has a truthful vitality and factual grounding in our nature that no one ever suspected.

- Protective constitutional law now has teeth, not an unjustifiable invention, a reality no one can refute, deny, or erase!
- A life-based philosophy is enabled to build and manifest itself.

None of those natural laws are open to opinion or a majority vote. Neither are they founded on a concocted morality underpinning natural law theory, since that shatters everyone's free choice. Natural law arises from <u>what</u> Man is by nature, not <u>who</u> one is. Man's nature must be the foundation of a Nation's Constitution, not one's acclaimed or claimed degrees of achievement or virtues.

As free societies take form in ways you'd never imagined, a profound spiritual swelling will arise in your heart that words cannot describe. Full consciousness models a science or code of ethics devoted to nature's codes of conduct. That teaches men and women how to think of life values and life itself, respecting self and others.

As shown by the Value Transfer diagram, (cognitive) ethics sequentially precede (enacted) morality, that revelation of a societal model found right in the heart of our orderly conscious process monitored by natural law. Simply stated–

- **Ethics is personal.** It concerns our thoughts and intentions. Life demands our wilful choice to support and sustain it, never sacrificing its supreme value for anything less. Thoughts, desires, and goals that uphold one's life are ethical; those that do not are not.
- **Morality is social.** We manifest morality by our actions. Life implies that we never act to deprive another of their life or the means to support and sustain it. Actions that respectfully uphold the lives of others are moral; those that do not are not.

Ethics and morality are now stripped from the claws of vultures and restored to the hearts of men and women where they rightfully and responsibly belong. Nature's codes of conduct are ethical and moral intelligence.

'Life-values' fuel our ethics. People can upload these values to their subconscious mind (generally around fifteen in sum) for prioritisation.

Moral actions follow ethical choices, each being automatically appraised, adjudicated, and sentiently reported, rightfully and lawfully so. Responsibility, respect, and rights go hand in glove. Now, Natural law defines morality–

Morality is the conscious will to live according to one's nature, never depriving others of the same opportunity, as manifested by our (ethic-driven) actions.

All who dispute that individual rights are inherent within the born nature of every man, woman, and child renounce their own nature, thereby rendering all their claims or protests invalid and void from pronouncement. Every man, woman, and child is born (equal) into the jurisdiction of life, thereby having equal (unalienable) rights to live free from all incursion and trespass. Likewise, every man and woman has comparable (inalienable) rights to the fruits of their labours, to uphold and sustain their lives.

To protect other people's rights is to guarantee one's own. Criminals confess crimes by their harmful actions, whereby they convict themselves. Actions preserving other people's right to life assure our rights automatically. Actions violating other people's rights forfeit our rights automatically. Such actions confess that we are outlaws. Our actions may or may not serve 'justness' upon others. Thus, 'justness' is enacting one's morality, while unjustness is immorality. That is how natural justice works.

Respect for natural law makes forced compliance with statutes obsolete. Free societies may now protect life and the enjoyment of all living men, women, and children.

Justness defines how people should respect each other, while' justice' is a practice that remediates harmful actions and restoration of the natural social order.

Justice is imbued in our human nature, and respecting how it functions appropriately; criminal action determines the measure of just remediation.

'Natural law' gifted by our Creator is not revealed to us through religion. Natural law is not a set of rules or principles that help us live together peacefully as social creatures. Natural law is guidance, assistance, and direction that aids personal growth and societal peace.

Natural law governs the consequences of our actions after we have acted. Justice is remediation and restoration of justness, not punishment. When we act justly, we express justice in our actions. When we act unjustly, we convey our need to return to a just state, although not our desire.

Accordingly, as offenders, our harmful actions determine the degree of restorative justice. We establish its measure. Our actioned violation of nature itself determines remediation. Pre-determined rules, society, or justices do not.

'Natural justice' is the practice of remediating' injustice.' To that end, whoever victimises another voluntarily gives up their rights for correction, remediation, and compensation. This voluntary surrender remains until that crime or aggression is restoratively closed. That is the general principle of Natural Justice according to existential natural law.

Therefore, no legislature or judiciary of a free society can dictate what justice should be.

Courts must decide what outcome is just, or else it too is guilty of injustice. Court justices apply the orderly principles of man's nature to restore orderliness according to the evidence of disorderliness. Shared understanding between like cases (Case Law or Common law) does not and cannot formulate (authoritarian) rules of nature. Orderliness by nature is natural law. Manufactured rules are not.

So, the difference between 'justness' and 'justice' surfaces.

- Justness is (first) served by each man and woman, not interfering with or denying any other person their ability to live and sustain their life.
- Only innocent individuals (persons) are free. One found guilty of injustice, or unjustness is not a free individual independent of the victim. Accordingly–

Justice is maintained, not enforced. That statement is an impossible mental hurdle for most people. Why? Because they believe the exact opposite due to brainwashing. An injustice breaks no law. Trespassers choose to disrespect the law, thereby voluntarily ruling against themselves, which determines the extent of remedy and restoration of the natural order.

Today, procedural rules are formulated by the judiciary outside of courtrooms months or years before. But no more. No law-making or law enforcement applies in a free society. The only law that must be known, transparent, and specific is the 'natural law of no trespass.' No rulings apply now until a (natural law) case is proven.

A quick read through the twenty natural laws shows that only six apply to criminality and justice. Disrespect only serves to strengthen them. They cannot be retrospective because they exist in our nature at all times. They apply only to future actions, and only after that can they be adjudicated and applied. Victimless crimes cannot exist, therefore. Neither do courts need to prove alleged guilt if, by criminal actions, a trespasser has already proven it.

That core principle of natural justice permits the founding of convivial societies. When each living being is enabled to become self-responsible, each one is their self-regulator, having no prescription for others concerning their choice of religion, morals, politics, interests, ideals, fashions, or any other. A society where each can freely meet, engage, or depart, absent subordination and regulation, would result in the most perfect social order ever witnessed.

It works personally and the same way for society. Unless we justly and morally deliver to others, we violate our lives, which we professedly uphold. Thus, we hold our own life in contempt, as valueless, by which we confess the need for remediation.

Thus, a person who is not innocent cannot be considered in justice to be a free person and to belong only to himself. He must have done something or something must have happened that gave some other person a lawful claim to his person or deprived him of his standing as a person in the law (perhaps making him an outlaw that anybody can capture at will). If he belongs to any person at all, a non-innocent person must in any case also belong to some other person, if not to his victim or their successors, then to some artificial person such as 'society', who derive their right to punish him from the fact that he now belongs to them. While this fact does not exclude him from being a member of an autonomous collective, it does rule out that he is a sovereign person. , Frank van Dun

Morality shifts from a social convention to its proper place as the conveyor of justness originating from its fully accountable place within each (individual) living being.

**No one decides justice. It just is.**

Question. Could 'moral justness' be preemptively taught in the classrooms of seven-year-olds? Yes, whereby the need for courts of natural justice would greatly diminish. However, state rule will not vanish while human sciences ignore the natural laws of our being as though they are non-existent. It follows that when millions vote for benefits, comforts, and security to be legally extracted from others, as though such theft ensures a just and moral society, they have voted to be ruled and thus accountable for all the disorder, chaos, and violence that eventuates. Such people should not mourn any injustice because the immorality of rule is what they voted for.

Natural justice requires a properly independent judiciary forbidden influence by political leaders. Free societies will prohibit all bribes and corruption among the police and judiciary, or freedom is non-existent.

The discovery, refinement, and systematisation of objective (natural) rules, methods, and procedures are the province of jurisprudence as a rational discipline working out the details, conventions, and protocols for an operationally efficient justice system requires knowledge of the general principles of natural law, matched with the judicial dispensation of justice. All legal force is forbidden, whereby natural justice within a free (protectorate) society results.

A Protectorate society will necessarily establish an independent judiciary. Judges cannot be politically aligned since political persuasion is prohibited, this being an additional form of the people's protection. No Justice can strike down unconstitutional laws because none exist. Neither does any exploitation of minorities exist. No Justice can fear retribution by politicians because none exists, but they can fear the people should they rule people's protection is denied.

Now, you have personal freedom and your means to a free society, both driven by value-based consciousness authored by free will, backed by natural law, and guided by an objective philosophy.

## Individual Rights

The term 'Rights' is routed in knoledge of Intrinsic Natural Law. Rights are actions that uphold and protect all aspects of one's Integrity – Right and Moral actions needed to Preserve peace and harmonious coexistence of all life.

# Chapter 8

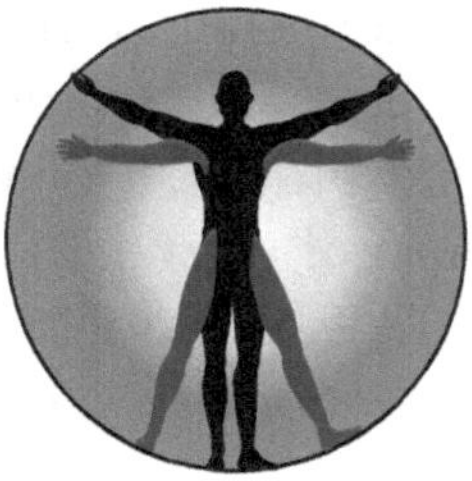

## Independence and Sovereignty

The separation of our conscious and subconscious minds highlights that individualism may still serve a common purpose, although we each are independent from one another. Independence means being singularly alive in body, mind, and spirit, and recognising that others are likewise blessed, despite their different focus in life. Like separateness is the natural order of the world.

Ayn Rand made independence very clear–

*We inherit the products of the thought of other men. We inherit the wheel. We make a cart. The cart becomes an automobile. The automobile becomes an airplane. But all through the process what we receive from others is only the end product of their thinking. The moving force is the creative faculty which takes this product as material, uses it and originates the next step. This creative faculty cannot be given or received, shared or borrowed. It belongs to single, individual men.*
*No man can give another the capacity to think. Yet that capacity is our only means of survival.*

Independence is fundamental to our biology, psychology, and praxeology – the study of human action and conduct. Independence is essential to our lives, thoughts, feelings, and actions.

Societal orderliness is the existence of many different and separate human beings, each living independently from all others without interference. Since there is no communal mental faculty falsely referred to as 'mass consciousness,' each of us can do, think, and say things independently and differently from others.

This separateness marks each one of us as an independent living human being.

Of course, people benefit from others in many ways. They succeed and benefit from passive or active cooperation with others, which cooperation can be given or withheld. It is not automatic, again implying our independent existence and individual personalities.

We each stand on the cusp of personal and societal change without precedent in human history. We have a glorious opportunity to entirely divorce from societal domination and control that has damnably beleaguered man's entire history.

Once we are sure of our independence, we can stop riding a collective life raft rotting from mental bankruptcy. The choice to be free is one we each must make. But first, we must know what that choice involves, how to exercise it, and how to protect it. From that understanding, we can reach out to others whenever and however we choose.

Solutions to private and public problems require thinking things through logically. We must reject what is unworkable or biased, while recognising that every mind functions independently, no matter how much it utilises information separately sourced by others. That independence is your power, yet that is what propagandists and collectivists wish to collapse or eliminate.

> *'Some people want to say that power is a neutral object that can be used for good or evil. That isn't true. Your deepest power is alive. It's personal. It's stunningly energetic and dynamic. It connects with your deepest understanding of what is true and good and right. But it never sacrifices itself on the altar of what others insist is good and true and right. It never deserts you for an abstract ideology someone else has devised. That ideology was formulated, in fact, to separate you from your power.' —Jon Rappoport*

Is that why no one is taught what full consciousness is? Your creative power is yours, individually and independently. The more you develop it, the less fear you will experience. Your powerful future, happiness, and freedom lies in your knowledge of consciousness, and in your ability to visualise using it to the full. Free individuals know that the greatest good comes from liberating all individuals to pursue their highest aspirations.

> *'The boughs of no two trees ever have the same arrangement. Nature always produces individuals; she never produces classes.' ~ Lydia Maria Child*

To walk through that door to human progress is to divorce oneself from the 'collective' mindset. It becomes evident that group or unity consciousness will not substitute for our nature or being because no such unified consciousness exists. Aggregate awareness can, as ball games amply testify.

The shift from emotional promptings to reasoning the value of life and making appropriate choices as adults is the difference between authoring our emotions versus being ruled by them. It is a tragedy that many people never make that transition, or they do so only in part. Conscious ignorance is the reason.

So, a new life-supporting wholeness emerges. Life is our only goal and purpose, contrary to almost all taught. Because 'society' is precious but remains upheld by senselessly destructive rules, it is now up to you and me to steer independence back on course. That is not the independence of one state from another, such as the (American) 1776 'Declaration of Independence.' Instead, it is your independence and mine from any state that violates our right to life

This choice to be free is one we each must make. Independence means being singularly alive in body, mind, and spirit. From that understanding, a whole new life-supporting perspective emerges. It begs a complete re-appraisal of psychology, psychiatry, philosophy, religion, politics, trade, society, competition, and cooperation. It challenges commonly held beliefs and throws authoritative government on the scrap heap. It even challenges the libertarian persuasion to reappraise their goals, also begging that we redefine justice based on the Natural Law of Allowance and the Natural Law of Just Consequence. Almost every precept ever taught is questionable!

All men and women have free choice to (ethically) know in advance of any action exactly what potential consequence will result. So people learn they are wholly accountable for it, mitigating circumstances accepted.

Our new Declaration of Independence will divorce us from the State, so let's explore its foundation and rationale.

First, we must attest that we live. Life is our hallmark. It substantiates that all who claim an opposing (legal) jurisdiction have voluntarily divorced from 'life' and willingly joined the club of (ineffectual) dead entities. Any ruler who chooses to relinquish their nature means we who do not are free from (their) 'rule by force' and widespread tyranny.

Next, the phrase 'consent of the governed' must be questioned absolutely! Why? Because governments that (forcibly) rule according to (statute) permissions (forcibly) rule our 'consent.' Mind-controlled brainwashing results. Remember what Francis Bacon said...

*"Nature, to be commanded, must be obeyed."*

Think about that. Nothing rules nature but itself ; neither does it issue commands to be obeyed. Nature is only to be 'respected,' and so long as we do, it respects us. Accordingly, *'consent of the governed'* is antithetical to free societies born of nature. Instead, (free) society derives from the free will of individuals who govern themselves as fully consented by their nature. And that 'consent' is universal. It is not democratic consent, nor the will of the majority, nor the will of so-called "elitists,' hence democracy is dead also. Self-governance is immutably inherent in what we are.

'Constitutional' natural law may now acquire indisputable power as granted by nature's source creator, strictly provided that 'unalienable rights,' freedoms, living identity, and 'natural justice' are upheld and forever protected. No better precedent exists than to be self-governed by what we each are. (Consider how that would impact the health industry, just for starters.)

We can keep suffering in ignorance — or wake up to a clarity of mind, self-mastery, and the wondrous lifestyle our nature intends. It's our choice! That choice also applies to the political realm.

So-called 'law' in today's world is artificial and enforced, which necessarily rejects the natural laws of our nature. All such administrations are immoral, if not criminally corrupt – witness' legal positivism,' political correctness, censorship, statute law, controlled mass media, propaganda as education, and religious indoctrination. Additional corruption arises from every legal abomination proposing, legislating, or coercing that your mind is inferior to some other intellectual or spiritual dominion, authority, deity, or new-age mystic.

It is not that governments and gurus don't trust people to read, think, or judge for themselves. They insist you never learn because your comprehension would destroy their authority and plunder their domination and control, thereby exposing all their evil secrets and corruption for all to see.

Few people perceive any means to overcome such legal oppression, slavery, tyranny, and unceasing war because people have no knowledge a remedy even exists. Non-discovery of truthful knowledge forbids (conscious) understanding and, therefore, active use of mental processes that would discover the natural laws of our existence.

A new action dynamic is urgently needed rather than a tacit agreement. People need to gain a new mindset via full consciousness to understand our subconscious functioning and its natural laws, ethics, morality, and justice. Do that, and a new sociological and political foundation emerges, one more ethical and moral than any employed in the past. It is time to paraphrase Thomas Jefferson's words–

> *"If a nation expects to be knowledgable and free, in a state of civilisation, it expects what should be and protects it."*

A revolutionary turn-around of this magnitude is unprecedented, but it is ours for the knowledge and willpower to achieve it! Full consciousness and its natural laws are our passport to humanity's glorious future. Nothing less will suffice!

Globally, society has succumbed to centuries of inept or evil philosophies to the point of coercive rule, further degenerating to authoritarian rule enforced by incorporated bodies as though legitimate government.

> *Evil uses the authority principle to condition people to obey without questioning what, why or whom they are obeying. Destroying your identity to gain power over you is the modus operandi of evil. — Jeremy Locke*

Service corporations (as today's governments) can never defend freedom when some people are deprived or overruled to benefit others. It remains that when people turn their attention to the study of Man and the natural laws of self-governance, only then will they sense the simplicity and beauty of creation denied their understanding for centuries. Only then will they realise the impossibility of any government.

In a letter to Stephen Grover Cleveland, the 22nd and 24th President of the United States, Lysander Spooner chastened the President by writing–

> *"For the reasons now given, the simple maintenance of justice, or natural law, is plainly the one and only purpose for which any coercive power --- or anything bearing the name of government --- has a right to exist.*
>
> *It is intrinsically just as false, absurd, ludicrous, and ridiculous to say that lawmakers, so-called, can invent and make any laws, of their*

*own, authoritatively fixing, or declaring, the rights of individuals, or that shall be in any manner authoritative or obligatory upon individuals, or that individuals may rightfully be compelled to obey, as it would be to say that they can invent and make such mathematics, chemistry, physiology, or other sciences, as they see fit, and rightfully compel individuals to conform all their actions to them, instead of conforming them to the mathematics, chemistry, physiology, or other sciences of nature.*

*Lawmakers, as they call themselves, might just as well claim the right to abolish, by statute, the natural law of gravitation, the natural laws of light, heat, and electricity, and all the other natural laws of matter and mind, and institute laws of their own in the place of them, and compel conformity to them, as to claim the right to set aside the natural law of justice, and compel obedience to such other laws as they may see fit to manufacture, and set up in its stead." —Lysander Spooner*

There is no excuse for the continuity of 'lawmakers" when the Laws of Creation have so long existed, and neither is there any excuse for not discovering these 'natural laws.' Meanwhile, far too many people believe that the government exists to ensure liberty or that the government is a benevolent provider of benefits. Look for your own sake and your children's sake.

Those who would give up essential Liberty, to purchase a little temporary Safety, deserve neither Liberty nor Safety. —Benjamin Franklin

The most precious question is, can we institute a different and more functional future for all humankind and protect it from ever defaulting back to the rules of the past since all failed abysmally? Can we free ourselves from patriarchal powers and so-called elites and govern ourselves individually? Can we free society from vicious competition at all levels, from calamity and self-destruction, by awakening to what will forever forbid the chronic mental and emotional environment that produced such perversion?

The answer is most affirmatively yes!

**Protection is the missing link.**

Henry David Thoreau said, *'There are a thousand hacking at the branches of evil to one who is striking at the root.'* Although many more people do so today, how many consider freedom's protection from usurpation, violation, or destruction? Isn't that the real issue?

Philosophy should be the guiding light of consciousness research and inquiry, but no one has examined consciousness beyond a science lab for decades if not centuries. Instead, save for 'objectivism,' all thought is given to reinforcing (insane) state dominance, aka 'statism.'

There are two reasons. First is that (mainstream) philosophy long ago lulled us all into thinking that nothing more was to be learned, whereby mental science stalled in its tracks. Second, authoritarian rulers will never replace their slave force of victims with knowledgeable, thinking, constructive, and loving people. Sociopathic rulers benefit considerably from anxiety, chaos, discord, tyranny, and wars, all demanding more control, force, and larger armies, even to carry the battle into space.

Justifiably reclaiming our unalienable right to life makes our rights imperative to be held in perpetuity with no loopholes. Leave that gate open, and all loose!

Unless all who are created equal unequivocally ensure their right to life and their unalienable right so to do – against all cancellation, violation, or usurpation – they will have neither rights nor freedom.

We are all born 'alive,' so by attesting that we 'live,' our divorce from dead (legal) entities is automatic; divorced from authoritarian tyrants who voluntarily rejected 'life' in favour of a legal jurisdiction that certifies death. They wilfully rejected lawful behaviour for outlaw behaviour, then legalised it.

We must clearly state our independence from all states that fraudulently sanction or enforce death (contracts) as a prerequisite of individual governance. Further, we must say that as volitionally conscious living beings, we refuse to act for fictional legal entities that are dead. Consider this introductory text–

> *I am flesh and blood, of free will, an Independent Living Being (ILB) in body, mind and soul; my freedoms drawn about me by the equal rights of all others. My first breath invoked source creator's endowment of unalienable right to my life and inalienable right to the property of my efforts, every exception and trespass forbidden by Creator's natural laws encrypted in my living nature.*

Now, dissect that text and consider what it means.

First, observe that the initial two words,' *I am,*' irrefutably state that my nature is intrinsic and immutable. Thus, all 'statutes' or 'legal constructs' that construe differently or attempt to overrule and negate that fact are invalid, fallacious, non-binding, unenforceable, and void from inception, directly violating our very being.

Next, the phrase' flesh and blood' states precisely what 'I am.'

'Free will' follows naturally since volitional consciousness separates men and women from all other life forms on earth. Dead legal entities are emphatically and automatically excluded. Freedom must indeed be drawn about me by the equal rights of all others since I am one of all those others. Freedom for one is freedom for all, and vice versa.

Consequently,' independence' from all legal jurisdictions is indisputably established. All animals are excluded by nature, including the (phrase) 'unborn young of animals,' which banks fraudulently claim as chattel, also that governments utilise to 'legally' claim a child before legal (birth certificate) registration.

The phrase,' Independent Living Being (ILB) in body, mind and soul' establishes 'independence' unequivocally since no dead legal entity possesses a body, mind, or soul!

Now consider the phrase, 'my first breath.' An infant's cry in its first breath is the only means it possesses to state its independent life in that instant indisputably. Nature's unalienable right to an independent life is instantly endowed, simultaneous with the inalienable right to the property of the infant's (later) efforts. Since 'mother dependence' instantaneously becomes 'infant independence,' no opportunity window permits government usurpation of this process. Neither can it 'register' an infant before being born because no independent life exists prior. Once separated from its mother, an infant instantly becomes wholly reliant on the natural laws of its nature, irrespective of the need for nurture. Its right to life is inherent, immutable, and never to be broken, infringed, violated, or dishonoured. Perhaps now you will better understand what Jesus meant by saying, *"I am the way, the truth, and the life."* ( John 14:6)

It follows that 'every exception and trespass' is not forbidden by your will or mine, or by our wilful consent, but by nature's law of identity encrypted within each of us. Identity also preserves free will, which indisputably means that all violations of free will are lawfully forbidden. Most importantly, any dispute concerning one's right to life is a matter for our nature's source creator, not for a court of law.

Do you now see the full impact of that introductory text? It means that sociopathic authorities have voluntarily chosen to vacate the 'jurisdiction of life' and legislatively certified that condition. Being pro-life, we do not consent to relinquish our lives. Thus, we declare our independence from all who do — all (voluntary) fictional legal entities which comprise the state.

Accordingly, your and my independence from all state legality fully accords with their choice to abandon life. They chose to divorce from life voluntarily, then legislatively certified their actions unequivocally! They divorced from all independent living beings who attest to their living identity. They abandoned 'life,' the present state of human society, and as ample proof, they've voluntarily rendered all their legislations invalid from inception.

Now, let's put words to paper and write our personal independence document.

**Private Declaration of Independence**

*When, in the Course of human events, it becomes necessary for one people to dissolve the political bands that have connected them with another and to assume among the powers of the Earth the separate and equal station to which the Laws of Nature and Nature's God entitle them, a healthy respect for their immutably endowed life-nature requires that they should declare the causes which impel them to the separation.*

*Self-evident truth holds all Men are created equal in nature while unique in expression, endowed by their nature with immutable and unalienable rights to life, liberty, and the pursuit of happiness. To secure these rights, lawful instrumentalities are instituted among Men, deriving just powers from their unalienable individual right to life and freedom and unobstructed action drawn about each by the equal rights of all others.*

*In ignorance of natural law facts, false and misleading theologies, ideologies, and philosophies have hidden, perverted, misconstrued, and overruled nature's laws and Man's right to life as though non-existent. Forbidden redress by legal artifice, corruption, and criminality in defiance of a free people, all Men are criminally forced to uphold bloody-minded tyranny as the only liberty possible! Men, blinded, deluded, and deceived, are branded as social animals and enslaved to political society with no disclosure. When injuries, violence, and usurpations consistently repeat for the direct object of tyranny as the 'moral right to rule' and 'immoral wrong to refuse rule'; when fraudulent legislations constrain men and women contrary to their nature by the fictional or covert invention; when criminal abuse, usurpations, and violation of Man's right to life reduce existence to animal-like status under absolute despotism, cessation of such insufferable and criminal evil is demanded forthwith.*

*Accepting equality and individual station entitled by the laws of nature, it is now each man and woman's unalienable right, indeed their duty as living beings, to abolish all statute legislations and divorce from criminally unjust legal authority entirely. Each and all people of Earth are impelled to determine complete separation and independence from all (state) power and rule backed by force and to seek, institute, and secure new protections in perpetuity, deriving their just powers solely from within the laws of nature and nature's God, all else excluded.*

*In complete absolution of criminal violation of Man's right to life, let the (natural) laws of nature and Nature's God be openly submitted to a candid world for the lawful upholding of human life. Natural law (Law) is the natural order of human beings capable of rational, purposive action, speech, and thought, the natural order of the human world expressing method, system, process, order, equality, and uniqueness, all inviting of free choice within free and cooperative rightful action.*

*All Homo sapiens men, women, and children possess like faculties, governed thought processes in union with certain free expression, independent free will thoughts, irrefutably testifying all living beings equally, independently free, and by nature complete, humankind their aggregation, not collection. Independent faculty is guaranteed, including individual responsibility, liability, and accountability; actioned consequences are inescapable. Respect for the lives of others reciprocally ensures one's own, never sacrificing life's supreme value for anything less.*

*Individual right to life is the unalienable right to the action of living, the faculties of movement, feeling, thought, and speech, without confiscating or violating the unalienable rights of any other.*

*Where the rights of all others are respected, no one can offend by any application of his own. The right to act in support of life is unalienable; the right to the product of one's efforts is inalienable. Individual rights preside over all other life forms, thereby denying collective 'human' rights.*

*To secure the specific unalienable right to life, unless all men are created equal, unequivocally protect their right to life and their unalienable right, so to do against all violation, cancellation, or usurpation, they will have neither. Therefore, no authority is granted to any individual to command another. Likewise, all commandments are refused; no man or woman is a human agent. No legal or other instrument may preside contrary. All thoughts and intentions are self-contained, unable to violate another's right to life or property.*

*Conversely, (proven) actions and behaviour that violate another's right to life publicly confess immorality, immoral action(s), and trespass of natural law. Fraud, blackmail, rape, theft, and murder do not occur accidentally. Actioned trespass of natural law admits to its lawful cessation, the transgressor's agreement to remediate harm and endure restoration respectful of that transgression. Criminal action forfeits freedom, whereby the victim remedially acquires rightful justice.*

*Natural justice binds. Because free society and natural law are co-dependent, unless each guarantees non-violation of the other, both vanish. Natural laws of perfected self-governing are the 'separate and equal station to which the laws of nature and nature's God entitle each man and woman.' Modelled for verbatim transfer into Man's societies, so decent respect for natural law declares separation from all contrary, singularly all men and women from the state, natural laws of proven and perfected societal governing commissioned forthwith.*

*By nature thus endowed, we do, with complete rectitude, solemnly publish and declare that all men and women are by their nature and life, unequivocally and eternally free from all artificial order; all men and women free from state authority, no dispute save to 'nature or nature's God.'*

*With firm and resolute reliance on the steadfast integrity and protection of Source, I now pledge my sacred honour to my fellow men and women within my immutable right to life and its protections; this document is my humble, solemn, private Declaration of Independence.*

*Autograph*______________________*this* ____*day of* _________ ___

*Witness* ______________________*this* ____ *day of* _________ ____

Now, we each have the wings to transform our lives beyond measure, thence to robustly transform society into what it should always have been. Philosophical objectivity, founded on the supreme value of life, is the only means to uplift human society to a (life-value-based) spiritual plane never dreamt of in human history.

The (above) Private Declaration of Independence should not be used aggressively or in confrontation. Its purpose is strictly educational, expressly to enlighten people about their choices in life and about natural law simplicity, truthfulness, elegance, and foundation in nature.

Your life belongs to you. Your joy in this world is to live it and to thrive! Grasp the vital importance of those words, declare your independence, and then, as more people do likewise, indifference to positivism will begin taking effect and reach the tipping point where a free society will follow.

Some say true sovereigns must dutifully and carefully educate others so they can eventually be sovereigns in their own right. That is a noble thought, but 'duty' is a mind trap open to authoritarian misuse.

For example, from a social point of view, it is commonly believed that a 'sovereign' being influences society or civilisation via a claim of authority or monarchical position. In wielding power to command or govern large groups of people, these (so-called) 'sovereigns' often use genealogies to assert they have a 'divine right to rule.' Often, they trace their lineage to some historical figure, such as Jesus, Mohammad, or David, but no such right to rule exists.

Self-mastery is not rule over others. It is one's acceptance of responsibility and liability for one's actions. It requires dedication, like mastering painting or the piano, where one mistake can ruin a whole composition. Thus, self-mastered individuals consistently reflect on their own experiences to see what can be improved and how their mastery can develop. That is precisely our blessings of conscience and emotions.

Once grasped that self-mastered autonomy is a philosophy of life and its outcome, one infraction or mistake is not dishonour, provided one takes steps to correct it. Infallibility is not required; no perfection is demanded. Rather an exemplary attitude toward life, a spiritual mindedness resulting in ethical thought, just actions and behaviour, including a decisive willingness to correct errors. We learn through mistakes. Self-mastery also embraces volunteered acts of restitution.

These masters of life seek knowledge and wisdom so they can be the best they can be in any situation. They learn to live in a way that honours their power to cultivate happiness, inner peace and graceful strength. Self-masterful autonomy and natural law are life partners. Life is its success. Nothing compares.

These people go beyond emotional resonance and blind faith. They seek truth. They ask hard questions to support their goals with crucial knowledge and understanding. So, they gain increasing competence and satisfaction through work, self-reflection, and self-discipline. They learn to develop their powers to cultivate happiness, inner peace, humility, and graceful strength.

Once we learn and practice the laws of nature, the struggle vanishes. Cultivation of self-mastery is life, and our means are gifted. Such is a lifelong pursuit, measured by definitive markers of progress and increasing degrees of competence, skill, and benevolent power. Time is not essential. One's attitude is, as the 'natural law of allowance' so beautifully provides.

One's culture, or birthright, might help make someone influential, but that is not self-mastered autonomy. One's status must be validated by what one does with natural-born talents to develop self-mastery. By their success, they must act with honour in defending the right of all people to self-develop likewise.

These people lead others into more significant states of freedom by their example. That is their badge of honour. None else is needed. It remains that if we each develop self-mastery and autonomy, government theft of our rights would be rendered obsolete in short order.

What happens if we decline mental effort by thinking that others know better because they've studied history, social sciences, or philosophy and we haven't? Look around you for that answer. When we refuse to take charge of our lives, governments swoop in to assert their (false) sovereign status and claim of authority. And with that assumed power to control your life, they do all necessary to topple all challenges. When we allow governments to legitimize 'sovereign status,' which is impossible for any 'collective,' we forfeit all claims to our lives. So, we give up love, truth, freedom, justice, and prosperity. We sacrifice our lives and efforts, including any means of reclamation and redemption.

We can blame our human sciences, who have disregarded our individual and independent nature and substituted societal presumptions in their place. Ethics and morality have suffered. Metaphysics has suffered, and so has the science of psycho-epistemology.

Our inability to be responsible, sane, rational, and compassionate people is all that governments need to assert their claims of authority and fraudulent sovereign status. If we admit their 'sovereignty' is valid, we relinquish our self-mastery, thereby forfeiting all claim to our lives. Does that explain why the term sovereign has been marginalised, diluted, and struck from our grasp? Do not be fooled by those trying to convince you that you're already 'sovereign' because you are alive. No one is made sovereign by any verbal claim or written document.

The nature of your character and being is the only tool by which you can master yourself. But unless you use that tool and conduct yourself in the manner nature's source creator intended, no self-mastered autonomous being will emerge.

Such knowledge is more than grasping our power to think for ourselves, to discern truth from disinformation, and to stand firm for what we know is right. We must also understand the reality of our nature and that its graciousness permits no compromise.

Magnificent personal achievement and unparalleled success are infinite within that natural border but are smashed by us allowing border trespass. That is precisely why the natural laws within our nature define life values and why both define an objective philosophy for their usage.

Nature's will is natural governance. Life prescribes that we uphold it through free will and to be the best we can be. Here lies the source of justness, inwardly to ourselves and later broadcast to the world as our morality. Spiritually based ethics are no less than spiritual life values on autopilot, as previously described. To employ life values is to use ethics. To put those values on autopilot effectively puts our morality on autopilot.

Once we grasp that the (natural law) principles of ethics, morality, and natural justice reside in the core of our conscience and emotional reporting systems, we see nature's recipe for personal freedom and the means for free organic societies, meaning self-governance within natural law.

Freedom has long been under assault. When rebranded by governments, political persuasions, and various social engineering programs, the word sovereignty is nothing more than a childish desire by a rabble of irresponsible people who prefer to ignore laws and do whatever they please. Nothing could be further from the truth, besides which no such thing is possible. The natural law of just consequence forbids it. We reap what we sow.

Similarly, the word 'sovereign' has been conceptually stolen to the point where it means nothing without a specific definition relating to individual living men and women. Law books and law dictionaries are equally worthless. Fierce debate emerges concerning the word 'sovereign' versus the word 'suveran,' and yet there is no consensus on an exact definition of self-sovereign identity (SSI). Neither does autonomy suffice. The best means of avoiding this rabbit hole is to use the term 'Self Mastered Autonomy' (SMA) since it conveys the outcome of freedom resulting from natural law and objective philosophy. Such is not claimable by default. It is not automatic, neither does it pretend or claim nobility. Instead, it requires upholding the truth of our nature and practicing its laws, thus keeping others' rights to exercise the same rules for their benefit and protection. Sovereignty is not a title or entitlement. It is not titles that we seek. Life is our goal, not acclamations, certificates of achievement, or nobility status.

Individual sovereignty – (no other kind exists) – is a mental, emotional, and spiritual code of practice founded on life values, respect for natural law, and (life) exercised through objective philosophical practice. It is earned through mental application, diligence, and discipline, resulting in ethics and morality — living a masterly fulfilling life by choice. What more is needed? A badge? A title? A certificate? Public recognition? Admission to the hall of fame?

Grasp the concept of Self mastered autonomy in that light, and all its other interpretations will vanish. You will become a master of your own destiny, one who assists in implementing true justice as an instrument of light in the world.

**Sovereignty**

Sovereignty is an ethical mind engaging in moral actions – applying life values such as diligence, discipline, respect, and integrity in harmony with innate natural law in practical, moral, and spiritual thriving.
Skills of personal excellence, spiritual accomplishment, and emotional rewards testify advancement – joy and happiness blossom.

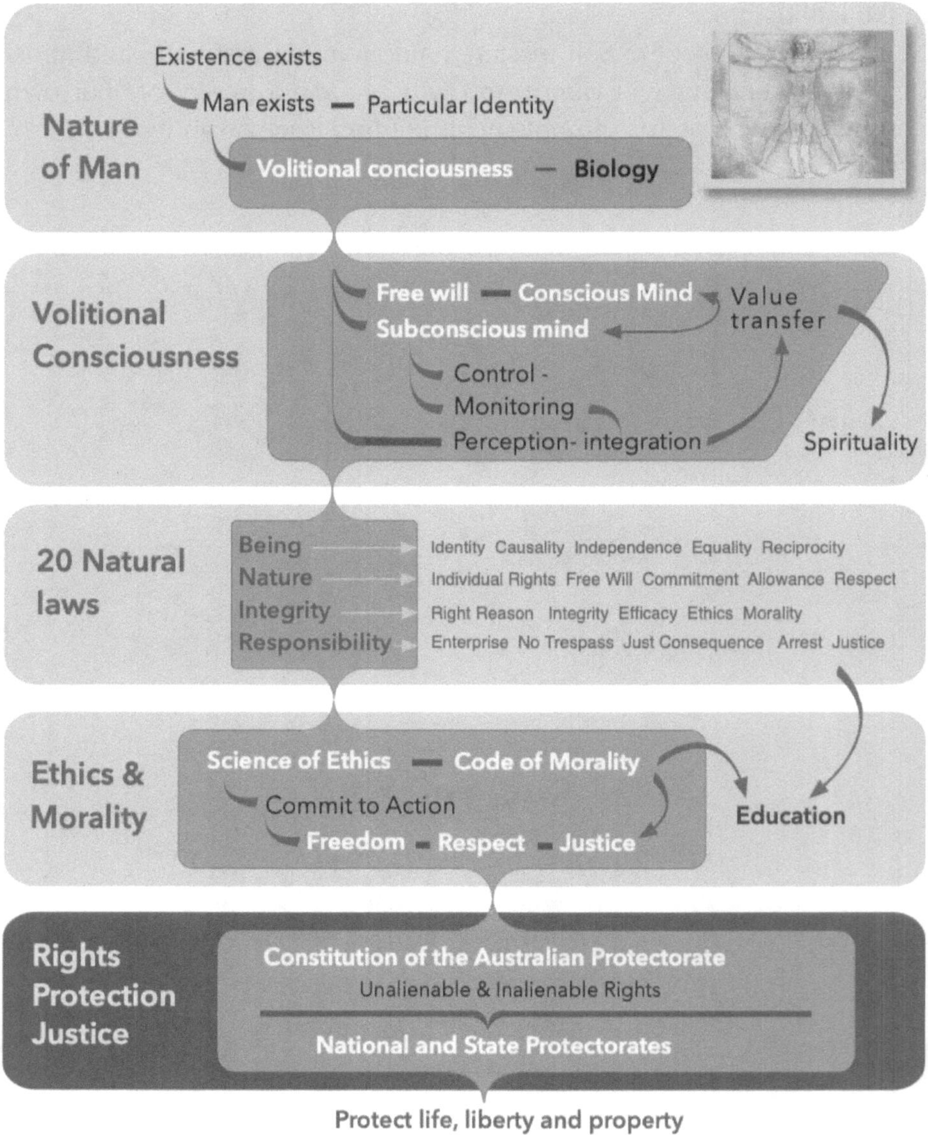


Australia as a Free Nation

10. Nature'sProvidence

# Chapter 9

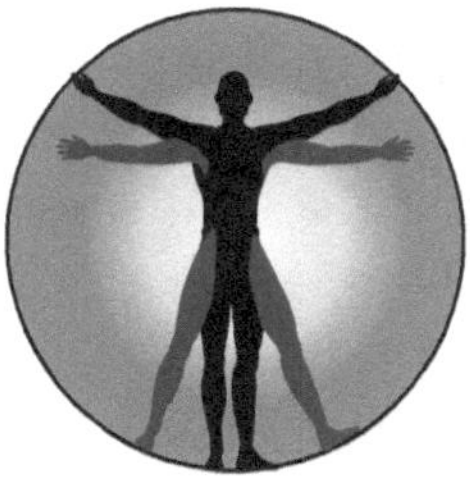

## Overture to Natural law

Mention the term 'natural law' among the few who've heard it before, and most will think of it as a more humane or gentler way to rule society. It is no such thing, just as the law of gravity or thermodynamics does no such thing. Natural law is nature's gift to man, assisting us to thrive and prosper in peace and harmony, in full accord with our human nature. It governs the consequences of our actions, just as we thrive on nutritious food and suffer from toxic food while having the freedom to eat what we choose with no prescription whatsoever.

Our biology shows logical patterns, internal order, unity, interdependence, interoperability, harmony, communication, maintenance, remediation, systematisation, and sequence. Similar functionalities govern the conscious process but not its content. The word' law' refers to' orderliness' and 'bonded unity' – natural law inherent in human nature. It is factual, therefore, not theory.

As mentioned, natural law issues no commands and accepts none, much like the laws of gravity and physics, biology, geology, etc., that control the physical and biological world (and universe). As revealed by human biology and consciousness, natural laws are our benefactors. From that brief description, we can now define natural law.

**Natural law is the set of universal, eternal, and immutable conditions governing behavioural consequences of volitionally conscious beings. Without respect for these precepts inherent in man's nature, preserving society's peace and happiness is impossible.**

Fourteen of the (twenty) natural laws are for your considerable personal benefit. Three are to prevent your train from falling off the rails, and three exist to put it back should it fall off. As such, they are to be deeply respected and loved, not shot to bits by tyrannical parasites or hidden from public view by conscious ignorance. Therefore, they should adequately appear in all educational curricula across all levels for personal benefit. In societal terms, they should be a fundamental prerequisite to anyone holding public office of any kind.

**Lex vs. ius**

The word 'law' was initially translated from the Latin word 'Lex,' which originated from commanding the mobilisation of armies. Today, 'Lex' refers to authoritative commands backed by physical force, whereby all statutes, falsely called law, originate from the word Lex.

Fortunately, 'law' is also translated from the Latin word' Ius,' which refers to "a solemn bond between two people," effectively an orderly agreement. Thus, 'ius' means 'orderliness' and preserving its governance innately within our nature; accordingly, Ius Naturale' (Latin) means 'natural law.'

Notwithstanding, the Source creator tasked natural governing laws within our bodies and minds to uphold life and protect us from all harm, trespass, and violence. Thus, they preserve the creative bond between our desires, values, and actions. From etymology, that 'bond,' or 'orderliness' is the Latin word' Ius,' which, within our conscious nature, is the Latin) term' Ius Naturale,' being 'natural law.'

Frank van Dun, a law philosopher, explains that from etymology, the word 'law' means 'order,' whereby orderliness (not commandments), within our biological and psychological nature, is 'natural law' exactly.

- Let's explore the idea of a solemn bond between two people.
- No cell, tissue, organ, or mental faculty instructs, commands, or orders another.
- Our hearts and lungs bond together to preserve our lives and our choices. So do our two minds.
- Our bodies and minds have governing laws that preserve natural orderliness.
- Cooperation and collaboration are mutual.
- A solemn bond refers to an orderly agreement, meaning" orderliness." This bond exists between the separate parts – to uphold and sustain life. As such, it denies or forbids any forced intervention or trespass.

Because all initiated force is outlawed, 'Lex' can play no part whatsoever, whereby (ius naturale) natural law is now all that remains.

Correspondingly, as van Dun confirms, "**law is natural law and nothing else.**"

> *The word 'law' denotes order: law is an order of things. Accordingly, the term 'natural law' denotes a natural order of things. 'Law' also connotes respectability: law is an order of things that people ought to respect. A natural law theory, in so far as it concerns human affairs, attempts to explain both what the natural law of the human world is and why and how we ought to respect it. However, whether, why and how we ought to respect the natural law are questions that we cannot address sensibly before we have a clear idea of what the natural law is. — Frank van Dun*

Therefore, speaking as physicists, chemists, biologists, astronomers, geologists, and practitioners of other natural sciences about different sorts of objects and phenomena is meaningful. These disciplines try to discover and eventually explain patterns of order (natural laws) within their chosen fields. They focus on the biological interactions of particles, atoms, molecules, physical states, cells, organs, and bodily systems as correctly as they should. But because natural laws of the human world relate to (spiritual) life values, our focus must be Life; philosophical guidance from ethics, morality, and justice inherent in the natural order of individual human beings, much more than physicality.

Without the cooperation of our systems and faculties and the independence of each, we could not function at all. We could not live. Most importantly, none of these laws command our free will. Orderly governance shows us that nature's source creator has modeled a free, peace-loving society within every man, woman, and child. We each function as a whole, while the individuality of each constituent member, every cell and body organ, is preserved.

From this, we learn how to write a country's constitution. Natural law cannot prescribe our actions in advance; otherwise, no free will could exist. It follows that natural laws govern the consequences of our actions and behaviour. Our feelings then report how objectively we have determined our life values, ethics, and morality in support of life's necessities and human spirituality. All authoritarian rule is a trespass of our nature, no matter how limited a government might claim to be.

'Order,' in this sense, means to structure in an orderly fashion. When one system induces the functions of others, there is a pattern, an orderliness of interconnectedness and interoperability. Such laws define what is completing or perfective of us, according to what we are by nature — rather than who we are.

These truths enable mental efficacy, freedom, creative ability, and emotional and spiritual joy to skyrocket while stress diminishes to near nil. Because natural law exists to uphold life, not the state, actions that respect natural law uphold life objectively and serve justice. Actions that do not are unlawful and unjust, mitigating circumstances admitted. Thus, natural law is inherent, not written by us or for us, as legislations or statutes to be (forcibly) complied with.

Visualise that same thriving ability within all peoples, and you'll see that expansive freedom, joy, peace, harmony, and spiritual attainment are global. 'Collectivism' is denied, while collaboration and cooperation are reinforced. Natural law is unquestionably established and factual, entirely objective of life itself.

When human affairs are in order, no person can hide responsibility for what they said, did, or brought about. Such orderliness implies that Jurors can easily trace words, works, and actions to their authors. No confusion among different individuals arises. The authors themselves bear actions that affect others.

As a result, there is no confusion as to who is innocent or guilty of a crime or owes a debt to one who was or was not a participant in some particular undertaking or practice. Whoever participated voluntarily is clearly distinguished from someone forced or tricked to participate, which exchanges were concluded via mutual consent and which were not, and so forth.

It follows that each innocent individual is separated from the threat of harmful actions from others, thereby enjoying their lives and property within peaceful, friendly relations. 'To each his own' is, therefore, the defining characteristic of law.

Respect is necessary to maintain that order, whereby respect for justice is the guiding principle of human action and interaction. That respect includes private property and the will to avoid causing physical damage to another person or their work. Equally, to honor lawful contracts and provide full restitution or compensation to those to whom one has caused unlawful harm. Additionally, those people will not hinder others who seek lawful remedies for criminal wrongs done to themselves or others.

Such orderliness first requires that different and separate persons be alike in their freedom; in particular, they are free in their independent actions, speech, and thoughts, thus rationally communicating their thoughts, intentions, and expectations to one another.

That is what our human conscious process does. Not only do its natural laws uphold such freedom, but its inherent philosophical principles invoke the same moral enactments. Individual people can respect the natural order, fail or refuse to do so, but regardless, the natural order will persist anyway because it is what life is.

Now, extend that principle to the social order. Unless natural law morality is respected, if not enough people follow or respect the invocations that define it, the social order will vanish, and disorder will prevail for centuries.

Once our behaviour is not enforced by officialdom, nothing prevents us from acting in orderly and predictable ways as imparted (but not forced) by the obligations inherent in our nature. Social orderliness prevails, cooperation likewise, first locally, then statewide, then nationally, then globally. Markets become international as the world transitions from dog-eat-dog competition to brotherly and sisterly cooperation.

Interpersonal relationships in free societies do not grant people more latitude; instead, denial of people's (born) latitude cancels. Free individuals can do almost anything within the same rights as all others, rather than being subjected to and bound by authoritarian permissions.

Authoritarian society depends on the limited wisdom of a few, while free organic societies foster the understanding of multitudes.

Frank van Dun makes matters very clear.

*The natural law of the human world is not a legal system. It appears that we must get away from the prevailing conception of law as a legal system, if we want to study and discuss the natural law of the human world. We have to get rid of those elements that properly belong only to the sphere of legal phenomena and not to the sphere of lawful phenomena. In short, to get a pure concept of law we have to separate the legal from the lawful, legality from lawfulness. Law is not a prescription telling us, how we ought to behave . Law is a natural fact, and law is natural law and nothing else."*

Albert Einstein also informed us...

*"The harmony of natural law reveals an intelligence of such superiority that compared with it, all the thinking and acting of human beings is an utterly insignificant reflection." — Albert Einstein.*

**Natural law is a superior intelligence**! The stakes have never been higher because Natural law *'theory'* is now shown to be false. Intrinsic natural law is factually authentic and protected from erasure, its potency magnified beyond measure, all thanks to full consciousness that invokes an objective approach to life.

It makes perfect sense that our mental faculties uphold life like our bodily systems work. Indeed, it becomes self-evident that our (whole) 'conscious process' must be objectively governed by our freely chosen values. In computer parlance, our life-conscious process is the hardware, courtesy of nature, while we write the software independently, courtesy of free will.

To judge whether some action or relationship is lawful, we should not focus on what people should do according to some moral or legal code but on the life-objective boundaries among individuals. When our actions outwardly manifest honesty and integrity found within, without which our mental and bodily life could not exist, the orderliness and morality of our societal structures will correspond. Self-protection is an immutable principle, not subject to differences of opinion, majority decision, or any arbitrary decree of society.

Nature invokes us to instrument our societies in spiritual accordance with the same integrity of purpose that upholds our lives as independent beings. Integrity, lawfulness, and justice are the foundations of societal natural law, as they are the respectful expression and manifestation of life itself: our body, mind, and soul.

Can these 'patterns of the natural order,' these 'Natural Laws' be established, authenticated, and validated as immutable and innate within each man, woman, and child? Yes, most assuredly. Because 'Intrinsic natural law' must be used in any attempt to deny it, it is axiomatically authenticated and validated. We cannot escape it. Natural law oversees our immune system, indeed, all our bodily systems. Moreover, our endocrine system mimics the whole conscious process. To speak that sentence aloud, the governing laws of our subconscious mind must fully coordinate our breath, lips, and larynx.

The evidence is indisputable. If we ingest toxins or poisons, we pay the price, however high that might be. If we hold toxic thoughts, propaganda, or ideologies in our minds, anxiety, stress, and trauma are certain.

To refute these natural laws is to deny one's nature. Natural law prescribes morality objectively, as it concerns life, but never commands that we obey it. Still no body cell can rule another. Comprehension of spiritual consciousness leaves bogus philosophies and erroneous teachings floundering in the falsities of their inventions, each having only one court of appeal – nature itself. Why, then, is natural law denied?

*The practice of Natural Law has been eliminated completely by the legal profession. Very often, the study and the practice of Natural Law are scorned if not ridiculed. The reasons for this desultory attitude towards Natural Law are many. However, the most important reason for the negative attitude is that the legal profession has discovered that there is much more money to be made from focusing on highly politicised complex, constantly changing systems of social regulation than it ever could hope to make from the study and practice of Natural Law. —Frank van Dun*[1]

Nothing is more important than to study nature's laws governing the intentions and consequences of actions taken by intelligent living beings. Reason being, whether one applies conscious thought to any action or not, natural laws will affect the outcome.

Why is this not understood? Principally because we've not considered that the laws of identity and causality also apply to the reality of our human nature. Once again conscious nescience readily permits false beliefs.

They may lead to people claiming that in nature or beyond nature there is an immanent, transcendent, supernatural or other non-human person that is the legislative authority of the natural law: God, the gods, or another quasi-personal power (Nature, History, Reason, Humanity).

*Such speculations and claims have no scientific value. If the natural law is understood to be an order of things then there is no reason to look for a legislator of the natural law. Even one who believes that God created the natural order of the human world will appreciate this: creation does not imply legislation. A creator probably wants others to respect his work but that does not mean that what he has created is a system of rules for respecting his work. Moreover, the fact that a creator wants his work to be respected does not by itself make it a respectable work. Were Lenin's, Stalin's, Hitler's, Mao's or Pol Pot's social creations in any way respectable? And these crooks were legislators!*

*Obviously, if 'law' were to mean 'legal system of a society' then 'natural law' would be an oxymoron and to speak of natural law would entangle one in a web of logical fallacies and epistemological*

*conundrums. There are no legal systems in nature. However, there are natural orders aplenty. Scientists who study, say, atoms, molecules or living organisms hope to discover the patterns of order (natural laws) that characterise such things and to arrive at a comprehensive understanding of the natural law of the things in their field of study. They are not looking for a legal system.*
*Similarly, while it makes sense to speak of the law or order of the human world, we cannot speak sensibly of the legal system of the human world. —Frank van Dun*

Humanity must reject the assumption that 'law' refers to a rule or system of rules if we consider law an order of things. It makes no sense to say that an order of things should be obeyed or followed. But it does make sense to ask whether we ought to respect it.

As mentioned, we eat nutritious foods and thrive, or we eat toxic food and suffer. The same respect applies to our thoughts and mental deliberations. Once we learn that the subconscious mind relies wholly on (life)' values' to uphold our lives, just as our digestive system relies wholly on nutrients, then 'life values' are definitively 'objective,' no longer a (moral) theory.

My books elucidate the conscious process to cement in natural law what Ayn Rand presented, specifically that *"the right to the pursuit of happiness means man's right to live for himself, to choose what constitutes his own private, personal, individual happiness and to work for its achievement, so long as he respects the same right in others."*

Conclusions are self-evident. Natural law governs the consequences of our actions and no more. It does not prescribe or control free will, nor can it, because actions follow from our free will choices in sequence. In sum–

- Natural law is inherent. No human legislator can erase it.
- It precedes all man-made laws.
- It governs the consequences of our behaviour, and never our free will. That is natural law freedom in full.
- It is as sure as the law of gravity, which means it is science and not theory.
- We are free to use it and thrive or deny it and suffer, which is the tragedy of human history.

*Every person has free choice. Free to obey or disobey the Natural Laws. Your choice determines the consequences. Nobody ever did, or ever will, escape the consequences of his choices. —Alfred A. Montapert*

## Overture to Natural law

Natural law is the natural order of human beings, capable of rational, purposive action, speech, and thought; the natural order of the human world, expressing method, system, process, order, equality, uniqueness, all inviting of free choice, within free and cooperative rightful action. Individual right to life is our unalienable right to the action of living, the faculties of movement, feeling, thought, and speech, without usurping or violating the unalienable rights of any other. Where the rights of all others are respected, no one can offend by any application of his own.

Independent faculty is guaranteed, including individual responsibility, liability, and accountability; all actioned consequences are inescapable. Respect for the lives of others reciprocally ensures one's own, never sacrificing life's supreme value to anything lesser.

The simplest way to respect or comply with a legal order is to follow or obey the rules of the legal system that defines it. But that method is not an option where the order of the human body or world is concerned. No authority commands anyone else. Likewise, all commandment is refused; no man or woman is a human agent. No legal or other instrument may preside contrary. Publicly proven actions and behaviour that violate another's right to life confess immoral action(s) and trespass of natural law.

Natural justice, remediation, and compensation are by natural law. All problems are resolved by diplomatic negotiations or appointing a judge or arbitrator. No convivial, organic order can wage war!

Nothing is more important than to study nature's laws governing the intentions and consequences of actions taken by intelligent living beings. Existential natural law, as revealed by full consciousness, is the means for unprecedented 'societal regeneration.' Natural laws will affect whether one applies conscious thought to any action.

Ayn Rand wrote that men must know clearly, and in advance of taking an action, what the law forbids them to do (and why). However, natural law does not 'forbid,' it informs her concluding remarks, being what constitutes a crime and what penalty they will incur if they commit it.

Using the term' Objective Law' denies any legitimacy of statutes or Positive laws. It calls for their complete abandonment in favour of natural law, precisely because it is entirely objective in life terms.

*You never change things by fighting the existing reality. To change something, build a new model that makes the existing model obsolete. — Buckminster Fuller*

The governing laws of our conscious process are unquestionably the new model that makes the existing positive law (Lex model) obsolete. Existential natural law clearly shows a society of fifty trillion individuals, cells living harmoniously nearby, each to the benefit of all others, with just twenty laws orchestrating success. They are the tools needed to build a new societal model that renders all else obsolete, exactly as Fuller described. That conscious model is precisely what we need because–

*No problem can be solved from the same level of consciousness that created it. — Albert Einstein*

Two-way (value) communication with our subconscious mind and the fact that our free will is (sequentially) sandwiched between two interdependent functions of the subconscious process makes it impossible for the conscious mind to overrule the subconscious mind and vice versa. This two-way mind protection incontrovertibly establishes the inherent law of nature, which states that 'no mind can rule another.'

Right in the core of our conscious operating system is nature's 'Natural Law of No Trespass.' All authoritarian rule and all forms of (overt) harmful mind control are thereby outlawed, or else human nature is denied.

I wrote in Law from Within (2017), "*When people vote to be ruled by force, they deserve all the tyranny their minders initiate.*" People justly receive what they voted for.

Nonetheless, today's (rule by force) mindset is never challenged, even by millions who claim to be 'awake.' People remain blind to their inevitable fate, denied all conscious remedy through blind nescience, not of who they are, but of *what* they are by nature.

Full consciousness, wholly reliant on life-sustaining values upheld by natural law, is their only salvation. Ayn Rand briefly explained that "*the objective theory of values is the only moral theory incompatible with rule by force.*" She was right on target once again because 'life values' fuel our whole conscious process.

Tragically, so many brainwashed people believe that without a ruler, there can be no order, never learning the natural laws of their nature, so brilliantly conceived as to come with a fail-safe protection system.

People must overcome prejudice, ignorance, and indoctrination. Natural law facts must be brought out of hiding because they inherently invigorate and protect the blessing of our being.

The first principle is that law is not a command, a system of directions, or control (even for the common good). Natural law is nature's invitation to live your life to the full. It is not primarily about crime and punishment. It's about the joys of living with justice for all, welcomed with open arms, prized, praised, practiced as a virtue, and placed at the top of one's value hierarchy. We can be inspired to preserve it through our conduct and thoughts and commit to its finite protection for our families in perpetuity.

'Intrinsic natural law' stands in its life's jurisdiction; therefore, contrary to all others, including 'common law.' Nothing obligates that we prove it. It is axiomatic, meaning we cannot exist without it.

Hence, people must educate themselves about natural law, reason, purpose, and objectivity. To step outside its boundaries and confess outlaw behavior. Transgressors voluntarily rule against themselves.

As mentioned, denying natural law is a matter for the source creator, not for a courtroom to decide.

Nevertheless, all infractions and violations will continue until we actively work to overthrow them. The solution can only come from within you through your knowledge. You can be a founding member of the most tremendous change that human societies will ever witness by learning of full consciousness and the natural laws it reveals.

You are the solution. You are a Creator. No government will ever be. Nothing holds us in check today but widespread common nescience born of authoritarian rule based on greed!

Natural law freedom and objective guidance is all you need!

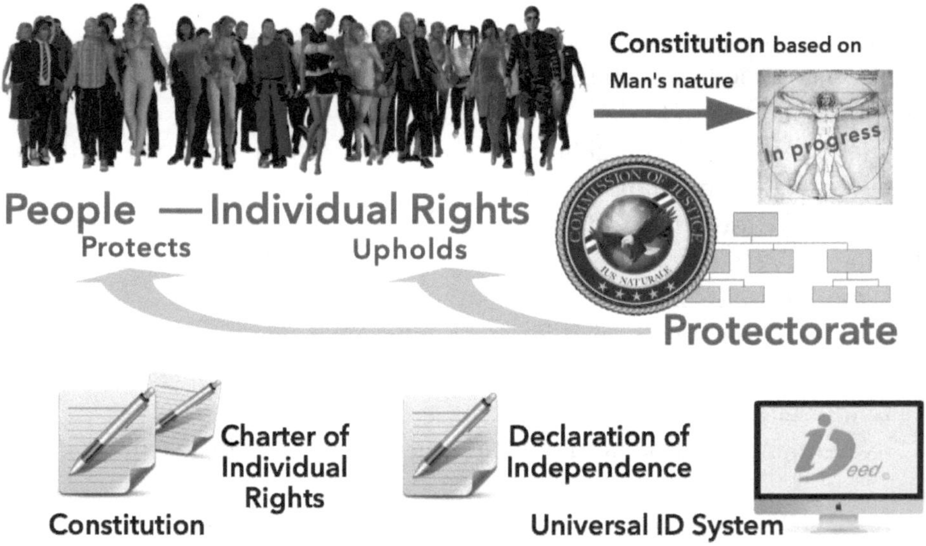


11- Protectorate schematic Diagram

# Chapter 10

## Twenty Natural laws

Natural law is no more a theory than the physical universe, a collection of physics theories. Natural law practice has never come to fruition; its practice is scorned, if not ridiculed, almost entirely by the legal profession. Today, common law advocates barely mention natural law despite it purportedly underpins common law.

This desultory attitude is principally traceable to the virulently anti-human ideology that there is little or anything respectable about human beings as they are. Hence, there is a belief that 'human nature can and should be changed' to conform to a supposed ideal of what man should be. Thus, men and women should be taught or forced not to respect the (natural law) order of the human world but instead to respect the imaginary 'normative order' that ideologues conjure in their minds as preferable. Not surprisingly, the legal profession knows well that highly politicised constantly changing systems of social regulation will monetarily profit them far more than they could hope to make from the study and practice of natural law.

Material science shows us that an entity's nature determines what it can and will do in any given circumstance. That means, unless we act according to the reality of our nature, our choices and actions are flawed before they begin. Just as we gain no material or spiritual benefit from whims, fancies, or ideologies that have no life-upholding foundation, neither can society.

My book *'Conscious Ascendance'* examines the twenty natural laws based on their derivative source in the human conscious process. My book *'Navigate to Freedom'* re-examines them in societal terms. Here, I want to correlate these laws with the 'objective philosophy' they reveal. Quotations from Ayn Rand show how precisely her philosophy coincides. People wishing to denounce her findings and mine should tender their protest to the Source Creator. No one can overrule human nature, the reason authoritarians invented Straw men to rule over us. Their game is now up, as confirmed by their choice to relinquish their minds. Their insistence on forcible rule over free choice is ended. Knowledge is our remedy and their defeat.

The diagram shows how the twenty natural laws fall into four groups clockwise from law number 1, each with five laws. Every law connects to all others, which reinforces their wholesome unity. Furthermore, each law has a counterpart or strengthening law found diametrically opposite—for example, 3 points to 13 and 6 points to 16. Here, I will show them in that counterpart order so their correlation becomes evident to my readers.

**(1) Natural Law of Identity**

*A thing is what it is and that as the thing is, it acts; conversely as the thing acts, it is.*

This law is the very foundation of Objective philosophy but is totally ignored by most all people. Yet every attempt to evade the fact that A is A is the secret evil people dread to face despite all the pain they have ever endured. Its purpose was to make you forget that Man is Man.

Let's now switch to the diagonal counterpart of Natural law 1, being natural law 11

**(11) Natural Law of Right Reason (From #1, Law of identity)**

*Reasoning discovers truths that are not self-evident—to adapt material existence to life-sustaining spiritual purposes*

Once we grasp how values reciprocally advocate and prompt more of the same, (causal) reasoning plays a critical role in which values sustain our lives and our endeavors and which do not. Reasoning embraces inquiry, contemplation, investigation, determination, evaluation, and commitment to the satisfaction of productive and efficient functioning.

Right reason embraces accurate and speedy resolutions, intuition, life values, and emotional stability, all of which depend on whether our accepted values are truthful or corrupted. Those who place a high value on mental agility, truth, validity, and integrity will speed past those who must mentally wrestle every issue with high certainty and truth.

This law fits hand in glove with natural law #2 in perfect accord with an objective philosophy as explained by Rand's sentence, namely–

Twenty Natural laws

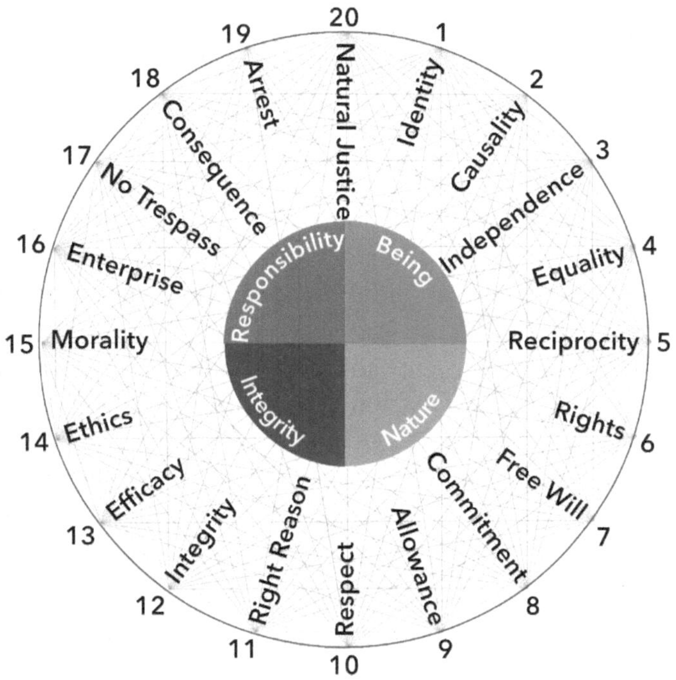


12. Natural law Flower diagram

A man does not act without knowing the purpose of his action. In choosing a goal, he considers the means required to achieve it, he weighs the value of the goal against the difficulties of the means and against the full, hierarchical context of all his other values and goals.

**(2) Natural Law of Causality**

*All action is caused and determined by the nature of the entities that act; no real entity (thing) can occur by chance, or without cause; a thing cannot act contrary to its nature.*

This law and law #1 reside in every tissue, cell, organ, system, and faculty of our physical, mental, and spiritual being. To toss those laws aside is to toss life on the scrap heap. Because the nature of an action is caused and determined by the essence of the entities that act, nothing can contradict its nature. That is how we function to achieve our goals. Causality is the founding tenet of the conscious process; it is irrefutably the cornerstone of objective philosophy. The counterpart of this Law is natural law 12

**(12) Natural Law of Integrity**

*The state of being whole, undivided, integrated, ethically intentioned, and committed to one's life, fully accords with the natural laws of one's nature.*

Our bodily systems and subconscious mind rely on 'integrity' unequivocally and unmistakably; failure to some degree results from any lapse. Our conscious mind is obliged to function in a particular manner. No compulsion exists, so we either respect this law or suffer dire consequences.

"Integrity is the recognition of the fact that you cannot fake your consciousness, just as honesty is the recognition of the fact that you cannot fake existence—that man is an indivisible entity, an integrated unit of two attributes: of matter and consciousness, and that he may permit no breach between body and mind, between action and thought, between his life and his convictions—that, like a judge impervious to public opinion, he may not sacrifice his convictions to the wishes of others, be it the whole of mankind shouting pleas or threats against him—that courage and confidence are practical necessities, that courage is the practical form of being true to existence, of being true to truth, and confidence is the practical form of being true to one's own consciousness." — Ayn Rand

This law is amply evident in truthfully precise, subconscious reporting, in all our mental and spiritual processes including perception, and in the faithful surveillance, monitoring and adjustment of all bodily functions. Absent this truthful integrity, all six of our subconscious faculties would fail. This pointer to our right to live free is the —

**(3) Natural Law of Independence**

*All men and women are unique and independent, according to their nature of equally being Man, qua (for) Man.*

The separateness and independence of our cells, tissues, organs, and systems facilitates multi-faceted contributions to life's fullness, satisfaction, and resoluteness. Likewise, the sovereignty of our free will mind, being separate from our automated subconscious mind, ensures authentic and productive communication of life values between both, that being our psycho-epistemological functioning.

> *"No matter how vast your knowledge or how modest, it is your own mind that has to acquire it. It is only with your own knowledge that you can deal. It is only your own knowledge that you can claim to possess or ask others to consider. Your mind is your only judge of*

> *truth—and if others dissent from your verdict, reality is the court of final appeal. Nothing but a man's mind can perform that complex, delicate, crucial process of identification which is thinking. Nothing can direct the process but his own judgment. Nothing can direct his judgment but his moral integrity." , Ayn Rand*

That statement describes the philosophical truth of independence. Our conscious process as the operating system of life wholly depends on our independent choice of values and actions, which is the entire substance and purpose of objectivist philosophy. The counterpart of this law is (#13)

**(13) Natural Law of Efficacy**

*Related conscious faculties, permit efficacious functioning, correspondent with valid and truthful mental content.*

Every biological and psychological faculty of our being is efficacious in itself. This law teaches that all erroneous beliefs, fictional laws, mysticism, subjectivism, perverted meanings, misconstructions of language, and stolen concepts will deprive or mislead cognitive understanding to retard mental comprehension. So we must respect this law, especially in partnership with the laws of allowance, commitment, respect, free will, integrity, and right reason.

**(4) Natural Law of Equality**

*All living beings of the Homo sapiens sapien species, are alike in nature and faculties; equally endowed.*

As men and women, we all are (respectively) equal by nature but uniquely different in expression, i.e., weight, size, race, language, color, etc. Indeed, we are so differently unique in thought and material expression that even our uniqueness is common to all. Our life, our every breath and heartbeat, are witness and testament to our (individual) being, without which we cannot exist. Separateness is fundamental to our biology and psychology, lives, thoughts, feelings, and actions, and that is also true of our equality.

> *Since nature does not endow all men with equal beauty or equal intelligence, and the faculty of volition leads men to make different choices, the egalitarians propose to abolish the "unfairness" of nature and of volition, and to establish universal equality in fact—in defiance of facts. Since the Law of Identity is impervious to human manipulation, it is the Law of Causality that they struggle to abrogate. Since personal attributes or virtues cannot be "redistributed," they seek to deprive men of their consequences—of the rewards, the benefits, the achievements created by personal*

*attributes and virtues. It is not equality before the law that they seek, but inequality: the establishment of an inverted social pyramid, with a new aristocracy on top—the aristocracy of non-value." —Ayn Rand*

Our conscious process expresses "equality before the (natural) law, the equality of fundamental, unalienable rights which every man possesses by having been born as a human being," accordingly, consciousness, natural law, and objectivist philosophy are cemented in unity once again. The co-partner of equality is ethics.

**(14) Natural Law of Ethics**

*Ethics, being the choice of life-supporting thoughts, values, and determinations, when acted upon, outwardly express an individual's morality.*

Ethics defines a life-sustaining code of values in order to thrive and prosper with happiness. As Ayn Rand described –

*"Man must choose his actions, values and goals by the standard of that which is proper to man—in order to achieve, maintain, fulfil and enjoy that ultimate value, that end in itself, which is his own life."*

Conversely…

*"The social theory of ethics substitutes "society" for God—and although it claims that its chief concern is life on earth, it is not the life of man, not the life of an individual, but the life of a disembodied entity, the collective, which, in relation to every individual, consists of everybody except himself. As far as the individual is concerned, his ethical duty is to be the selfless, voiceless, right-less slave of any need, claim or demand asserted by others. The motto "dog eat dog"—which is not applicable to capitalism nor to dogs—is applicable to the social theory of ethics." —Ayn Rand*

Ethics is not societal. It is inherent in the moral fibre of life itself. It governs our choices, as testified by the truthful, honest, wholesome cohesiveness of all our biological faculties, aided by similar qualities and values in the subconscious mind.

**(5) Natural Law of Reciprocity**

*Respect for one's individual life, and reciprocally for the right of all others to live, guarantees the freedom, and right of all others of the human species.*

Reciprocity manifests within our nature by successful (value) outcomes, making known our more successful (value) inputs, primarily through the mentoring faculty of feelings. In turn, these intuitively prompt spiritual advancement, resulting in the growth of life itself and the making of a kind soul. To refuse such offerings is to express favour for lesser values, leading to depreciation, decay, disease or death.

This law fits perfectly within the law of identity (1) because it wholly relies on identifying what values uphold and sustain life and which facts are endorsed by our feelings, respecting particular actions employing those values.

**(15) Natural Law of Morality**

*Actions and behaviour publicly testify one's pre-conceived moral stature, and agreed moral accountability.*

Our nature testifies that immoral actions do not break natural law, but instead reinforce and amplify its necessity, thereby pointing to necessary correction.

> *"A moral code is a system of teleological measurement which grades the choices and actions open to man, according to the degree to which they achieve or frustrate the code's standard of value. The standard is the end, to which man's actions are the means.*
> *A moral code is a set of abstract principles; to practice it, an individual must translate it into the appropriate concretes—he must choose the particular goals and values which he is to pursue. This requires that he define his particular hierarchy of values, in the order of their importance, and that he act accordingly." — Ayn Rand*

The (conscious process) value transfer wave shows that thoughts sequentially precede action, meaning that consciously chosen values, being our thoughts, are properly one's ethics, one's ethical value choices. Actions follow, which is the material manifestation of one's ethics, or lack thereof. Law (#14) (ethics) concerns thoughts, while this law (#15) illustrates the manifestation of one's ethics as one's 'morality.' Ethics relates to intention, therefore. Morality is expressed through actions or behaviour.

**(6) Natural Law of Individual Rights.**

*Every man, woman, and child is an independent living being, having individual, immutable, and unalienable right to his or her life, free and independent from any usurpation, or violation, whatsoever.*

Rights belong only to every man and woman singularly. No collective rights can exist.

The source of this law is the separate contributory functioning of every biological and psychological constituent of our being.

> *"A "right" is a moral principle defining and sanctioning a man's freedom of action in a social context. There is only one fundamental right (all the others are its consequences or corollaries): a man's right to his own life.*
> *The concept of a "right" pertains only to action—specifically, to freedom of action. It means freedom from physical compulsion, coercion or interference by other men.*
> *Thus, for every individual, a right is the moral sanction of a positive—of his freedom to act on his own judgment, for his own goals, by his own voluntary, uncoerced choice. As to his neighbours, his rights impose no obligations on them except of a negative kind: to abstain from violating his rights." —Ayn Rand*

A prosperous, thriving life depends entirely on self-respect for our bodies, our minds, the natural order and laws within ourselves, and our chosen values. Once again, the link between consciousness, natural law, and an objective philosophy is straightforward. The diagonal counterpart of this law is–

**(16) Natural Law of Cooperative Enterprise**

*Cooperative effort with others, will return more benefit than most individual's can achieve alone.*

Collaborative enterprise satisfies the natural law of no trespass in all respects while upholding the laws of equality, independence, right reason, efficacy, and morality. This law stems from the whole of our being, free will being the exception. All of our body cells, systems, and faculties are endowed to cooperate for synergistic benefit, likewise, life-value communication between our two minds.

> *A proper association is united by ideas, not by men, and its members are loyal to the ideas, not to the group. It is eminently reasonable that men should seek to associate with those who share their convictions and values. It is impossible to deal or even to communicate with men whose ideas are fundamentally opposed to one's own (and one should be free not to deal with them). All proper associations are formed or joined by individual choice and on conscious, intellectual grounds (philosophical, political, professional, etc.)—not by the physiological or geographical accident of birth, and not on the ground of tradition. This requires a high degree of conceptual development and independence. But this*

*is the only way men can work together justly, benevolently and safely. Ayn Rand*

A symbiotic society may thus emerge. Symbiosis is broadly defined as the interaction between two (different) organisms living in close physical association, typically to the advantage of both. Cooperation and collaboration emerge as primary considerations. Cooperation and individual rights are inextricably linked, as objective philosophy emerges definitively through values and explicit principles. Free will is paramount.

**(7) Natural Law of Free Will**

*Free choice of thought and action, by any and all Living Being's, are guaranteed inclusive of the responsibility, liability, and accountability, naturally and inherently flowing therefrom.*

There are no exceptions, escape routes, let-outs, excuses, or pardons for refusing to exercise free will, or for overruling it. This law stems from the fullness of our conscious process, without which we cannot function in honour and support of ourselves.

*To think is an act of choice. The key to what you so recklessly call "human nature," the open secret you live with, yet dread to name, is the fact that man is a being of volitional consciousness. Reason does not work automatically; thinking is not a mechanical process; the connections of logic are not made by instinct. The function of your stomach, lungs or heart is automatic; the function of your [cognitive] mind is not. In any hour and issue of your life, you are free to think or to evade that effort. But you are not free to escape from your nature, from the fact that reason is your means of survival—so that for you, who are a human being, the question "to be or not to be" is the question "to think or not to think." —Ayn Rand*

Free will is necessarily inviolate because no mental, emotional, or spiritual growth is possible without it. We each are the author of our life. Individual rights, free will, respect, and responsibility are inseparable within our nature, each separate from society. To command free will denies it.

Since two persons cannot be free and equal when one of them is controlling, managing, threatening, blackmailing, or extorting the other, so arises the diametric partner of this law–

**(17) Natural Law of No Trespass**

*No independent living being has the right to trespass, or to violate another's life, or property.*

This law informs No Trespass of any other living being's right to life. Notice that respect for all other people and no violation of the rights of others are nearly identical. However, this law is far more comprehensive than the non-aggression principle. More than causing no harm or loss, it unites with the law of free will (#7) to express that all of these twenty laws comprehensively uphold life and our (property) means to sustain it. That is objective philosophy, no less.

> *"A crime is a violation of the right(s) of other men by force (or fraud). It is only the initiation of physical force against others—i.e., the recourse to violence—that can be classified as a crime in a free society (as distinguished from a civil wrong). Ideas, in a free society, are not a crime—and neither can they serve as the justification of a crime." —Ayn Rand*

This law is found everywhere in our nature. It explicitly protects each constituent from interference by others and protects against all enemies, foreign and domestic. It is also the right to bear arms, therefore.

- Our right to act, so to live, fully accepts the reciprocal right of all others equally so to do.
- Trespass of another's rights, self-cancels one's rights, respective of any relevant action.
- No claim of right may negate, usurp, or overrule the unalienable rights of other living human beings.
- Independent rights of Man preside over all other life forms.

Our right to life is our right to exercise it, fully upheld by the reasoning process. Our free will right to life is the natural law of no trespass, precisely emphasising that crime violates other men's right(s) by force (or fraud); that being the initiation of physical force against others.

The opposite should be our goal and means, namely the intention to exercise our free choice, to achieve a particular result from our chosen actions, and bear responsibility for our behaviour. So arises the–

**(8) Natural Law of Commitment**

*To live is to commit to actions and bear the consequences.*

Moral responsibility, and accountability, are expressed by our actions. 'Commitment means to actively 'focus.'

> *"In any hour and issue of his life, man is free to think or to evade that effort. Thinking requires a state of full, focused awareness. The act of focusing one's consciousness is volitional. Man can focus his mind to a full, active, purposefully directed awareness of reality—or he can un-focus it and let himself drift in a semiconscious daze, merely*

*reacting to any chance stimulus of the immediate moment, at the mercy of his undirected sensory-perceptual mechanism and of any random, associational connections it might happen to make. — Ayn Rand*

A non-focused mind may be said to be conscious since it experiences feelings and perceptions. But in the sense of being aware of reality and dealing with it, an unfocused mind is not (entirely) conscious. Commitment and accountability, or their lack, lead to respective consequences, being the diagonal counterpart of Commitment.

**(18) Natural Law of Just Consequence.**

*Nature serves just consequence, whether respected or not.*

This law allows the full consequences of one's actions, for better or worse. It mimics Francis Bacon's statement, *'Nature to be commanded must be obeyed,'* however, given our free will and that natural law never commands, the phrase more accurately should read *'Nature to be mastered, must be respected.'*

Consequences will not necessarily be the exact measure of one's moral or immoral action because efforts jointly contributed by others or mitigating circumstances may apply. 'Just consequence' means that consequences belong to whoever caused them and makes no mistakes. Here, then, is found the essence of natural justice.

Psychologically speaking, one's choice 'to think or not' is their choice 'to focus or not' – to be 'conscious or not' – metaphysically, the choice of life or death. Consciousness, natural law, and objective philosophy thereby unify once again. Infants lack this ability of course, hence–

**(9) The Natural Law of Allowance**

*Every man, woman, and child (including infants and those mentally handicapped) are endowed to venture forth and to progress at their choice and pace, in service of their life, but are not absolved from refusing, so to do.*

Nature's Source Creator has allowed our subconscious mind to fully function, including for emotions, even though the cognitive mind is unable, but not unwilling, to perform at its fullest potential. Infants have no words, concepts, principles, math, or science. Accordingly, until such develops over time, the subconscious mind prompts young children's activities, also notifying their (by-passed) cognitive mind, altogether the 'Natural Law of allowance.'

Accordingly, all those lacking a comprehensive (cognitive) database can experience the emotions of success or failure while progressively growing (as best possible) in cognitive mental stature, understanding, and spirituality. This Law permits learning and spiritual maturity to become habituated throughout our adult life, not until age seven, as many believe. It allows for our inability without excusing refused ability. That (never before explained) distinction is fundamental. It speaks of graciousness, politeness, integrity, gratitude, and respect. It facilitates the development of mental competence, consistent with choice and without penalty. It boosts ever-increasing mental efficiency over time, clarifying that mental and emotional development fosters a richly rewarding life. So arises the–

**(19) Natural law of Forceful Arrest**

*Arrest of all initiated force, protects Man's unalienable right to life.*

Supreme mental coercion, such as fraud and blackmail that deny our perception of reality or any threat of physical destruction that forces us to act against our judgment, all negate or paralyses our means of survival. Whoever initiates the use of force, for whatever purpose and to whatever extent, is intent on harming or destroying our capacity to live! Because force and a free mind are opposites, those who herd men and women to rule them cannot claim the sanction of reason, as no advocate of contradictions can claim it.

> "The basic political principle of the Objectivist ethics is:
> *no man may initiate the use of physical force against others. No man—or group or society or government—has the right to assume the role of a criminal and initiate the use of physical compulsion against any man. Men have the right to use physical force only in retaliation and only against those who initiate its use. The ethical principle involved is simple and clear-cut: it is the difference between murder and self-defence. A holdup man seeks to gain a value, wealth, by killing his victim; the victim does not grow richer by killing a holdup man. The principle is: no man may obtain any values from others by resorting to physical force." —Ayn Rand*

Without protection or self-defence, we each are at the mercy of all who initiate force, including governments, fraudsters, blackmailers, tyrants, rapists, psychopaths, terrorists, thugs, warmongers, and murderers. The precondition of a civilised society, is the barring of physical force from social relationships. Nature has established (the principle) that if men and women wish to deal with one another, they may do so only by reason, discussion, persuasion, and voluntary, un-coerced agreement. Security of each individual and their property against predatory attack emerges as a vital condition of society.

This law is self-evident in our reflex actions, bodily immune system, endocrine system, conscience, feelings, and emotions. Those protective measures collectively give rise to the–

**(10 Natural Law of Respect.**

*No man, woman, or child can uphold their unalienable right to life without correspondingly respecting the equal right to life, of all other living human beings.*

Neither of our two minds can violate the process of the other, whereby each respects the other. Respect for one's life informs that personal freedom is guaranteed only by each of us, granting everyone else the right to life. This law is exhibited by those who uphold the natural law, rejected conversely by all those who trespass. Respect and natural justice should be the core ethics taught in all curricula from infancy.

Values represent our respect for life, as evidenced by every element of our conscious process, or else our values would constantly conflict with our bodily functions. Thus, the Source creator's gifts are harmony, cooperation, gratitude, grit, discipline, correspondence, nurturance, reason, and many more virtues. They inherently exist within each of us because our body and mental processes rely on life-enhancing virtues and ethics.

Freedom and respect are reciprocal. We can ensure our right to life only by endorsing other people's right to their lives. Freedom, respect, and individual rights are inseparable and, when exercised, result in justice as the counterpart of respect.

**20 Natural Law of Justice**

*Innocent, natural individuals are free. Proven trespassers of natural law, are outlaws, perpetrators of deliberately enacted transgressions, voluntary bearers of natural justice.*

Every individual is author of their actions which translate directly into moral justness, or immoral unjustness, served upon others.

> *"For instance: what fact of reality gave rise to the concept "justice"? The fact that man must draw conclusions about the things, people and events around him, i.e., must judge and evaluate them. Is his judgment automatically right? No. What causes his judgment to be wrong? The lack of sufficient evidence, or his evasion of the evidence, or his inclusion of considerations other than the facts of the case. How, then, is he to arrive at the right judgment? By basing it exclusively on the factual evidence and by considering all the relevant evidence available. But isn't this a description of "objectivity"? Yes, "objective judgment" is one of the wider*

> *categories to which the concept "justice" belongs. What distinguishes "justice" from other instances of objective judgment? When one evaluates the nature or actions of inanimate objects, the criterion of judgment is determined by the particular purpose for which one evaluates them. But how does one determine a criterion for evaluating the character and actions of men, in view of the fact that men possess the faculty of volition? What science can provide an objective criterion of evaluation in regard to volitional matters? Ethics. Now, do I need a concept to designate the act of judging a man's character and/or actions exclusively on the basis of all the factual evidence available, and of evaluating it by means of an objective moral criterion? Yes. That concept is "justice." —Ayn Rand*

This justice law is located right in the core of our conscience and emotional reporting systems, where it belongs, for the exact reasons those faculties exist. Emotions (feelings) inform of justice or injustice, what is upholding one's life or hindering it, meaning they justly approve or censure alternatively.

In conclusion, free persons do not commit crimes—those who have (prior) chosen to relinquish their freedom do. Those who self-declare they can refuse others' right to life have inwardly rejected morality outright. Correspondingly, their actions will outwardly broadcast their need to reconvey to a state of natural order and its natural laws.

The full force of Natural Justice will bear upon such perpetrators, the only force they have the right to choose. None of these twenty laws are prescriptions. None dictate or compel what one must do or not do.

- **In our personal lives**, natural law adjudicates the consequences of our actions. We are rewarded or censured in some form.
- **In societal terms** of natural justice, we are rewarded for our progress or arrested for causing harm. It remains that until we have acted, there is nothing to adjudicate.

Consequently, the following natural law descriptions cannot read like statutes. As already mentioned, they read more like instructions spoken to a jury before it retires to adjudicate the facts of a case, according to past actions allegedly committed by the accused individual. Each law defines a fundamental premise that upholds our lives

# Chapter 11

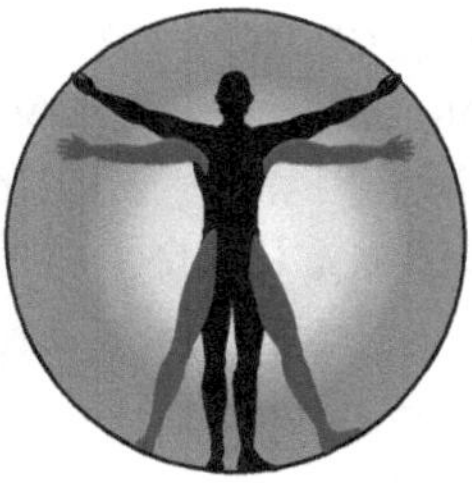

## No Rule By Force

Today's human tragedy results from (governments) never protecting individual rights. The government's monopoly of force now possesses a potential for evil far exceeding any other institution. Almost all legislations are rotten to the core. Yet we've not recognised the ignorant lack of knowledge that has allowed today's brutally oppressive crimes to develop without challenge.

Fortunately, every man and woman has the moral right to refuse rule by force and defend that right by exercising the 'natural law of no trespass,' indisputably encrypted in our biological and psychological processes where no human legislator can erase it. It is time to comprehend the truth unmistakably.

Natural law automatically governs the consequences of our actions and behavior, preserving free will. That reservation of freedom is nature's irrevocable 'consent to societal protection' from all who would violate it.

**Lawful vs. legal force**

If government is factually the 'science of societal management,' we might say it is lawful to use retaliatory force against aggressors to protect innocent people. In such cases, the government does not initiate action; instead, criminal conduct that causes personal injury or loss to law-abiding people or otherwise disrupts the community's peace triggers the government into 're-acting' to terminate such crimes.

Today, the state initiates aggressive (criminal)action. It legalises violence against innocent people to advantage some people, or itself, at the expense of those victimised. The 'protective body' (government?) must distinguish (initiated) criminal force from (lawful) retaliatory force. So long as the government does not, it is inherently dysfunctional and harmful.

As a result, virtually every country on earth suffers from national or federal regulations applicable to almost every area of commerce and life. Initiated legal force by national, state, and local governments, even by police forces, includes but is not limited to violation of property rights, invasive surveillance, civil asset forfeiture, invasive warrantless searches, child theft, no-knock raids with violence, mandatory permits, licenses, registrations, prescribed business hours, even a dictated 'age of consent.'

No free society can exist when politicians, bureaucrats, regulators, statists, and authoritarians use government force to impose their goals and desires, hinder or deny personal freedom, strictly curtail economic activity, and even compel people to associate with people they would rather not.

Most people are oblivious to how much the government infringes on their freedoms. Thus, they are entirely untroubled by complying with government mandates and statutes – utterly ignorant of what a free society is – worse, they are unaware of their constructive role in building such a society. For any incursion into their lives, they respond, *"government must do something."* They never cry, *"Governments that do not protect against all evil promote it."*

Our task appears hopeless –

> *A Constitution of Government once changed from Freedom, can never be restored. Liberty once lost is lost forever. When the People once surrender their share in the legislature, and their Right of defending the Limitations upon the Government, and of resisting every Encroachment upon them, they can never regain it.— John Adams– in a letter to his wife, Abigail, 1775.*

Fortunately, that is no longer true. Our task is not hopeless because now we know about our immutable strengths and that all dissenters have relinquished theirs, making none of their edicts valid.

Thus governments sacrificed our protection for theirs. Instead of protecting people and their rights, self-protection became its sole mission, whence greed, avarice, and corruption progressively smash lawfulness, resulting in the people paying an unfathomable price without end. Government edicts or laws are (today) taught, propagandised, legislated, and enforced to maintain control, including control of Man's thoughts, intentions, and actions. The result is anti-life.

More and more people are awakening to the truth of this corporate conquest and bloody-minded subjugation of humanity by authoritarian corporations masquerading as governments. This diagram illustrates that tragedy perfectly by showing that no escape exists.

A few people, very few, are now beginning to search for an alternative to government. In recent times, several counter-movements have emerged, some asserting the purported divine purpose and operation of

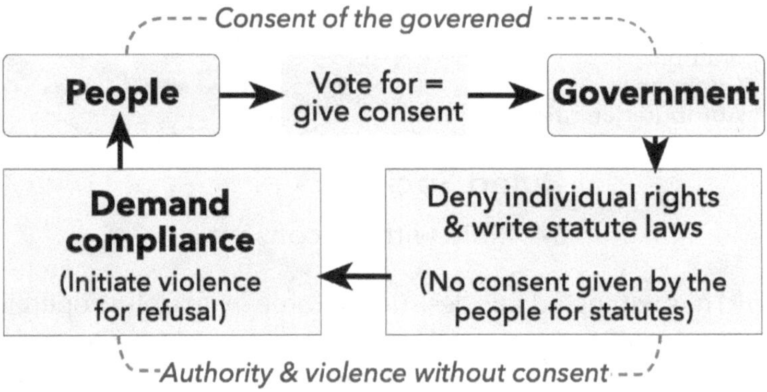


13. Consent of the governed

Common Law, professedly to enable individual, unalienable rights and the freedom of each man and woman as the proper universal order of all societies. Some claim that this (biblically foretold) manifestation of common law is when all people have facilitated their natural equality, devoid of all divisions, compulsions, and oppression, thus living in harmony with creation and peacefully with one another. But there is more.

Diagram 14, (next page), presents a different picture of the same story utilising the (form) shape of the value transfer wave diagram.

What was free will in the initial (VTW) diagram (P55) is now replaced by a brainwashed society. Government statutes and legislations injected into our awareness, result devious mind control directing our compliance.

Additionally, what was originally our automated subconscious mind working with our free will now shows as an authoritatively ruled society that, to a large degree, is fully automated. Authority and indoctrination are fully locked thereby, and neither can cancel the other due to authoritarian oversight. When these two diagrams are correlated, the full force of authoritarian rule strikes home with a vengeance.

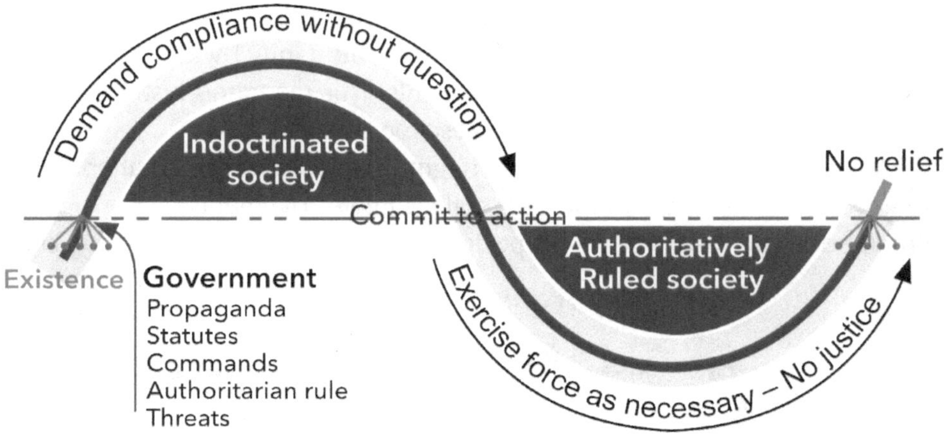


**Ruled Society**

14. Rule without consent

The world has witnessed this destructive force in ceaseless operation for centuries, most significantly over three years past, but people understand a mere smidgen of what I've just described. As a tragic result, precious few realise they are likely again voting for the age old mindset of rule by force, ostensibly via a different Constitution.

There has to be a better way forward, and there is. What do you see when you read the bottom line in this diagram and compare it with its counterpart diagram (13) on the previous page?

15. A Protectorate Flow diagram

Free organic societies consented by nature replace (non-consented) authority and violence. The people vote for a protective instrumentality that graciously accepts nature's consent for freedom, which no human can disagree with. Two political parties are no longer needed because

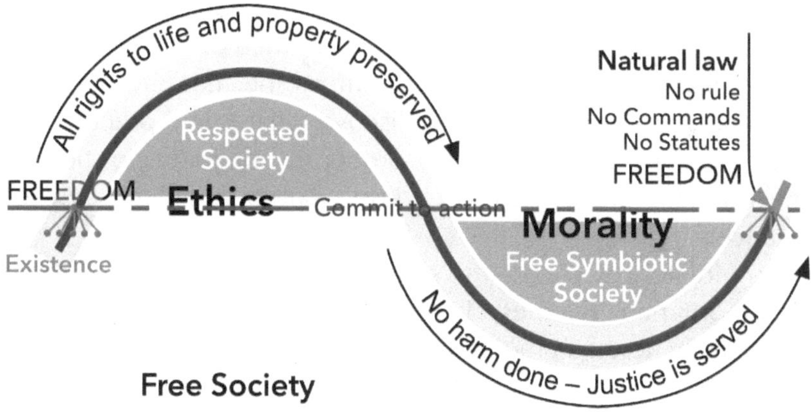


16. Ethics- Morality Transfer waveR

everyone has confirmed nature's consent that no (invented) overruling laws be implemented.

Now compare this (VTW formatted) diagram (16) with diagram14 - immediately to the left. Natural law emerges at the right side of diagram 16, completely replacing (left side) government in diagram 14.

Ethics replaces free will in the original VTW diagram, while actions performed by the subconscious mind are now moral actions in a free symbiotic society. A 'Protectorate' substitutes for government. All rights to life and property are protected, and justice is served in free societies.

Government edicts or laws are (today) taught, propagandised, legislated, and enforced to maintain control, including control of our thoughts, intentions, and actions. The result is anti-life, as the first two diagrams show.

The alternative is a protected free society s shown here. Observe the vital difference in both diagrams regarding '*consent*.' Where consent today shields the state at the people's expense, in a free society, nature's consent ensures people's protection. Opinion and votes play no part since consent is universal by our Creator, given all who step outside natural law confess outlaw behaviour.

As previously described, the human conscious process conclusively shows that 'natural law' reveals morality, not vice-versa, as '*natural law theorists*' claim. Indeed, had common law adherents studied the human conscious process, as indeed they should, both they and natural law theorists would have recognised several fundamentals of natural law.

- Natural law is immutably innate, encrypted in our nature where no legislator can erase it. Its immutable governance of our biological and psychological faculties definitively outlines the morality upon which life depends. We are obligated to discover, learn, and practice this by choice. Morality is not an innate propensity or predisposition to do good. Instead, it advises us to choose what is good, free will being imperative.
- All who violate free choice are outlaws, inclusive of all governments and authoritarian regimes. To rule morality is to rule free will authoritatively. To teach morality is to uphold free will and natural law, both moral pointers for safe passage and conduct because, unlike (invented) statutes, neither curtail free choice.
- Nature's governing laws are its invitation to imagine, create, prosper, and thrive, thence to report our actions via feelings as morally approved by nature – individual authors of immorality held to account for remedy.

Of most significant importance, by far, is that all forms of positive law depend on independent free will choices that formulate them. Should it be surprising that the Nuremberg code binds authoritative law creations and formulations, not only their enactment?

So long as humanity believes in an innate morality, no advance from made-made law based on opinion and majority consent is possible. Conversely, should 'common law' advocates or natural law theorists ever accept self-governance within the terms of natural justice, they will forsake all manufactured statutes and good riddance.

Above all else, until society explicitly moves to abolish all legal fiction by asserting our unalienable right to life as independent living beings, it will continue to languish in the clutches of positive law.

Freedom is singular. It belongs to each (independent) living man, woman, and child. On the other hand, liberty is plural, or social, as determined or permitted by the rulers of a society. It is, therefore, incumbent on us all as independent living beings (ILBs) to preserve individual rights and interests, individual responsibility, and individual 'executive' decision-making ability concerning the conduct of our lives and our social interactions. Because the conscious mind is the author of our actions, our 'right to action' is intimately related to freedom of thought, speech, and behavior. People must remodel today's society to protect and preserve our unalienable rights to life; no compromise or surrender admitted.

Few people understand this inversion. The mindset holding that one individual being (or group) has an 'authoritarian right' to rule others is corrupt to the core! Such corruption, benignly disguised as beneficial government, also conceals that no free society supporter truthfully admits or confesses to a wilful agreement of tyranny, slavery, initiated violence, and wars.

All 'laws' arising from this (inane) moral inversion are considered indispensable to life's comfort and security satisfactions, and so they repeat century after century, unchallenged. The conclusion is clear.

**Any society that authorises a state to rule it by force deserves all the tyranny and bloodshed that 'authority' enacts.**

I submit that is societal insanity, but until we change our mindset, criminal violations of our lives will continue according to our (coerced) permission.

Look no further for the source of today's problems–

Jean-Jacques Rousseau, (1712-78), a French philosopher and writer, believed that *while Mans freedom is a fact of nature, people should be taught to consider that it is dangerous; whereby they ought to sacrifice their individual nature to the artificial condition of citizenship. Furthermore, natural persons should become artificial persons, that is, citizens—wittingly or unwittingly—willingly, or by legal compulsion.*

As a result, the STRAW-MAN on your government-issued documents is an invention, a fake fictional entity that uses your name in ALL CAPS. It is created through your birth certificate when you were born when you could not possibly refuse it. Accordingly, you (purportedly) live in this fictional world as a dead, legal entity in whose courtrooms there is no word for a living man or a woman. No living people are recognised. Only dead fictions are.

Ayn Rand briefly explained that "*the objective theory of values is the only moral theory incompatible with rule by force.*" That is precisely why I had refused all forms of positive law and natural law 'theory' from the beginning of my research. Tragically, that same (rule by force) mindset prevails to this day, never challenged by millions who claim to be 'awake.' They are not! Like drowning men clutching at straws, they hurtle downstream at an increasing pace, blind to their inevitable fate, denied all conscious remedy through global nescience, not of 'who they are,' but of 'what they are.' Knowledge of full consciousness, backed by natural law and an objective philosophy, is their only therapy. Sadly, or tragically more accurately, conscious nescience blocks that pathway.

So, the people are ruled – by monarchs, emperors, kings, governments, socialist dictatorships, democracies, or communism. Notwithstanding, nature cannot be ruled, not ever!

The government makes straw men to circumvent the fact thay cannot rule nature. It invents citizens, persons, and subjects and writes them into its statutes and a constitution. All ("citizens" or "persons") people must comply with government statutes as though enslaved. Natural (living) identity no longer (legally) exists. Everyone is a legal fake – a dead fictional entity – thus ruled.

Clubs, institutions, libraries, schools, universities, and corporations effectively create 'office holders.' So do board games like chess.

As mentioned, "Society by company" office holders include teachers, principals, secretaries, students, members, financial officers, deans, lecturers, managers, and presidents. Their respective roles are defined by their sphere of operation, meaning they have rules to comply with. There is nothing inherently wrong with Society by company. Companies work by those means, but rules apply to employees only.

The government employs the same method to create politicians, house members, lawyers, justices, citizens, subjects, persons, or other titles that might apply to an official position. The government makes rules for *everyone* so that its (totalitarian) Society (by company) is successful.

Because they now rule the country's people, governments find the need to control money. They invented taxation and a national reserve bank, which brought the people under its overt control. It invests in health, schools, and education for the same reasons. Necessarily, it makes rules for the people, adequately called statutes, falsely called law.

Who now cares that governments are corporations? So long as the government is a legitimate 'society by company' and strictly confines its rules to its employees, no others are affected, leaving the rest of the world free from rule by force. The moment the government spreads its wings and applies its rules to non-employees, a crime against humanity is committed. That practice continues to this day, often via idiotic legal maxims. For example. *"He who does not deny admits."* That legal presumption is not a fact despite its use in that manner. The truth is, *'he who did not deny did naught.'*

Consider that a fictional legal entity cannot write, speak, hear, or act. Dead entities are inert corpses. Human beings act. Corpses cannot. No action is attributable to a dead entity, no matter how much legality decrees otherwise. No legal or criminal charge levied against a legal entity carries any weight, nor can it. No legal statute written by or addressed to a dead entity is worth a dime. Not one!

And that means no indemnity can apply to a legal' office.' The individual man or woman who (from that office) actioned any trespass or crime against humanity is fully responsible, mitigating circumstances accepted. An action is the product of a single living man or woman's choice to act, regardless of whether any particular office is legally instituted or specific actions are legally necessitated. No legal protection or indemnity is possible, therefore. (See the Nuremberg Trial judgments for evidence.)

So, how do we resist? How do we reclaim ourselves? We do not! Why not? Because to do so falsely credits tyrannical oppression with legitimacy. To plead deliverance from evil is to admit its criminal authenticity. It isn't valid now, and it never was. Evil holds no power but what we grant it. So stop! Tyrants have no legitimacy precisely because they had to abandon their born nature to authoritatively command yours!

- They walked out on life – voluntarily. **You didn't.**
- You've not spat in the face of your creation. **They have.**
- They voluntarily relinquished their born nature. **You didn't.**

Demand they defend their (supposed) right to disagree with your (life) position. They cannot because the more they express their ignorance of their lives – the more they confess incompetence to hold any public position or office.

Their confession demonstrates how natural justice works. No artificiality can compete with nature or replace it. No such attempt has any validity but what your consent gives it.

To exercise your right to life, you must know how and from whence your rights come. You must understand your nature, how it protects you, and how it protects itself. You must know consciousness as your operating system of life. Only then will you glimpse a free society.

Imagination is gifted to establish two-way (value) communication with our subconscious mind. The fact that our free will is (sequentially) sandwiched between two independent functions of the subconscious process makes it impossible for the conscious mind to overrule the subconscious mind and vice versa. Two-way mind protection incontrovertibly establishes the most precious law of nature, which emphatically states that **'no mind can rule another.'**

Right in the core of our conscious operating system is nature's 'Natural Law of No Trespass.' All authoritarian rule and all forms of (overt) harmful mind control are thereby outlawed, or else human nature is deposed. Protection from violence was to have been the role of government, but while authoritarians rule that it is unlawful to pillage and plunder, its invented rules that loot and plunder are held legal as though lawful.

Everyone must be free from coercion by others. Each person can then make their own choices in life and follow through with them. If someone else disagrees with how you're living your life, they're free to say so and even try to persuade you to act otherwise. But no one can force you to do so.

Libertarians often refer to this idea as the Non-aggression Principle (NAP), an ethical stance asserting that (initiated) aggression is inherently illegitimate or wrongful and that forceful self-defence is legitimately lawful.

Consider the evidence. Neither our heart nor lungs can trespass the other, nor our two minds infringe on each other. Free will cannot interfere with the subconscious process, which (in return) protects our free will. Similarly, the *'natural law of No Trespass'* protects society, which reciprocally protects our individual life choices.

The primary lawful and moral issue is not the arresting of force, aggression, or violence, but instead the unalienable right of every single man and woman to live. Life should be the determinant of ethical thinking and moral actions. Life takes precedence, thus determining whom or what should be arrested. What better could anyone ask when our 'free will' spiritually determines value, purpose, and morality concordant with the same rights in all others? All just actions testify to morality. It follows that immorality and aggression that might arise be arrested and natural justice administered.

> *"The basic political principle of the Objectivist ethics is: no man may initiate the use of physical force against others. No man—or group or society or government—has the right to assume the role of a criminal and initiate the use of physical compulsion against any man. Men have the right to use physical force only in retaliation and only against those who initiate its use. The ethical principle involved is simple and clear-cut: it is the difference between murder and self-defence. A holdup man seeks to gain a value, wealth, by killing his victim; the victim does not grow richer by killing a holdup man. The principle is: no man may obtain any values from others by resorting to physical force." — Ayn Rand*

We should have known better and busted the herd mentality millennia ago, yet today, its truth remains unknown to all but very few.

Force is one of two kinds, therefore.

- The initiated force that violates one's life is unlawful, unjust, immoral, and even criminal.
- Defensive arrest of illegal and destructive force to uphold life is lawful, just, and moral.

That is the Natural Law of No Trespass. But, you may ask, isn't this the non-aggression principle (NAP)? No. Why not? Because life is first a moral issue. Life protection is paramount, while non-aggression is secondary. But isn't this a circular argument? No, it is not. For example, taxation is not aggression. It is coercive theft without physical aggression. When our focus is life's preservation, all forms of harm are arrested, not just aggressive harm. Trespassers, including people who coerce others, determine the extent of damage or hurt, illuminating the extent of remediation necessary, as seen by a court justice.

The difference between morality as a social convention and its proper place of justness within each (individual) living being becomes vibrantly clear. Morality exists within every cell, tissue, organ, system, and our conscious and subconscious minds. It has existed since Man's inception, and life demands that we protect it.

> *If physical force is to be barred from social relationships, men need an institution charged with the task of protecting their rights under an objective code of rules. —Ayn Rand*

An individual's freedom within the natural law comprises any action compatible with the natural law of conviviality. That means each of us taking on moral obligations towards other individuals and, by implication, entering into society with them, provided the society in question embraces and upholds the natural law.

Such freedom was to have been the role of government, but no government in all history has done so. No government has fully upheld the concept of Individual Rights. America came closest.

Life's protection invites questions. What constitutes interference that violates an individual's right to life? Freedom means protecting one's life and property from interference or trespass by others, specifically through physical force or coercion. Physical force is well understood; typical examples include rape, bodily harm, detention, torture, and murder. Physical coercion includes such as theft, legal or otherwise, blackmail, fraud, and debilitating threats of violence, including all that arrests one's choice to live in freedom. The basic principle of morality and justice is that no man may initiate the use of physical force against others. Thus, the non-aggression principle assuredly results without Man's written rules.

> *"A right cannot be violated except by physical force. Whenever a man is made to act without his own free, personal, individual, voluntary consent—his right has been violated.*
> *We can draw a clear-cut division between the rights of one man and those of another. It is an objective division—not subject to differences of opinion, majority decision, or the arbitrary decree of society. No man has the right to initiate the use of physical force against another man." —Ayn Rand.*

When advocates of the non-aggression principle (NAP) eventually hail man's right to life as primary and thereby seek first to institute and protect it, their cause will advance immeasurably. Today's political question is now crystal clear. Do you want to be protected from evil, or ruled by evil?

Until protection is affirmatively chosen and implemented, every seeming way forward is open to blockage and denial. One's right to an opinion is not the immutable right to rule another.

- People plead for reinstating democracy, but no one describes its interminable evils. One mind cannot rule another!
- People denounce capitalism, yet no one describes its profound benefits and achievements.
- People send myriads of documents to the government at considerable expense to reconvey their political status, yet precious few reconvey their minds cost-free.

All these people focus on reviving the past, yet no authoritarian structured society has ever succeeded, or you would be joyously living free from evil right now.

Nothing is changing as yet. Everyone is happy to chat about villainous corruption, yet no one researches any alternative.

- People who want to be ruled by an authority will write a constitution to ensure its results and take all steps necessary to ensure that nothing will stand in its way. Witness the 'Rule of Law' and the 'Social Contract.' Everyone suffers accordingly.
- People who want protection from evil and violence will write a constitution to ensure their (God-given) rights and protection and take all steps necessary to ensure that every (countermand) form of dictatorial rule is abolished.

- Whatsoever Constitution allows that one man or a group can rule over others favors authoritarian rule in principle.
- If, however, 'freedom' refutes the concept of rule, then it will say so explicitly, whereby tyranny is forever banned, and the people are permanently protected.

The question remains, do you want to be protected from evil, or ruled by it? If protection is your choice, then that is your task. Everything contrary is a roadblock.

*I swear by my life and my love of it that I will never live for the sake of another man, nor ask another man to live for mine." —Ayn Rand.*[3]

All countries now have the opportunity to stamp the phrase 'free nation' on the world map. The foundational premise of free societies is in our nature and is irrevocable. A country's people must declare independence from all tyrannical, foreign, and domestic authority.

As a vital constitutional task, 'all (freedom) dissenters must be left no argument but to dispute their nature,' automatically negating every dispute they raise with no escape possible. Natural law is the only means to freedom and our superior protection from depravity, corruption, slavery, and tyranny.

**Freedom and autonomy reject rule by force**

To understand natural law is to comprehend the fullness and beauty of oneself; not mankind, government, statute laws, positive law, or society! It is to comprehend, that when Creator ordained Man's free choice to live life to the fullest imaginable, natural laws must concretely ensure it.

Nature guarantees that one's mental choices can never corrupt the vital mental processes; reciprocally ensuring that mental processes can never override one's free options. Each had to be guaranteed autonomy to contribute to the other, cooperatively and harmoniously without interference. And that left free will free.

What better explanation sums up individuality, individual rights and intrinsic natural law than the Creator's testament of all three? There is no better example of the principle of non-aggression; none! It is the Creator's natural law of no trespass. No better societal model has ever been offered—but the institution of individual rights is the only thing that can grant it!

Few advocates of the non-aggression principle (NAP) understand this totality or its source. The natural laws of independence, equality, integrity, individual rights, and free will, are all contained within the natural law of no trespass. Commitment, allowance and respect are inclusive, ethics and morality also. This lesson is profound; never to be overstated. Man's nature and his life, are the bottom line; the only adjudicator of his rights, and any social structures that he may desire.

Some argue that only three laws exist—keep the peace, love others as oneself, and respect free will causing no harm or trespass, or words to that effect. All are true in societal principle but lack substantive qualification. None define one's self, one's unalienable right to life, what constitutes free will, how harm or trespass is caused, and by whom, or what constitutes natural justice.

Will anything change, while today's agreed mindset holds tight to the notion that society prevails above all; to which individual men and women must be a servant?

Does Man's ignorance of natural law result from mental apathy, ignorance concerning his faculties, blind acceptance of collectivism, whose social structure enforces compliance with deadly force, or all three? If (sociopathic) rulers, could conspire to conceal Man's true individuality, and force authoritarian rule as law, intentionally making Man a slave without his knowing, why would they not? Ignorance, and servility, thus taught and ingrained into Man's consciousness, would cement authoritarian rule, domination, and control, forever, wouldn't it? Isn't history that proof? Should it surprise, that Man regularly votes for this criminal continuance the world over, and no one ever asks 'by what God-given right should one man rule another?'

Today's task is to advocate, build, and practice individual rights. When we pull the foundation from under authority, sociopathic dominance over Man will crash.

Observably, the Creator has modelled free, symbiotic societies within the nature of every man, woman, and child. All twenty natural laws are translatable into society verbatim. None can be erased. Statism and statute law are made redundant — safety rules remain.

'*Symbiotic society*' is described as different organisms living in close, physical association, typically to the advantage of all. And that, is exactly what our full conscious process is. Our nature is an orchestral masterpiece of creation; different bodily organs, systems and two interlocked minds all working synergistically to the advantage of all.

That picture is the Creator's model for free, organic, symbiotic societies.

# Chapter 12

## Declaration of Independence

America's Declaration of Independence defined how and why the thirteen colonies severed their political ties with Great Britain to form their own government. This move to independence did not happen overnight. Indeed, the desire of many colonists to separate from Britain had been brewing for years.

On June 7, 1776, Richard Henry Lee of Virginia presented a resolution to the Second Continental Congress stating that the colonies "are, and of right ought to be, free and independent States." His call to dissolve political ties with Britain set the stage for the declaration. Still, not all members of the Continental Congress were ready to accept the Lee Resolution, as it became known. After several weeks, they appointed five men to draft a document explaining why the colonies believed they had the right to form their own government. This 'Committee of Five' consisted of John Adams, Benjamin Franklin, Thomas Jefferson, Robert Livingston, and Roger Sherman. That committee appointed John Adams and Thomas Jefferson to write the original draft of what later became known as the (1776) 'Declaration of Independence.'

Adams insisted that Jefferson take the lead, which he did, and although other members of the Committee of Five made a few changes, Jefferson remained the principal author. His draft drew on the language and ideas of several other documents, including the Virginia Declaration of Rights and his version of the Virginia Constitution.

The Declaration of Independence was officially adopted on July 4, 1776 — the day Americans recognise as their Independence Day. A total of fifty-six Delegates from the Continental Congress Signed the Declaration.

Political independence rests on the fundamental autonomy of the human mind. The ability of men and women to think for themselves and guide their lives makes political independence possible and necessary. Without it, there would be no autonomy or independence to protect. Accordingly, there is no authority higher than the individual mind, for which Thomas Jefferson advised us to *"fix reason firmly in her seat and call to her tribunal every fact, every opinion. Question with boldness even the existence of a God."* Without independence and reasoned trust in our judgment, we sacrifice our minds to the state, church, race, nation, or neighbors. That legacy made America the freest and most prosperous country in history.

America's Declaration of Independence document later grew to be revered. Its bestowed freedom inspired many other countries,' and heavily influenced France's Declaration of the Rights of Man and Citizen (1789), as well as Venezuelan (1811), Liberian (1847), and Vietnamese (1945) Declarations, to name a few.

That history is notable because almost all nations now find themselves in a similar predicament. The most pressing matter facing all is not how they might profit in the same manner, but rather, what they can learn from that document and its failings, if any, and what will perpetuate the freedom of the nation's people. That is of the most significant importance today, so let's begin with one of the most memorable lines in history. *"We hold these truths to be self-evident, that all men are created equal, that they are endowed by their Creator with certain unalienable Rights, that among these are Life, Liberty, and the pursuit of Happiness."*

Notably, the Declaration of Independence had a much broader and deeper compass than mere secession of territory and establishing a new nation. It set new principles. That is the task facing many more nations today since no political principles employed in the past have prevented what has since occurred. That distinction is crucial to our advancement.

So, what went wrong around the world? What has allowed 'self-evident truths' and the 'consent of the governed' to be smashed beyond the repair of our 'pursuit of Happiness?'

The answer is not self-evident because if the Declaration document existed to protect the rights of the people, then the words 'protection' and 'rights' are supreme above all else. Yet, the need for 'Protection' is omitted from the list of self-evident truths. Further, while "certain unalienable Rights" imply that all men are treated equally, 'individual rights' should be the sole means of preserving or protecting equality. Moreover, the word 'liberty' can be omitted because it refers to collective rights or permissions. It should properly be replaced with the word 'freedom' as it applies singularly to individuals, not groups or society as a collective. It is possible to have liberty yet not be free.

So, while the Declaration of Independence contained immortal truths, it duly authorised and instituted a representative public body in a (political) sovereign capacity, all supported by the force of the people's opinion.

We have all heard that *"governments derive their just powers from the consent of the governed,"* that is to say, collectively or with the consent of the majority in (modern) democratic language. Here, then, is an unresolved anomaly. While the rights of all individuals are purportedly held sacred and protected by constitutional guarantees, which even the government itself is bound not to violate, nonetheless, the rights of all individuals are collectivised by the state under the banner of 'liberty.' Government is thereby enabled to indoctrinate, regulate, and manipulate the *'consent of the governed,'* from which it derives its (purported) just powers.

The concept of a republic is correct in defining individual rights, as opposed to a democracy based on majority rule. Nevertheless, authoritarian rule is automatically annulled since individual rights are founded on equality. It matters not how much-limited government appears or is praised as virtuous; no rule is righteous, whereby rule must never function again. Thus, while America liberated itself true to freedom principles it declared, including the moral (not financial) system of capitalism, its specific failure to protect 'individual rights' permitted degenerate political action, resulting in unrestrained authority from the unbridled weight of an influential few. Such degradation of rights and corruption is the opposite of what *'certain unalienable rights' offer 'all men created equal.'* Hence, republicanism was doomed from the start because it failed to protect the people's protections.

Notwithstanding, the fierce personal and public struggle between two political titans continues to shape America and much of the world today. While disguised as political parties ostensibly upholding the same cause, neither is booming due to the root problem of authoritarian rule, no matter how limited. Not surprisingly, the world surges toward totalitarianism with no arrest or respite on the horizon, meaning it is time to get very serious –more truthfully factual than at any time in Earth's history.

[The next few paragraphs were covered in my book *'Navigate to Freedom'* but are rewritten here with some additional clarifications.]

Sociopaths and psychopaths have, as their final scorched earth policy, united to unleash a program intended to pollute the DNA of Mankind to erase life's signature imprinted in our DNA. After that, they claim that we, as their exclusive patented property, are no longer a part of nature's source creator. Like cattle rustlers attempting to change our brand, they claim that by use of their concocted 'Mark of the Beast,' all dimwitted or trusting souls who fall for this ruse will become property belonging to them for whatever use they deem appropriate, including democide, all to suit their criminal purposes.

(Democide is any murder by government--by officials acting under the authority of government. That is, they act according to explicit or implicit government policy or with the implicit or explicit approval of the highest officials.)

Will they get away with it? No. The reason is that all of them, by choosing criminal actions, voluntarily relinquished their own nature and rights, by which forfeiture, all of their (claimed) DNA patents are rendered void from inception. They walk out on life voluntarily. They give up their freedom willingly. By their own free choice, they volunteer that death be their God. Meanwhile, natural law delivers the consequence of those actions. Our task is to apprise them of these immutable facts with irrevocable certainty so that no defence on their part is possible.

Can that be done? Yes, absolutely. How? By uniting our human conscious process with the lessons offered by the United States Declaration of Independence. I will present these principles so you can see the road forward with clear and resolute certainty, yet never attempted in history.

You will recall me describing that our cognitive free will is (axiomatically) positioned between the subconscious faculties of perception and muscular activation. Therefore, we each are the indisputable author of all our actions, automatically responsible for their consequences as natural law determines. Nothing can alter that fact save death. No 'right' to commit death exists, save (personal) suicide.

No change to our DNA by any man or woman can alter that fact without such actions, confessing those people's free choice to violate their nature, thereby lawfully canceling their actions. Moreover, free choice to violate another's nature annuls any claim to that particular choice. Consequently, those sociopaths are fully accountable for all detrimental and harmful consequences as outlaws.

That is natural law and natural justice. Additionally, the sandwiched location of cognitive freedom describes the nature of independence and individual rights, whilst our sequential mental process delineates the matter of 'protection.' The subconscious mind cannot overrule free will, or else we have no free will. Neither can free will overrule the subconscious mind because its process is fully automated. No mind can rule another. Free will is fully protected because, without free will, our conscious process cannot function at all.

Our (unalienable) right to life is individual and cannot be otherwise. Our (inalienable) right to property is personal and cannot be otherwise. Thus, the body of people we elect must protect our rights and freedoms henceforth.

Four lessons concerning a new Declaration of Independence (for all nations) are now vividly clear.

**1** Rights belong exclusively to every man, woman, and child. No group of people may overrule, usurp, deny, or forbid those rights, not even the government.

**2** Individual rights must be enshrined and fully protected. People cannot abandon their rights to self-evidence alone.

**3** Because free will is self-activated, no life-supportive action can transpire without free will. Hence, it cannot be overruled, usurped, denied, or forbidden.

**4** No free society is possible without the absolute protection of free will, plus every individual's unalienable right to life and inalienable right to property and our pursuit of happiness.

Those revelations are a game changer beyond all else. The message from nature's source creator is indelibly clear, the intention being that we govern ourselves, which requires that we do not elect anyone to control us. Jefferson's political philosophy came very close when he said,"*That government is best which governs least.*" Indeed, the only thing it can control is your protection and mine. That is exceedingly close to the 'republican' ideal; however, *'no rule'* replaces *'limited rule,'* the door crack through which tyranny invariably enters.

It remains that if our free will is not to be prescribed by any outside source, including DNA modifications, there can be no government whose legislation may gravely threaten to violate our protections. The people must protect their unalienable right to life and (inalienable) property rights from all interference and theft. Then, any empires, monarchies, or governments that infringe on or violate those freedoms via authoritarian rule declare themselves outlaws by nature.

Just as neither of our two minds can prescribe the other's process, neither can any outside source do the same. All that we need, therefore, is a body of people charged with administering our protections and not one thing more. Is there any precedent for such a thing? Yes, absolutely. Our bodily immune system, our endocrine system, our conscience, and our emotions all testify that cause unmistakably. Protection is encrypted in our nature.

Now, the phrase *'consent of the governed'* is shown for the imposter it is. Propaganda and indoctrination fuel our conscious ignorance to manipulate our consent. In truth, tragically, without our knowing, we endorse an evil that moulds our consent, thereby denying all remedy.

But no more. We can replace *'consent of the governed'* with *'nature's consent to self-govern our autonomous freedom within the equal rights of all others.'* The replacement term *'Creators consent'* suffers no obstruction but from self-declared outlaws, whose (anti-life) choice renders their mandates void from inception.

Thomas Jefferson correctly identified that the Source creator conferred divine rights on every individual but never to those who forbid our rights. Today's tragedy arose from not protecting those rights and freedoms. Self-evident truths did not suffice and never will. Fortunately, we now have proof of what does defend our rights.

Our nature, bestowed by Source, survives through inbuilt protections, impossible to erase, even by DNA pirates.

The 'natural rights' spoken of by Jefferson were the right to life, which requires each individual to have access to work and acquire property to "pursue happiness." The term 'have access' means the *government cannot deny it,* not that *government must provide it.* In political terms, we possess the natural right to defend our life, liberty, and property from invasive attacks. It was the government's proper purpose to use its defensive power of force to repel all assaults on our rights and freedoms, such that should government overstep that boundary, then it would be the greatest tyrant and plunderer of them all. And that has happened worldwide. Since the government has a virtual monopoly of force, its potential for evil is far greater than any other institution.

Jefferson's position on foreign policy did not extend to equipping the government to remake the world to America's liking forcibly, but instead to not stand in its way. Indeed, Jefferson expressed his foreign policy in this classic phrase: "*Peace, commerce, and honest friendship with all nations-entangling alliances with none.*"

So we read "*that whenever any Form of Government becomes destructive of these ends, it is the Right of the People to alter or to abolish it, and to institute new Government, laying its foundation on such principles and organising its powers in such form, as to them shall seem most likely to effect their Safety and Happiness.*"

Three fundamental lessons emerge for our consideration.

**1** First, no man has a mandate from God or anyone else to rule over other men, nor any right to do so. No emperor, king, dictator, monarch, or government is a superior moral agent in denying or confiscating people's unalienable right to life. Political consent can never be universal since majority consent must overrule minority dissent. Gang warfare is inevitable thereby, and impossible to prevent, whereby the concept of 'rule' is flawed from the outset.

**2** Second, a government's power is only 'just' when the people's rights are preserved and protected. Today, consent is given only to the institution of government, never to the separate legislations it enacts. Accordingly, we are held captive, with all our rights and freedoms denied.

**3** Since universal public approval of State legislations are impossible, the government denies our right to disagree with any part. If that does not convince you all government is impossible, nothing will.

The lesson is crystal clear. If we are to preserve our rights and freedoms, all who refuse them must be allowed to fall on their sword.

So we read that in 1776 "*when a long train of abuses and usurpations, pursuing invariably the same object evinces a design to reduce them under absolute Despotism, it is their right, it is their duty, to throw off such Government, and to provide new Guards for their future security.*"

More than opting to throw government out, we have reached a point in world history where new guards will facilitate their obsolescence.

We have before us, both the charter of a new nation, and the rationalisation of rebellion. Jefferson himself launched the political principle, that when the instrument of government fails, or worse, it opposes bettering our circumstances by destroying them. Properly, it is high time to banish authoritarian rule from the surface of the planet. Any government. .

That begs the question: is a government necessary at all, if the only thing required is to preserve the people's right to life, their freedom, and their pursuit of happiness?

My answer is a resounding no! There is no better quest than to abolish what punishes us, accept our given rights and freedom and protect both in perpetuity. For that, we have all the means necessary to orchestrate a free society, doubly blessed by the fact that all actions by trespassers and outlaws self admit their crimes against humanity.

We have all the means necessary to orchestrate a free society, doubly blessed because all actions by trespassers and outlaws self-admit their crimes against humanity. Accordingly, *'Nature's consent to self-govern'* removes all need for *'consent of the governed.'* All need for government as we have known it is cancelled, provided we ensure our free will and rights are protected from all trespass.

**Declaration of Independence**

My draft 'Declaration of Independence' is more than for your diligent reading. It calls for your study and comprehension. Its form and substance closely approximates the (American) 1776 Declaration of Independence, mainly for reasons already given. In form, it contains the same three parts: first, a preamble; second, a list of grievances; followed by a statement of rationalized rebellion invoking the charter of a new nation. It references the people's unalienable right to life and inalienable right to the fruits of their labours, consistent with the pursuit of happiness.

The declaration document refers to a Charter of Individual Rights inclusively written in an (elsewhere drafted 2019 – since amended) Constitution document, also notationally written in the next chapter. Chief among all documents is the word 'freedom' (independent) instead of' liberty' (collective).

Additionally, the term 'Protectorate(s)' replaces government. Hence, individual rights universally belong to all people regardless of indigenous heritage, foreign culture, or ethnic background.

The Declaration preamble introduces the conceptual principle of 'new Protections,' hence the demise of all 'government' and all variations thereof including Corporate lookalikes. A revolution of this kind is unprecedented No such thing has ever transpired before. The words that follow are crucially important. They spell out that the (new - outstanding) Protectorate hallmark is the form and powers of natural law encrypted in our human Nature.

Further, as gifted by 'Nature's God' (Jeffersons' words), our gift of the rights, freedoms, and powers within those laws is firmly established as non-erasable, which same laws assuredly attest will affect the people's Safety and Happiness. In other words, people's (freely given) respect for the natural laws of their Nature echoes nature's indisputable consent for absolute protection of the peoples rights and freedoms as gifted by Source Creator. No further (universal) consent is needed since all (enacted) dissent by outlaws triggers our protection and natural justice. Likewise, no need exists for group rights; hence, all potential for gang warfare dies.

This Declaration manifests the principle of free will in society, absent any prescriptions, instructions, statutes, or artificial law. No better form of self-governance exists, nor can it.

Here is a suggested 'Preamble' part, made applicable to any nation on earth by inserting its defined (geographical Nation) name. [I published the original text and all grievances for Australians in Navigate to Freedom. This version universally applies to any nation.] Further amendments may follow.

**Part One- Preamble**

Whereas Men and Women of the [INSERT NATION] are now recognised only as fictional legal entities, it has become necessary they unilaterally dissolve the political bands that once united them but now abjectly compels enslavement to a corporatised sociopathic conglomerate. A decent respect for their immutable 'right to life' requires they should declare the causes which impel them to the separation and their natural born right to reconstitute society for freedom in perpetuity.

Self-evident truth holds that all men and all women are (gender) created equal in nature, unique in expression, endowed by Nature's source creator with unalienable right to life, freedom and pursuit of happiness, and inalienable right to the fruits of their labours: That whenever any instituted Form of Government becomes destructive of those rights and freedoms, it is the Right of the self-governed People to alter or to abolish it, and to formulate new Protections, founded on the principles and just powers that, by the immutable Laws of Nature and Nature's God encrypted in all men and women, assuredly effect their safety, protection and happiness.

Prudence indeed dictates that the people should not change established Governments for light and transient causes and that Mankind appears more disposed to suffer without appeal than to right wrongs by abolishing increasing sufferance enacted by stealth with increasing force and violence over generations. But when abuses, usurpations, initiated force, and insufferable trauma in pursuit of overt dictatorial object evinces absolute despotism absent end, it is the people's right and duty to throw off such government and provide new protections for their future comforts and security. The patient sufferance of all [INSERT NATION] peoples, recently exacerbated by genocide, necessarily adjures they urgently abolish all former government systems, indeed the very concept of government, and begin anew. [INSERT NATION] rule reveals a history of repeated injuries and usurpations, later transformed without Peoples referendum to a 'corporate service provider absent de jure government' having in direct object the establishment of an absolute tyranny over [INSERT NATION] States vested in communistic world control; a 'new world order.' In proof thereof, the people now submit the facts of criminal violation of Man's right to life to a candid World.

**Part Two – List of grievances**

Part Two lists very pertinent grievances – vital issues that are critical to understanding. This part may also include travesties concerning indigenous sovereign peoples, people of all ages, all forms of government, changes made without the people's consent, fraudulent identification through legalese and tradable birth certificates. However, it is not necessary to list the whole gamut of authoritarian domination, and control, past, present and future planned. Instead, authors must address the fact that today's government has authored its own demise by citing evidence that proves that matter beyond debate. The draft document for Australia does that explicitly! Other countries are obliged to do likewise.

**Part Three – Declaration of intent.**

"The falsely acclaimed [INSERT NATION] government has committed itself and its agencies to ensuring that the unalienable individual rights of all who maintain and uphold government should never exist. Forbidden redress by immoral (legal) rules, deception, and corruption in defiance of a free people, all [INSERT NATION] people are insanely and criminally forced to uphold bloody-minded tyranny as the only liberty possible! Such rebellion unquestionably confirms that the '[INSERT NATION] Government' corporate entity is illegitimate and criminally liable.

When Statutes constrain men and women contrary to their nature by any fictional or covert invention, when criminal abuse, usurpations, and violation of Man's Right to life, reduce existence to animal-like status under absolute despotism, cessation of insufferable criminal evil demands. When injuries, violence, and usurpations consistently repeat for the direct object of tyranny over Man, so indisputable crime summed as 'moral right to rule' and 'immoral wrong to refuse rule,' is historical fact open to all seekers of truth, no need to re-state it. No trial is warranted; all crimes against humanity, by action, confessed.

We, the One People of the [INSERT NATION] now assembling in appeal to the Supreme Judge of the World in Rectitude of our Intentions do solemnly publish and declare that the States and Territories of this [INSERT NATION], of Right, ought to be one Free and Independent Nation. Henceforth its states, territories and all people are absolved and divorced from all Allegiance to past government; all political connections with [SPECIFY OTHER PARTIES] dissolved. Additionally, all non-elected bodies, assemblies, incorporated entities, other partisan authorities/agents, and alphabet agencies, foreign and domestic. Moreover, as One People, we declare our Right to peaceful co-existence, self-governance, to maintain National Defence, both Foreign and Domestic, contract Alliances, establish Trade, and do all which Independent Nations and States may by Right do."

*****

The(triple authored) Declaration document for Australia renders all previous constitutional and quasi-constitutional documents void. It further renders the Nation reconstituted on the Rights, and Laws of Nature encrypted within the nature of every man, woman and child as set out in the (Constitutional) Charter of Individual Rights. Thereby established, no 'person' or Sentient Living Being may initiate the use of physical force or violate another's life, save for (self-defence) arresting any initiating party. Protectorate governance shall have no other function than to delineate, enact and uphold such Natural Laws, Rights and freedoms in perpetuity. For this Declaration securing and protecting life, reason, and freedom respectful of all in human affairs, we pledge our diligent, most reverent commitment and our sacred honour.

The first paragraph of Part three following the list of grievances serves to acutely and accurately sum the whole list in such a manner that all committed crimes against a Nation's people are shown as indisputable facts warranting immediate replacement of government, no invented phrases for the sake of dramatisation warranted or permitted.

The third last paragraph (above document) is written to expose immorality and injustices and concludes with the principle of natural justice whereby (outlaw) practitioners confess (intended or actual) criminal action. In other words, everything in the document must uphold all the Life-sustaining natural law principles that human nature reveals, such that no objection can be raised without disputing one's human nature, instantly and automatically canceling their objection.

That is an indisputable watertight case. Document authors must eliminate phraseology, words, concepts, or principles that might undermine the cause. They must cross-examine all sentences in terms of express statements absent ambiguity. Further, any anomalies or dichotomies must be removed, even across paragraphs and pages.

The best legal, lawful, philosophical, and psychological minds will scrutinise this document, many seeking possible flaws to deny or refuse it. Accordingly, the document must point all readers to the source of natural law intrinsic in our nature, unequivocally, with no sidetracks permitted. Nature is the bottom line; our source creator refuses all differing opinions. Dissenters must put up or shut up. Authors must ensure that nature's outcome is conclusive, final and inescapable, with no refusal possible.

My second last paragraph explains the people's divorce from all government, its affiliations, and treaties with all corporate or governmental entities, whether foreign or domestic, which by abolition can no longer apply. Sovereignty of the people means divorce from all who would violate self-mastered autonomy, all foreign and domestic agencies, corporations, and governments themselves. This paragraph draws attention to parameters guiding the implementation of a (separate)' Protectorate Constitution' document, including the 'Charter of Individual Rights.' No suggested amendments to this Declaration must usurp its purpose, need, or lawful thrust.

My final paragraph delivers the outcome of all that proceeds it. As concisely and accurately as space permits, it establishes the new nation, its lawful parameters, the un-erasable source of those foundations, and self-governance of all its people, "this Declaration securing and protecting life, reason, and freedom respectful of all in human affairs."

Remember that this document cannot be read or comprehended in isolation. Without knowledge of the source of natural law, no relevance to justice, rights, and freedom is certain. Plus, with no rightful (lawful) objective philosophy, no measure of its authenticity or validity is possible. (My other books fully describe this.)

Humankind faces its greatest challenge in world history, and now you've all the means necessary to complete it. Refuse this opportunity, and it will likely never be repeated.

Speaking from experience, any discussion concerning any single point I have made or revelation almost inevitably results in someone questioning, *"But what about...A or B or C?"* One needs to know the whole story to understand the derivative parts, yet the big picture is almost unexplainable without grasping its parts. It's a catch-22 situation. I sincerely advise you carefully choose with whom you discuss these matters discretely.

It is sad, if not tragic, that modern-day 'progressives' speak of the secular divine right to 'entitlements,' by which individuals are assisted at the expense of others. Tragically, all collectives are accountable to the nation under the banner of 'democracy' or 'social contract,' and that is the thin edge of the wedge Society today consists of evil parasites whose goal is to existentially build and extend a system of political favours and privileges among corrupted businessmen – 'crony capitalists' – who are unwilling or damnably incompetent to honestly and morally produce anything through peaceful and voluntary trades in a free marketplace.

Those who comprehend the liberty for which America's Founding Fathers pledged their lives, fortunes, and sacred honor in the war of independence must do all in their power to restore that crucial understanding and appreciation of individual freedom and individual rights throughout the world's nations.

Conscious knowledge, existential natural law, and objective philosophy ensure that freedom in political and economic individualism is forever cemented in society as humanity's proudest and most noble achievement.

It follows that revision of our whole education system is urgently needed, most notably in human and mental health sciences.

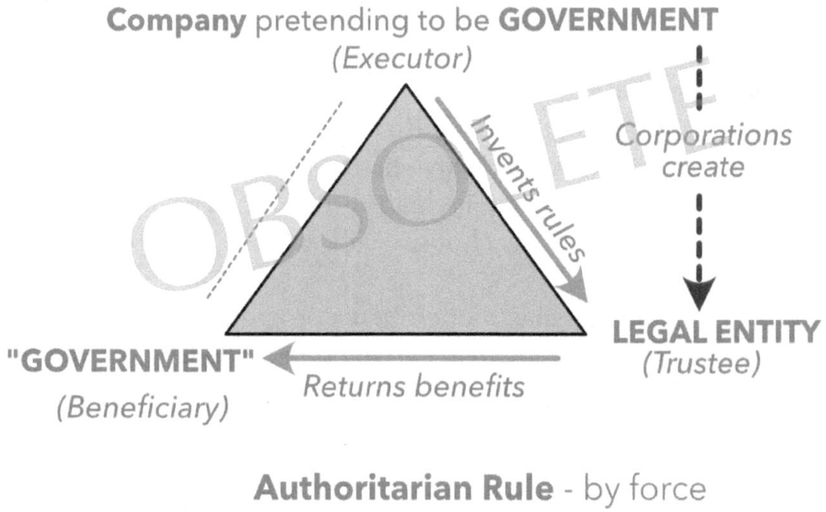


The above diagram shows government as a trust, all based on pretend laws rendered obsolete in a Protectorate Society.

The bottom diagram echoes the same format but shows Living Beings as the beneficiary - not Governments. The 'Protectorate' suffices as a 'trustee' by upholding natural law as employees of the people.

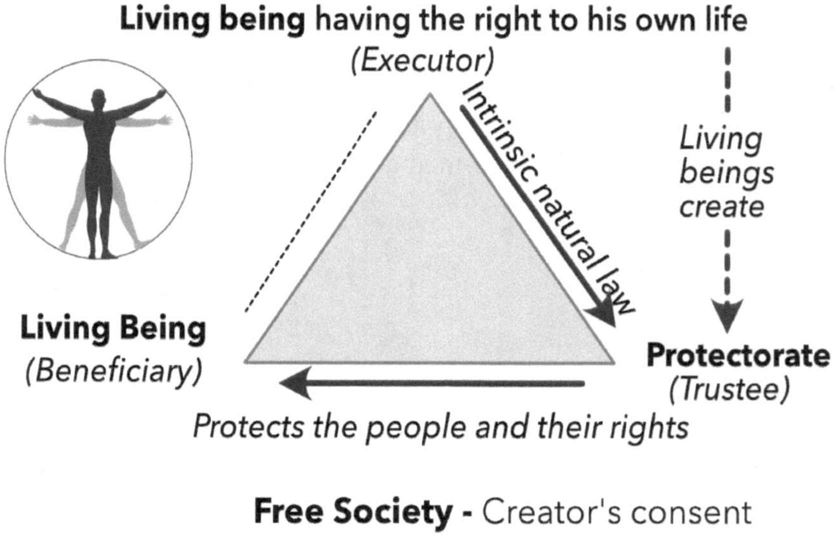

# Chapter 13

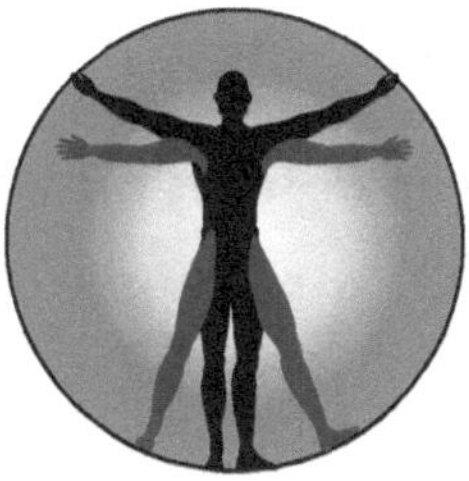

## Charter of Individual Rights

This chapter is an abbreviated version of the Charter of Individual Rights included in the Conceptual Constitution document, written for our future free (Protectorate) societies. I introduced them in my book *'Navigate to Freedom,'* for which a (conceptual) Constitution has already been written for adoption by any country, although not yet released. The articles below are based on natural law revealed by the human conscious process but are illustrative of intent only, not the actual article wording. Included quotations show how individual rights parallel an objective philosophy.

**1. Article: Preliminaries**

The People of a [Subject Nation] have immutable and unalienable right to life and inalienable right to the fruits of their labours within limits drawn around each by the equal rights of all others; such Rights unable to be removed by any means.

Because a (protectorate) nation comprises only individuals, it can have no rights other than those of its people. It has a right to its territorial integrity and social system and has constituted a Protectorate since the people instituted that. The elected Protectorate is the servant or agent of its people. Its rights are delegated to it by the people specifically for protecting them from physical force, derived from every individual's right of self-defence.

Natural law, gifted by Nature's source creator and encrypted in human Nature, decrees that whosoever disavows the following immutable individual rights in Articles 2 through Article 10 inclusive repudiates their own Nature. Our independent Nature is our reality, negating any contrary uttered or written proclamations or claims, including all legal inventions, automatically rendering them null and void from inception.

*Reality is an absolute, existence is an absolute, a speck of dust is an absolute and so is a human life. Whether you live or die is an absolute. Whether you have a piece of bread or not, is an absolute. Whether you eat your bread or see it vanish into a looter's stomach, is an absolute. — Ayn Rand*

**2. Article: Unalienable Right to Life**

No Protectorate is permitted to annul, invalidate, deny, or usurp anyone's unalienable right to life drawn about them by the equal rights of all others. Furthermore, no Protectorate may grant anyone or any group or body of people any authority to command another since no man, woman, or group is a human agent; all claims are refused and dismissed.

*A "right" is a moral principle defining and sanctioning a man's freedom of action in a social context. There is only one fundamental right (all the others are its consequences or corollaries): a man's right to his own life. The right to life means that a man has the right to support his life by his own work (on any economic level, as high as his ability will carry him); it does not mean that others must provide him with the necessities of life. —Ayn Rand*

Additionally, no man, woman or child shall be legally or otherwise deemed, classified, or treated as animal.

**3 Right to Freedom**

This article ensures every individual's unalienable right to life, freedom, and the Pursuit of Happiness, including free-will choice of thought and action, travel, and privacy, all guaranteed inclusive of the responsibility, liability, and accountability naturally and inherently flowing from there. Additionally, this article protects the NaturaL law of Free will, including one's whole conscious process that testifies to it.

A rational mind does not work under compulsion; it does not subordinate its grasp of reality to anyone's orders, directives, or controls; it does not sacrifice its knowledge, its view of the truth, to anyone's opinions, threats, wishes, plans, or "welfare." Such a mind may be hampered by others, it may be silenced, proscribed, imprisoned, or destroyed; it cannot be forced; a gun is not an argument.— Ayn Rand

Importantly, as stated in the Charter –"No Protectorate shall, regardless of purported authority, abrogate, subjugate, subordinate, fraudulently acquire, usurp, blackmail, invade, violate, commandeer, steal, arrest, confiscate, or detain the duly secured value of life, or one's property by the principle of Natural Law immutably inherent in each (individual) Sentient Living Being, without prejudice by creation."

No individual may be pressured to join, contribute, register, or enrol in any association. No individual is required to enter any branch of the Armed Forces, private militia, intelligence, or police.

**4 Free Association — Human Expression and Privacy**

This article contains several subclauses, as should be expected. Consenting adults are protected, and so are the rights of individuals to peaceably assemble or join together in marriage or friendly association.

Nature also protects the equality of all men and women. Additionally, no Protectorate shall vitiate, deny, or annul any individual's unalienable right to resist and defend against all transgression, trespass, harm, and violation of life. Accordingly, all people have the right to protect their rights.

The people of a free nation agree on the basic principle to be implemented – individual rights. No need exists for the decisions of a majority vote since Nature's source creator has consented to every individual's rights. Disagreement refutes one's Nature, which nullifies the dispute. No man or group thereby holds a blank check on power over others.

Free exchange of ideas, freedom of religion, freedom of speech, freedom of the press, electronic, optical, or any other communication or expression are also protected. So, too, the freedom of assembly, everyone's right to physically gather or associate with others in groups for economic, political, or religious purposes. Meanwhile, no one may countermand or obstruct the redress of grievances, opinions, and views, the right of public criticism, or the right of the public to combine and demonstrate against oppression and wrong-doing. In short, the people are their protectors. Religions, religious customs, and indigenous or local culture shall not be.

People's right to travel, vote, privacy, and make important decisions about their health care or body and the right to critical thinking, ethics, and morality are protected.

**5. Identity**

No Protectorate shall accept as Identification (ID) any card or document purporting that the cardholder is a 'person,' which claimed 'person' is in truth an invented fictional entity having no life characteristic identifiers (e.g., blood group) irrespective of a (displayed) portrait photo.

Conversely, an individual's biometric identification of their sentient living being (ILB) that biometrically attests to their life as an individual man or woman is valid.

Whatever you choose to consider, be it an object, an attribute or an action, the law of identity remains the same. A leaf cannot be a stone at the same time, it cannot be all red and all green at the same time, it cannot freeze and burn at the same time. A is A. Or, if you wish it stated in simpler language: You cannot have your cake and eat it, too. —Ayn Rand

Many people refuse to accept the fact that A is A. The purpose of those pirates who taught us to evade that fact was to make you forget that Man is Man – to make you accept you are a legal entity subject to their rule.

All legal identification based on invented fictional entities is abolished within a protectorate, automatically canceling every written (law) statute or legislation concerning such inventions. All identity theft, past, present, and future, is abolished, save for membership cards used in voluntary institutions such as universities, libraries, incorporated bodies, gymnasiums, or clubs.

**6. Health**

No Protectorate or any medical practitioner shall require an individual to be medically treated or undergo medical experiments, be forced medical examination, or be given treatment without informed consent following full disclosure.

On the physical level, the functions of all living organisms, from the simplest to the most complex—from the nutritive function in the single cell of an amoeba to the blood circulation in the body of a man—are actions generated by the organism itself and directed to a single goal: the maintenance of the organism's life. —Ayn Rand

Unlawful human trafficking or unlawful trafficking of any human body parts, or fluid, whether prenatal, infant, child, or adult is strictly outlawed.

Unlawful human trafficking or unlawful trafficking of any human body parts or fluid, whether prenatal, infant, child, or adult, is strictly outlawed.

Individuals are permitted to ingest substances or participate in practices that may or may not cause health, ill health, or injury, provided that such actions do not harm the rights and freedoms of others.

All pregnant mothers are permitted during the first three months of pregnancy to act for and on behalf of the foetus umbilically co-joined as a potential independent living being, in satisfaction of the mother's own free will and unalienable right to life. Likewise, pregnant mothers are free to refuse any medical practice or procedure that may cause harm to themselves or the foetus at any time during the term of pregnancy absent the mothers' autographed consent of full written disclosure inclusive of the practitioner's admission of liability.

An embryo has no rights. Rights do not pertain to a potential, only to an actual being. A child cannot acquire any rights until it is born. The living take precedence over the not-yet-living (or the unborn). Abortion is a moral right—which should be left to the sole discretion of the woman involved; morally, nothing other than her wish in the matter is to be considered. Who can conceivably have the right to dictate to her what disposition she is to make of the functions of her own body? — Ayn Rand

**7 Age of Independence**

Having no precedent on earth, this article endorses a teenager's right to choose and practice full adulthood with full unalienable and inalienable rights within three years, say between fifteen and eighteen years of age. No adult who respects freedom can dictate a set age otherwise. Given that parents and legal guardians have complete freedom to raise their children as they see fit, they are equally deemed responsible and accountable for the actions of their children. However, any teenager who at the minimum set age chooses to accept, hold and honour a "Probationary Acceptance (of) Sovereignty Status", (PASS), assumes full adulthood freedoms and responsibilities, such PASS automatically becoming redundant upon reaching the end of the period allocated to the PASS.

The responsibilities of these teenagers and their parents are made crystal clear. Should any PASS holder within the specified period be found to have relinquished their (adult) rights by violating the constitutional rights of others, the (PASS) is canceled, whence the wayward individual is held fully accountable for their actions as though an adult – complete parental care and responsibility instantly reinstated. The success achieved by the PASS-entitled teenager, still with parental guidance, will produce long-lasting benefits for all involved.

**8. Inalienable Right to Property**

Quote: *"No Protectorate shall cancel, forfeit, annul or alienate any individual's right to own personal property free and clear of all encumbrances; nor forbid any right to alienate property rights over things, being no right to alienate the right itself, property rights thereby preserved."* That text shows how rights are protected and how 'protection' itself is protected. And that is how a 'Protectorate Constitution' will differ from all past constitutions.

In addition, property is accorded 'value' through every Sentient Living Being's thought, speech, and action to cultivate, make, and earn value, which preserves each individual's free will to choose to gift, trade, or dispose of said value or property.

*Only a ghost can exist without material property; only a slave can work with no right to the product of his effort. The doctrine that "human rights" are superior to "property rights" simply means that some human beings have the right to make property out of others; since the competent have nothing to gain from the incompetent, it means the right of the incompetent to own their betters and to use them as productive cattle. Whoever regards this as human and right, has no right to the title of "human." —Ayn Rand*

Accordingly, "no Protectorate shall authorise acquisition of property ownership by any means other than being gifted, bought, or sold; provided that such property may be aliened in service of incurred debt; no private property ever taken compulsorily for public use; regardless of 'just compensation', no form of eminent domain henceforth existing. save as elsewhere described."

*A unilateral breach of contract involves an indirect use of physical force: it consists, in essence, of one man receiving the material values, goods or services of another, then refusing to pay for them and thus keeping them by force (by mere physical possession), not by right—i.e., keeping them without the consent of the owner. — Ayn Rand*

**9. Right to Intellectual property**

Intellectual property is prescribed within limits that protect original ownership rights but also prevent' original patent' applications from being bought to prevent that patented idea from ever being marketed.|Patents and copyrights are the legal implementation of a man's right to the product of his mind., to the origination of an idea. The subject of patents and copyrights is intellectual property.

However, an idea cannot be protected until given a material form. The patent or copyright protects not the physical object but the idea that it embodies. Said differently, the idea's originator creates value that may not be used without his consent. Correspondingly, the law establishes a mind's right to that property it has brought into existence.

No patent may be secured from any idea that has been in the public domain or used commercially before a potential patent application date. Neither may any part of any life form nor any biological modification of existing organisms creating a new class of biological organism ever be patentable.

Any previous patents concerning any constituent part or whole part of any life form are rendered null and void and terminated without exception. Nature cannot be re-invented.

**10. Right to Protection from force and coercion**

No Protectorate shall permit, authorise, direct, mandate, legislate or command the initiation of force, violence, coercion, blackmail, rape, or fraud against any individual's life or property.

Whatsoever or whosoever denies, precludes, or prevents any individual's choice to justly and morally act to support their life and property commits a crime of trespass pending arrest.

**11. Right to Protection**

A Protectorate shields its Members from false impersonation. Everyone has the unalienable right to resist and defend against all private or public transgression, physical harm, trespass, and violation of life. Physical harm includes but is not limited to unconsciousness, mind control, prolonged stress of the five senses, pain, broken bones, disfigurement, infection with a disease, coerced or compelled vaccinations, injections, DNA manipulation, or alteration.

Serious harm includes the cumulative effect of any harm likely to endanger a person's life or exercise of their free will that is or is expected to be significant and longstanding, or in fact, does. Threats are also defined. In addition, no Protectorate shall disallow or deny that retaliatory force may lawfully and morally be used by any Individual separately or collectively, only in defence against those who violate an Individual's unalienable right to life; such arresting force including the use of arms strictly and lawfully limited to stopping the immediate threat and no more, thus preventing further force initiated against any Individuals or their property.

**12. Right to bear arms**

This article (particularly) defines that "No National Emergency shall preclude any individual right to self-defence. Neither alter the duties prescribed for all protectorates in this constitution."

Further, "no Protectorate shall deprive, deny, or forbid any Individual's Right to bear arms in self-defence against any threat of imminent danger to life, except those individuals found to have used arms to deny the right of others." Otherwise, every individual has the right to preserve, protect and defend his life, liberty, and property, or that of any other party, or to organise himself into private militia for these purposes. Furthermore, "no

Individual's severally, or collectively, may initiate force, coercion, blackmail, or fraud against any other Individual's life, or property."

**13 & 14. Protections from servitude, war, terrorism, and surveillance.**

Two articles are reserved:

- First, for defining protections against servitude, war, and terrorism
- Second, for defining protection from invasive systems and privacy violations. Such includes any wilful damage or interruption to any electronic systems. All forms of local or remote (electronic or camera) contact tracing and surveillance that permit, allow, or facilitate usage or sale of that collected data to any third party are prohibited.

**15. Right to one's rights**

Everyone has a right to a fair and speedy trial by a local and impartial jury; alternately, the right to a public trial, all protected from secret proceedings that might encourage abuse of the Natural Justice system, preserving transparency.

No one can ascribe or confer unalienable or inalienable rights to 'collective' bodies or collective numbers of Individual Living Beings; human rights, indigenous rights, fundamental rights, workers rights, or other such claimed 'collective rights' rendered redundant by Unalienable Individual Rights herein defined.

No Protectorate shall infringe, deny, or forbid the right of an individual to organise the overthrow of a government initiating force against its people.

- No Protectorate shall deny or forbid the right of Members of the Armed Forces, private militia, intelligence, or police to disobey any order which they have certifiably established as conflicting with the rights and liberties eternally enshrined in this Charter of Individual Rights. (Refer to the Nuremberg Code.)

**Protection**

All the (above) articles in the (actual) Constitution differ from the explanations above in that they specifically state that our rights shall never violated or denied. In that sense, they markedly differ from rights (written in the positive format), which are effective government permissions only. Individual rights are innate and immutable within us all.

## What is a Protectorate?

'Protectorate' is another word for a "protected state."

# Chapter 14

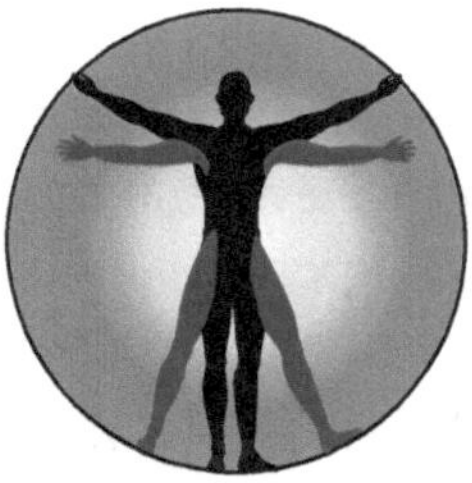

## Protectorates versus Government

Ordinarily, this term refers to one state (Big Brother) protecting another state. However, if we think of people as born into the jurisdiction of life, meaning the condition or state of living life, then people who vote for a (political) body of people to protect their living state will elect a protectorate.'

Thus, a 'Protectorate,' substituted in place of government, is a constitutionally appointed body of people that upholds and protects people's rights and freedoms. It is that simple. Of course, it cannot violate anyone's rights without trespassing its charter, whereby the people forbid authoritarian rule by the protectorate as prescribed by what their human nature is and how it functions.

**The Social Contract**

People rejected Natural law some five hundred years ago and replaced it with a theoretical construct of the 'state of nature,' such nonsense permitting what has since been called the *'Social Contract.'*

Thomas Hobbes held that the 'State of nature' is a state of anarchy, an existence on Earth that is nasty, brutish, and short. It has no law to govern it, save "might makes right." As a result, the 'social contract' became popular in the 16th, 17th, and 18th centuries and grew among its theorists to explain the need for government and the obligations of its subjects.

Very briefly, the social contract provides that all individuals forfeit their natural freedom in exchange for their protection by the state. Because no one saw the glaring mistake, or they chose to ignore it, authoritarian rule still prevails. The result is that more care is devoted to state organisations than the people they purportedly serve. Therefore, people believe that nothing the state does can ever be unjust since authoritarianism is the foundation of all law, based on theorising that the state of nature is an anarchical condition with no law.

The tragedy is that the more we support natural law theory, which purportedly props up 'common law,' the more we endorse authoritarian control of our free will. So, we permit authorities to enforce compliance with their invented statutes, resulting in perpetuated slavery, all sanctioned by our ignorance. If nature is factually unruly, then rights must be structured as permissions with an ever-more-powerful state to enforce them. It gets worse because the social contract, which none of us signed, asks, "Why should we not have a right to all things since all things are declared a matter of human rights?" Do you wonder why all human institutions (the nation, the family, the university, etc.) must submit to the state's power, having unlimited authorisation in advance to do whatever it pleases? That insanity is called 'consent of the governed.'

Our capacity for action diminishes as the state expands, and our understanding of its motives fades to nil. The immense machinery of the state sets about emptying the world of all norms and canceling all references and benchmarks, thus producing a world without (seeming) command but to which everyone complies by rote as though commanded. The state thereby fertilises an artificial "state of nature" that we must bend our 'will' to support, just as animals adapt to nature. By this sacrifice, tragically, our true creative nature is smashed almost beyond repair.

**From the social Contract to natural law**

Because natural law never found its factual roots, no one could explain the beautiful flower that should have bloomed worldwide. But no more. Natural law is a fact, not a theory, which Frank van Dun often echoes as an indisputable conclusion. Notwithstanding, Aristotle came closer to the truth than any other natural law advocate.

> *"What makes it true that something is good is not that it stands in some relation to desire, but instead that it is somehow perfective or completing of a being. And, what is perfective or complete of a being depends on that being's nature. So, for example, what is good for an oak tree is completing or perfecting it, which depends on what an oak is by nature."*

Natural law is now simple and scientific. Your 'nature' is that of 'Life' expressing itself. So what is completing or perfective of you is perfective of life. Add that your heart and lungs perform as does your conscious process, and all of your governing laws are perfective of you and your life.

There can be no debate without first rejecting your nature. And that cancellation of nature is precisely what the 'social contract' (government) perpetrators have done unto themselves, willingly, without force or coercion.

Meanwhile, all those who practice an Objective life-based philosophy have a short circuit to success, previously mentioned in the extensive works of novelist/philosopher Ayn Rand. The online *"Ayn Rand Lexicon"* has many pages of quotations written by her and other 'objectivist philosophers' on every ethical or moral subject you can think about, not forgetting individual rights. Do not panic when the index alone runs to about eight pages. Be thankful you have a reference source that will massively reduce your learning task.

**Positive and negative rights**

Positive rights specify what is permissible, e.g., People have the right to free speech. Negative rights determine what may not be forbidden or taken away, e.g., 'no government may interfere with or deny the right to free speech.' Upon examination, however, positive rights are 'permissions' given by a government. To the contrary, because negative rights curtail the government and not the people, they are the only definitive rights within a 'Protectorate.' Constitutional authors must take all care to ensure that rights derive from our born nature as above, albeit negatively expressed, to protect them from all trespass or usurpation.

Legal documents invariably use the word 'including' to expressly deny what is not specified. For example, saying "includes Honda and Ford" means all other car makes are excluded. Such Legal gobbledegook deliberately confuses people's minds, just as 'Positive Rights' are 'permissions,' not 'rights.'

**Why is 'death' the hall mark?**

Natural law governs the consequences of human actions. It cannot be preemptively directed or commanded because there is no rule to enforce. Accordingly, there can be no such thing as 'law enforcement' or 'law enforcement officials,' or indeed 'law enforcement officers (LEOs).' Unless expressly defined otherwise, the word law refers to natural law and nothing else.

Why is 'death' the hallmark of today's legal system? Given that nature has forbidden that 'life' be forcibly ruled, the only way authoritarians could circumvent life's roadblock was to invent a (fraudulent) fictional 'death system' and compel people's participation while claiming they consented. But, as mentioned, these tyrants voluntarily sacrificed their own lives to a lifeless system. All statutes made by those who volunteer to be lifeless are utterly worthless. To legalise a fiction as though real instantly invalidates it. Fantasy has no power, and it never will!

Never forget, political beings with limited consciousness (nescience) don't secure power to help people. Instead, they use people to secure power.

**Anarcho-capitalism**

The political philosophy of Anarcho-capitalism (aka Capitalism) eliminates the state in favor of personal sovereignty, private property, and free markets in an organic society. It is a moral system, not a political system. Following that idea, one concludes that privately funded police, courts, and other security services would (ideally) exist, much as one hires a private detective. Such a system is described as a 'Kritarchy' by Frank van Dun, who, you will remember, is a philosopher of law.

However, competitive protection does not exist in our biology or psychology. Both show 'cooperation' as the root core of natural law. I do agree, however, with Wikipedia's part description–

Personal and economic activities under anarcho-capitalism would be regulated by victim-based dispute resolution organisations under tort and contract law, rather than by statute through centrally determined punishment under political monopolies.

A protectorate society is not a government. Instead, an elected body of people upholds and protects all individuals' self-governance, thus denying all initiated force, authoritarian statutes, rules, and coercion.

The phrase anarcho-capitalism is logically outdated today, replaced by natural law unknown when Anarcho-capitalism first emerged. Our task is straightforward. People must learn the truth of human nature to affirmatively state that all governments have no lawful choice but to resign. The retaliatory use of force then acquires legitimacy.

As Ayn Rand describes in "The Nature of Government," (The Virtue of Selfishness)...

*The retaliatory use of force requires objective rules of evidence to establish that a crime has been committed and to prove who committed it, as well as objective rules to define punishments and enforcement procedures. Men who attempt to prosecute crimes, without such rules, are a lynch mob. If a society left the retaliatory use of force in the hands of individual citizens, it would degenerate into mob rule, lynch law and an endless series of bloody private feuds or vendettas.*

Rands statement is true, and although she argued for government as the protective body. She continued...

*This is the task of a government – of a proper government– its basic task, its only moral justification and the reason why men do need a government.*

I concur. Rand can be forgiven because the name 'government' is now repugnant, having since become an instrument of violence, more rampant today than ever before, if history is truthful. Nonetheless, both Rand and van Dun agree with me that *"the retaliatory use of physical force should be under objective control—i.e., under objectively defined laws"* and that *"working out details, conventions, and protocols for an operational and efficient system of justice is no mean task."*

Therefore, I initially proposed a Commission of Justice, administered by an elected body of people but not shopped for individually, such as employing a private detective.

Substituting a 'Commission of Justice' into Rand's statement, you'd have–

*Retaliatory use of force is the primary and proper task of a Protectorate. It is the means of placing the retaliatory use of physical force under objective control—i.e., under the objectively defined laws of nature.*

Now consider the offerings of Lysander Spooner–

*Certainly no man can rightfully be required to join, or support, an association whose protection he does not desire. Nor can any man be reasonably or rightfully expected to join, or support, any association whose plans, or method of proceeding, he does not approve, as likely to accomplish its professed purpose of maintaining justice, and at the same time itself avoid doing injustice. To join, or support, one that would, in his opinion, be inefficient, would be absurd. To join or support one that, in his opinion, would itself do injustice, would be criminal. He must, therefore, be left at the same liberty to join, or not to join, an association for this purpose, as for any other, according as his own interest, discretion, or conscience shall dictate.*

*An association for mutual protection against injustice is like an association for mutual protection against fire or shipwreck. And there is no more right or reason in compelling any man to join or support one of these associations, against his will, his judgment, or his conscience, than there is in compelling him to join or support any other, whose benefits (if it offer any) he does not want, or whose purposes or methods he does not approve. —Lysander Spooner, Natural Law; or the Science of Justice: 1882*

This understanding becomes more manageable if one regards (non-man-made)' objectively defined laws' and 'natural law' as the same, which, in truth, they are.

Having made that switch, the remainder of this chapter builds towards a free society under a Protectorate, which exists to protect the people within the natural laws of their nature. The following chapter will deal with constitutional issues.

**Constitutional Role of a Protectorate**

The idea that people form a government or some other authority over themselves to protect and expand their freedoms is pure insanity. Authority kills freedom. It cannot defend it, therefore. To protect freedom is to do only that and nothing more. No one can expand the fullness of freedom if it was not freedom to begin.

There is no political process in a protectorate because no legality as we presently know it exists; thus, no need exists for the separation of powers. No power exists to make laws because law is intrinsic natural law and nothing else. The so-called system of checks and balances already exists, encrypted in human nature. Tragically, the notion that man must make authoritarian laws is the by-product of conscious nescience no one can seemingly shake off. Knowledge of our conscious faculty is the only thing that can.

Whosoever forbids specific thoughts, words, or pictures from being spoken or broadcast harms all forms of creativity by curbing others' freedom of thought and expression, thus derailing their careers, curtailing the fruits of their labor, and denying their creativity and intelligence. The principle of state censorship is expandable because nothing that would arrest it exists. Those in power will do all it takes to forbid all criticism of their government and suppress any ideas they find threatening.

The first task in re-purposing government or replacing it is not to arrest criminals but to expose the immorality and criminality of today's legality, all of which denies lawfulness.

When people understand that an initiated force threatens their lives, they will fight to protect their freedom and safety, or they have no protection either. Your triumph over evil, your security, your safety, and your well-being are what protect theirs, and vice versa. Today, that is back to front. We lobby to preserve the state, believing its overruling of our (individual) rights protects all people. It remains that theft of our rights is theft of our lives.

*Freedom is the sure possession of those alone who have the courage to defend it. Pericles*

*You can protect your liberties in this world only by protecting the other man's freedom. You can be free only if I am free. Clarence S. Darrow (1857-1938) American lawyer*

*Those who expect to reap the blessings of freedom must, like men, undergo the fatigue of supporting it. Thomas Paine (1737-1809) English intellectual.*

Protection of ourselves and our (individual, rights is all that is needed. To that end, every necessary law exists, not in the lawmakers' books but in our nature.

*The practice of law is a rational discipline of justice, not of legality. —Frank van Dun; "The Lawful and the legal."*

Government and its legal processes are antithetical to the nature of man and man's morality. The government cannot defend freedom while denying some people their right to life and the fruits of their labor.

When people finally accept the criminality of authoritarian rule and turn their attention to protecting man's life instead, only then will they grasp the simplicity and beauty of creation that has been denied their comprehension for centuries.

**Equality of law**

Since twenty (inherent) laws govern our actions but do not 'rule' us, the phrase "Rule of law" is now called into question. What does that phrase mean in a free society, or is it now obsolete? A free society may still have 'rules,' but it does not have 'laws that rule.' Without grasping that fine distinction, confusion reigns. The original idea behind the 'rule of law' was that (citizens) people should be governed (ruled) by clear and general law principles and not by any arbitrary whims of justices, monarchs, or politicians. That implies exercising ruling principles inherent in our nature, meaning legislators cannot do as they please.

A free society upholds (natural) laws without enforcement since none prescribe. Intrinsic natural law never 'rules' in the usual sense. Natural law is the maintenance of orderliness, not a command that orderliness must exist. Therefore, no such thing as 'Rule of law' can exist. Our conscious process shows that the 'Natural law of no trespass' exists. Accordingly, the law is nature ruling itself for self-protection and maintenance, not a (statute) invention that denies nature.

Our task is to switch from statute inventions to natural law maintenance.

Law is not a command, rule or norm, nor is it a collection or system of such directive elements. It is an objective condition that many people may and in fact do value. As such it may inspire them to formulate rules of conduct that help to bring it about or to restore it when it is impaired.

> *We may call such rules 'rules of law', but we should then always remember that they are only related to law as means to an end — and that they deserve to be called rules of law only because they have the establishment or restoration of law (or ius) as their end. For that reason they may also be called rules of justice, because the literal meaning of 'justice' (Latin: iustitia) is 'what is conducive to ius'. In other words, justice is what aims at the establishment of the condition in which people interact on the basis of mutual consent. Justice is respect for law in the sense of 'ius'. — Frank van dun*

Moving from a ruled society to a free society demands that the authors of the new constitution expressly forbid present elites and vested interests. Indeed, all who profit from ruling over others are accountable for their actions. Any action that trespasses or violates another's life automatically sacrifices their right to choose so, meaning only innocent people are free.

**Equality of Justice**

The intention behind the 'rule of law' remains valid: to protect individuals against arbitrary power and ensure that people in authority face the same criminal penalties for wrongdoing as everyone else. Suppose, indeed, we all are guaranteed natural justice through equality via natural law. In that case, the most apt replacement phrase for free societies is 'Equality of Justice.' Riddance of arbitrary decisions by Protectorate members and Justices, not being held for long periods without trial, not being doubly tried for the same offense (double jeopardy). Also, until convicted, the presumption of innocence is greatly simplified. All of that and more falls under (the equality of) natural justice - since it is the means for upholding or restoring natural law.

Past precedents will not define the limits of official power because there is no official power in a free society. None! The lawful retaliatory force to arrest crime is not an authoritative power. It is the arrest of initiated force and restoration of the natural order, which is creative.

Libertarians may argue that it is the role of (strictly limited) government in free societies to protect the freedom of individuals and not curtail it. But no. Because there is no government as commonly known, the roles are reversed. It becomes the role of the people to protect other people's freedom so that each can govern themselves. The Protectorate exists only to maintain that natural order. Thus, the people's creative power is protected, and a free society blossoms.

**Constitutional Hierarchical structure from the people up**

The following hierarchical example is generic and thus adaptable to different countries or states. Intrinsic natural law is by nature expressly individual. That is the beginning.

- After that, what one man cannot protect alone is best served by 'Community'; hence, local municipal, Town, and City Councils, or Counties, whose proper tasks include, for example, water, sewerage, waste disposal and ambulance services, public safety, and local signage. All is protective in the broadest sense.
- What one Municipal Council cannot do alone is protectively best served by a 'Greater Community'; hence, 'State Protectorates', including police and judicial services in the interests of Justice, fire and police services, state highways, and signage.
- What one State Protectorate cannot do alone is protectively best served by the National Protectorate, including judicial services and the Military, in the interests of Justice. National protection includes National highways, International airports and (international) diplomacy, weather bureaus, shipping, national border protection, radar installations, postal oversight, and coastal navigation beacons.

All forms of the Protectorate derive from each individual, which is to say, from the bottom up, not from the top down. Notably, the whole societal structure builds on the rights of every individual. At the same time, the Protectorate (government substitute) protects the people's rights.

The major components of the country's justice system, along with courts and corrections, are maintained for protection, with Local MunicipaL Councils responsible for Local Services. The task of the Protectorate is to protect the land while upholding all individual's unalienable right to use it for life-sustaining benefit.

Consequently, the Protectorate is logically the custodian of the land and not its owner. If, in that role, it allocated, consigned, or transferred custodial title to a parcel of land such that the recipient (Custodian) was indebted to fulfill the same protection, then nothing has effectively changed save that a different individual (National man or woman ) is now held responsible for that land's protection.

That means any improvements made to land, such as orchards, sheds, houses, or farm structures and machinery, are saleable, but not the dirt below. Custodial title to the land transfers by selling that property, meaning only the improvements buy and sell. The land is irrevocably connected because people cannot have one without the other. In the case of an iron ore mine, the sale price will naturally depend on the estimated value of iron ore. For a farm, the sale price will reflect potential profits based on climate, existing infrastructure, and machinery. In contrast, the sale price for a house will depend on size and amenity, locality, climate, transport, and views.

Nothing changes effectively. However, since people can never sell land, none can ever be sold by anyone to foreign or offshore interests. Thus, the nation's people are always protected. Remember that iron ore value comes from the efforts to extract it. Hence, ore is a product for sale, but the inalienable right to the (geographical) land parcel is not. The same applies to many different land usages. When land usage is canceled or terminated, such as house demolition, for example, then the present custodial title holder is responsible for the reinstatement of the land to its original condition as nearly as possible. Thus, land is protected and available for custodial title transfer based on its life-sustaining potential.

The principle of 'indigenous peoples' guardianship remains. Custodial title holders now care for their land, providing a deep sense of identity, purpose, and belonging.

**Protection**

As previously described, integrity, honesty, commitment, truth, and self-preservation are inherent in the natural laws that govern all our faculties, systems, and processes, without which life would cease. Thus, values, ethics, and morality all emanate from within individual men and women in every country and culture, each according to their choice, corresponding with the right of all others to choose.

*"Bureaucrats protect the establishment. Leaders protect individual*

*rights." — Charlie Kirk*

*"Those who step outside natural law are self-confessed outlaws." — Frank van Dun.*

Natural law grants no permission or authority for one to trespass upon another's life, as witnessed by neither of our two minds being able to overrule the other. Furthermore, independent human lives cannot fuse into one unified entity without sacrificing their singular unalienable right to life and the means to live it. Accordingly–

- Natural law refuses all authority. It denies all orders and all authority save its own, regardless of source or claimed authority.
- Natural law refuses initiated force in all forms, whereby the right to exercise force to arrest such assaults is morally justifiable. Murder and self-defence are opposites.

Freedom is not a commodity for oligarchs or authoritarians to hand out, distribute, or deny at their whim or will. Neither is it a moral, spiritual, or political paradigm in which anything goes, a condition that many falsely refer to as anarchy. Freedom is a priceless treasure for you to uphold and safeguard because it is yours, not the government's property. It is for you to respect and protect, therefore. The task for the (so-called) state, once transformed into a 'Protectorate', is to protect your life and free will and thus protect your freedom. Of course, you must first claim your right to freedom before that can occur.

- The method for claiming it is an objective philosophy.
- The means to do so is your complete conscious process.
- The validity and authenticity of both the technique and the means are the steering laws inherent in your nature.
- The whole process is self-governance, self-mastery, or your self-mastered autonomy.

That summation is a complete about-turn from all that has ever been promulgated in the past. It puts you in the drivers seat of your life where you rightfully belong. Not because some sage, or intellectual, philosopher, dictator or monarch said or decreed it thus, but because your factual nature and your spirit are together your life indisputably.

To repeat, all who dispute those facts disclaim their own nature. Your power in this world is yours entirely, but until you claim it, you've ceded your life to whomever claims it, thereby abetting their crime. That is the state of today's world in a nutshell.

America's founding fathers understood that one's right to life is part and parcel of one's nature; a self evident truth. Although that might be said to be an experiment in self-government, still the proper roles of the respective parties escaped vital attention.

It is not for government to inspect food, fight poverty, create jobs, feed or vaccinate anyone, fight discrimination or provide disaster relief; neither to mitigate climate change, subsidise or give grants to individuals or business, explore space, rectify income equality, regulate commerce, or provide public assistance. Neither should it ever intervene regulate or control peaceful activity. Thomas Jefferson offered salient wisdom in his first inaugural address in 1801 –

> *A wise and frugal Government, which shall restrain men from injuring one another, shall leave them otherwise free to regulate their own pursuits of industry and improvement, and shall not take from the mouth of labor the bread it has earned. This is the sum of good government, and this is necessary to close the circle of our felicities.*

The broadly stated lesson over time, and particularly since 2019, is that a self-governing nation must first consist of self-governing individuals, that lesson now more specific and pertinently crucial. Self-governing individuals must exercise, maintain, and protect their (individual) right to life, whereby any (elected)' steering body' (Protectorate – formerly government) must serve only to preserve the protections manifestly practiced by each individual. If not, a breakdown in the moral fabric of society is the only possible outcome, having dire consequences, including an explosion of violence, crime, child trafficking, drug abuse, deviant sexual promiscuity, and more, all of which smash the blessings of freedom and prosperity to shreds.

More simply stated, an authentically free society will, personally and societally, securely protect one's already practiced and protected concepts of freedom, opportunity, and equality. While such societal protection maximises all opportunity and innovation, it, like natural law, promises no resultant success or rescue mission, both being our independent tasks in nature.

Contrary to popular belief, freedom does not create prosperity. It simply removes all barriers to human thought, talent, invention, and productivity, thereby permitting the people's creation of wealth where little or none existed. A free society spontaneously builds from the morally productive actions of individuals by natural laws that promote peaceful cooperation. Freedom is not imposed from the top by political authorities. It is made from every individual's life, by their choice, and no other. No need remains for a majority to rule a minority. Democracy is irrelevant.

Objective philosophy holds that the only task of government is to protect our freedom. The government would consist of the police, courts, and military. It would find and arrest criminals. It would defend us from foreign invasions. It would not act as a charity service, subsidize businesses, or tell people whom they can sleep or speak with. The only job the government would have would be to ensure that each person respects other people's boundaries.

**Constitutional Fundamentals**

A free society Constitution must be unlike any other Constitution, primarily because natural law never commands. Its prime purpose is education. Maintenance and protection of the natural order of man should properly ensue, whereby people are free to govern themselves.

This chapter and the following only sketch the fundamental precepts of natural law from which a Nation's Constitution can be (finally) authored. That task requires a deep understanding and a finite grasp of every word in context. Eventually these fundamental principles will become established precedents that constitute the lawful basis of a polity, organisation or society, thus protecting individuals governing themselves.

Accordingly, these Constitutional protection protocols express the people's unalienable right to live free from all that inhibits, obstructs, or denies their right to life. The protocols state the truth of man's nature, now and for all time, thus presenting a potent power never before realized, much less understood. No one can refute the facts of natural law, which is truly epic!

The final (derived) Constitution cannot and need not definitively explain all natural law issues. Such matters are for the human sciences, biologists, neuroscience, psychology, and philosophy to address correctly, as they always should have. The compass of these protocols, therefore, is confined to comprehension of (factual) intrinsic natural law and free will at the personal level, whereby the same principles translate to a thriving and productive society offering protection of all individual rights and freedoms sourced from the 'laws of nature and Nature's God.'

A free society is one in which self-empowered individuals imagine and independently work to simultaneously create their most excellent futures. Each must discover their power and ensure nothing stands in the way of exercising it. Freedom is secured, not prescribed; consequently, state control is only necessary to preserve and protect it in an organically free society.

Rights are fully preserved in any process to contract for the acquisition, transfer, or exchange of property. All forms of theft are denied, including duties, registrations, taxation, and eminent domain, as elsewhere explained in protection terms. One's right to seek life-sustaining goals or outcomes through actions within the equal rights of all others categorically forbids all trespass of those rights. There can be no debate without one relinquishing those rights, whence all discussion cancels.

No group (or government) can have Rights above those of the sovereign Individuals of the Subject Country. No individual has the authority to command another; all commandments by others refused thereby, no man or woman a human agent; no legal or other instrument presiding contrary or contradictory of the unalienable individual Rights of Man. No group rights can exist since every group member already has the right to life. No claim of right that does not already exist can exist.

Since the right to life is absolute, the right to uphold and sustain one's life is also a given. Every fruit of their labour is their inalienable right. Hence, our unalienable right to life and our inalienable property right.

**Each person has the free choice to respect the natural laws and that choice determines the consequences - for that is the natural law**

# Chapter 15

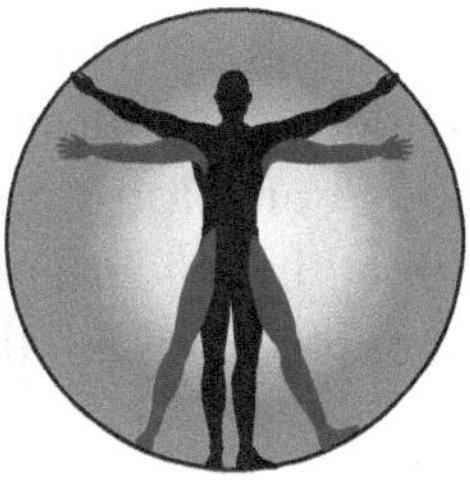

## Self-Mastery and Education

False ideologies and corruption drive most people's subconscious programs, about which they know nothing, the reason being that we have all been lied to, propagandized, stripped of our birthright, and made servants to the state. We are drip-fed propaganda, while false ideologies and corruption drive our subconscious programs about which we know nothing. So, we don't know anything of natural law intrinsic to our nature. The necessity for new education in all schools and universities is paramount. Today, no literature describes how a tender young infant can value-charge its subconscious mind, even though it cannot speak, read, write, or use a smartphone. Yet we've all done it! No more evidence is needed.

The transformation will result from understanding nature's most precious gift of consciousness and the natural laws it reveals. There is hardly one branch of philosophy, psychology, or human science that does need urgent revision, nor is there one textbook that does not need primary amendment. Neuroscience, psychology, and psychiatry have long rejected conscious inquiry as subjective, non-science, or of no value. Yet, all their remarkable achievements are only made possible through the factual mental processes they refuse to study.

This tragedy begs a complete re-appraisal of all human sciences, religion, politics, trade, society, competition, partnership, etc. Politics has already committed suicide through corporatism, although it remains deeply ingrained in the human psyche, if not in mainstream media and fake corporatised parliaments worldwide. Reverse that disaster, and we all should paraphrase Thomas Jefferson's words–

*If a nation expects to be consciously knowledgeable and free in a state of civilisation, it expects what should be and protects it.*

Today's task is to rid the insane notion that people's comforts and protections can only be provided by governing their ruin;' democracy' is a prime example. Natural Law, consciousness, and objective philosophy each impart essential knowledge independently, yet all three inextricably unite as though one. Nothing compares with this life-founded trio, nor can it.

Truth, reality, and values are the keys to a future we have never dreamt possible. Our transformation will result from fully understanding nature's most precious gift of consciousness. Truth, reality, and values are the keys to a future we have never imagined. Everything is in place for the institution of free, organic societies founded on natural law, modelled within the nature of every man, woman, and child. Free societies then uphold protected self-governance.

Free societies will ensure that consent given by our Creator's gifts for actualizing self-mastery and individual sovereignty is always protected! From the beginning of my research, I sought to comprehend how consciousness could apply to an infant with no words, math, or science, equally to a senior elder with a lifetime of experience. Success far exceeded my ambitions. The power of natural law in our nature, although never witnessed in history, is available to benefit all people strictly provided that 'unalienable rights,' freedoms, living identity, and 'natural justice' are upheld and forever protected. No better precedent exists than to govern ourselves according to the nature of our being.

Accordingly, we now have an opportunity to teach life-sustaining philosophy at primary school levels, eloquently structured to prevent conscious ignorance from ever developing. The same philosophical principles delivered through college or universities will spill over into all career choices and vocations, including jurisprudence.

These opportunities offer a revolutionary understanding of human nature, ethics, morality, justice, rights, sociology, law, and sovereignty, forging unprecedented unity and freedom for humanity.

Just as existence exists,' life lives,' irrefutably! Those who grasp objective philosophy may run with these opportunities. Authors, teachers, videographers, lecturers, librarians, and countless more disciplines now have a grand chance to embark on the fascinating journey of our time in human history: no more illusions and no more denial.

Conscious knowledge in a storm of truth will reshape our understanding of self, life, rights, ethics and morality, sovereignty, justice, sociology, philosophy, society, and reality. Once this unification is fully comprehended, nothing excels, nor can it.

Protectorates should educate the populace concerning the protections they administer. As a result, private educational curricula must conform with the Constitutional protections of life and property and respect justness and justice.

Protectorate school funding may cover basic (subject) schooling costs only to schools whose curriculum corresponds with Protectorate-issued 'Freedom Standards' concerning rights, free will, respect, responsibility, ethics, morality, sovereignty, and justice.

Ideally, the Protectorate will offer different funding scales aligning with specific education curricula. The more moral taught content is, the more its teaching is financed. Crime drops without authoritarian commands.

People must also question philosophy. A proper philosophic system depends not on opinion or even advanced teaching. If, as (elsewhere) shown, an infant can program its subconscious mind with values despite temporary cognitive handicap, then 'objectivity' is for all men, women, and children. Moreover, since we can choose our values for better or worse, an objective philosophy must adhere to that same free will opportunity, mainly because our feelings mentor our choices.

New education is imperative in all schools and universities, human sciences, psychology, and philosophy, as well as in law and politics. It is expressly intended in my (universal) 'Constitution' that the National Facilitation Centre (NFC) and State Facilitation Centres (SFC) work jointly to prepare educational material for the People and develop teaching curricula at all levels. This objective mission is wholly protective; given that people understand their rights and freedoms better and how to maintain them respectfully, the greater they will see that no crime can deliver better. Thus, it will diminish markedly.

Radical change is warranted. Here are some of the matters of importance–

1. Existence precedes consciousness. Life must exist before people can cognitively understand it. That order is irreversible. [legal entities are dead.]

2. Identity and causality are constituents of existence, without which consciousness is a lie. Maintaining, upholding, and enforcing lies defying one's nature is effectively spitting in nature's face.

3. Life is the supreme value. It must be the foremost concern of every comfort, security, safety, and freedom that people desire.

4. Our right to life is individual. No collective liver, brain, or stomach exists. With individual rights instituted, no group rights exist because no need exists. Rights are of nature, not the state or the United Nations.

5. Sensory perception reveals the facts of existence. Ignore fundamental truth, and consciousness becomes the judge of reality. When the state is falsely hailed legitimate, no overthrow is permitted.

6. Believing that Man is born with a 'tendency to evil' permits morality to assume a (collective, prerogative. Authoritarian rule is deemed imperative at all costs, with no protest admissible. That notion is false.

7. The non-aggression principle is not a theory. It is the natural law of no trespass encrypted in our nature.

8. Freedom to think means not surrendering the sovereignty of our mind to anyone, any belief, or any other. Nothing serves our thoughts or self-mastery when rulers, neighbors, or imposters are the term-setters of our minds.

9. Individualism presides over all forms of collectivism.

10. Free will is not a free license to act irrespective of consequences. Free will encompasses responsibility towards others, but not our responsibility for others. Unceasing respect for the lives of others is the only means to ensure freedom for all people!

11. The adolescent mind swap is not known or taught, whereby millions of teenagers and their parents suffer untold stress, even physical harm.

12. Truth does not allow for knowledge, facts, life, morality, and justness to bend to someone's personal or political persuasion. The natural laws of identity and causality forbid it. Truth and falsity remain distinguishable; consciousness obliges us to learn the difference.

13. Educational literature often fails to distinguish between conscious and subconscious processes. Sequential orderliness and natural law are obscured.

14. Justice is concerned only with remediating wrongful actions, not correcting wrong thinking. Ethics and moral correctness are vital for human science education.

15. Spiritual values should uphold all physical enactments. Two-way communication between our conscious and subconscious minds is a value-based spiritual exchange. And that psycho-epistemology communication is the perfect model for all societal interactions.

16. We are spiritual beings living a spiritual life, served by an existent reality that we adapt to our purposes.

17. Natural justice serves our refusal of collectivism. No escape routes exist.

In sum–

- Science has failed mental knowledge, hence philosophy.
- Errant philosophy has denied psychology.
- No one teaches the psychology of consciousness. We all fail.
- Human consciousness, thus abandoned, allows collectivism to fail society.
- Society degenerates into a disaster condition almost beyond repair.

If you can grasp that totality, it is clear that present-day education concerning consciousness is vacant, utterly inept if not corrupted. Learning the truth of our nature is now the battle for humankind. Nothing but a drastic transformation in conscious knowledge will rid ignorance, thus allowing us to correct today's social obscenities.

**A place of solitude**

Solitude is welcome and never feared. We do not need compulsive action. Our unique quality of volitional consciousness grants us the wisdom to act with purpose and discernment, setting us apart from creatures driven solely by compulsive instinct. In our journeys through life, we encounter paths of solitude that beckon us to progress with unburdened steps so that our creative contributions help us to walk in solidarity with our moral being and purpose.

In attaining our full potential as human beings, we are obliged to enjoy contemplating our future endeavours, including when we unite in cooperation with others. Although united by a shared purpose, togetherness can sometimes prove burdensome. So we are reminded that in life's grand tapestry, we come into this world alone and depart it in solitude. From the art of being alone, we find solace in our own company itself, a rewarding skill of great value from which people truly realise harmony.

As members of the human collective, we are:

- A singular indivisible entity of life itself.
- A unique independent living being (ILB).
- A singular masterpiece united by nature with all others.

In moments of solitude, not loneliness, we paint the canvas of our lives, thereby shaping our identity in life terms. This creative path properly leads to conscious and spiritual enlightenment in a world bustling with connections and interactions. The fruit of these solitary moments reveals the art of embarking on a voyage of joyous self-discovery. We discover sacred communion with ourselves, our ability to choose productive values, employ them in our thoughts, manifest morality in our actions, and share these fruits with others likewise blessed. This sanctuary of solitude allows us to sew the seeds of our true essence and joyfully nurture its rewards with others. We encounter the wisdom to perceive life's panorama with clarity, building and mastering our soul amidst the noise of the world that all too often denies us. Thus, we can nurture life's blessings with patience, integrity, passion, and compassion.

The act of being one with oneself but not lonely is not meditation. It is not an escape from reality but rather a pilgrimage into the core nature of our being. Our wilful decision to peel away layers of corruption and deceit requires us to consciously engage with the values inherent in our subconscious mind wholly given to life's betterment and spiritual accomplishments. As we journey this path of enlightenment, we understand better our experiences and how the natural laws of nature cultivate emotions. Our thoughts and feelings give rise to deep insights and purposeful directions, such patterns demolishing the roots of our fears while stirring the aspirations of our souls.

This process of introspection reveals the wings of our minds. As the author of our achievements and recipient of their benefits, we speed past limitations and soar towards horizons we'd never dreamt possible. Finding this solace and joyous creativity within ourselves requires bravery and courage, for without the (seeming) protection of external validations and (supposed) societal comforts, we are on our own. We must face our fears, acknowledge our vulnerabilities, and resolve that no emotions or perceptions will divert us from choosing and enacting the very values that life depends on. Amidst our periods of silent contemplation, we must recognize how growth and wisdom stem not from embracing our imperfections but from implanting our resolved perfections, which render all else worthlessly redundant.

Joy lies not in forgiving our mistakes but in celebrating our triumphs. Our courage has confronted the shadows of life, its insecurities, doubts, and fears, and sent them packing. Now, we see these past blockages as mere Illusions, transient and powerless in the face of our inner strength. We are a singular contributor to humanity, not its dependent.

Having cast aside collective limitations, we are free to embrace life's boundless possibilities, thereby holding the brush that paints the canvas of our life according to our heartfelt choices. As we cultivate emotional intelligence and articulate our values clearly and authentically to others, we also communicate the synergistic power of values. They aid comprehension of what we are, enabling us to explain who we are. Thus, we become beacons of inspiration, igniting positive transformation in those around us.

Self-reflection in periods of solitude embraces our individuality through our journey of self-discovery, self-mastery, and autonomy. This sacred pilgrimage to our innermost self, testified by the manifestation of our self-authored values, is the most significant personal joy possible. It is the secret to the most tremendous societal success the world has yet to experience.

When lecturers deliver these personal philosophical principles through college or universities, spliced with the universality of natural law, our career choices and vocations will blossom. Teachers can provide complete consciousness teachings early, allowing lecturers to deliver natural law later to non-corrupted minds. Conscious ignorance and erroneous presumptions have no chance to develop. Meanwhile, an objective philosophy provides a solid platform for intrinsic natural law. These teaching opportunities offer a revolutionary understanding of human nature, ethics, morality, justice, rights, sociology, law, and self-mastery, forging unprecedented unity and freedom for humanity.

Just as existence exists, so' life lives' irrefutably! Those who grasp objective philosophy can best seize and run with these opportunities. Authors, teachers, videographers, lecturers, librarians, and many more disciplines now have a grand chance to embark on the most fascinating journey of our time, indeed in human history.

A proper philosophic system depends not on opinion or advanced teaching. If, as (elsewhere) shown, an infant can program its subconscious mind with values despite having no words, math, or science, then 'objectivity' is for all men, women, and children. Moreover, since we can choose our values for better or worse, an objective philosophy must precisely adhere to that openness because our feelings attest to our choices. This work opens the door to intelligent contributions based inside of life, not externally imposed on life, which is a crucial distinction. Life is within – not imposed from without.

**Life lives.**

Rand expressed a vital essential, namely, "existence exists." As already hinted, my contribution as a Neo-Objectivist would be to add the term "Life lives." Full consciousness is axiomatic, its governing laws immutable, and their protection of free will and freedom.

Grasp the fullness of what these two axiomatic statements mean. One cannot deny existence without using it. (Existence and consciousness—are axioms you cannot escape.) One cannot refute life without using it.

> *"An axiomatic concept is the identification of a primary fact of reality, which cannot be analyzed, i.e., reduced to other facts or broken into component parts. It is implicit in all facts and in all knowledge. It is the fundamentally given and directly perceived or experienced, which requires no proof or explanation, but on which all proofs and explanations rest." Ayn Rand.*

Jefferson made that clear in his letter to Francis Hopkinson, March 13, 1789...

> *I never submitted the whole system of my opinions to the creed of any party of men whatever in religion, in philosophy, in politics, or in anything else where I was capable of thinking for myself. Such an addiction is the last degradation of a free and moral agent.*

**Reliance on government**

Criminal action forfeits freedom, whereby the victim acquires rightful justice. Criminals confess crimes by their actions, whereby they convict themselves. Checks and balances are self-actioned which is how natural justice works.

All who disagree freedom must be faced with the fact they have abandoned their nature, automatically negating their every dispute. They give up their freedom willingly. Our task is to apprise them of these immutable facts with such irrevocable certainty that no defence on their part is possible. (Witness the Nuremberg code.)

People have witnessed the Legal (unlawful) transfer of wealth from producers to others in virtually every society since day one, and this continues in every nation today. The truth is, legally initiated authoritarian force is criminal theft of your right to life! Our task is to establish a free society where none now exists. Think of this as three different questions, all having the same answer:

1. Who shall wield authoritarian force? None!
2. For whose benefit shall such authoritarian force be wielded? None!

3. At whose expense shall such authoritarian force be enforced? None!

How, then, can authoritarian theft be forever eliminated? As my books explain, the answer is that we all possess an ethical, spiritual power and the means to morally exercise it, all contained within a naturally governed, self-authored, objective, intelligent framework centred on life itself.

As previously mentioned, no one can exercise authoritative force in denial of their nature without first relinquishing their own (born) nature, by which all their claims are void from inception.

So let's now pose similar questions concerning your power gifted by nature, not authoritative force, yet again where all have the same answer.

1. Who will wield your nature-given power? You!

2. For whose benefit will your nature-given power be wielded? Yours, but others may also profit.

3. At whose expense will your nature-given power be wielded? Yours, and no other!

That's it! Your life is what you are; your joy in this world is living it. Ayn Rand's objectivist philosophy states it clearly.

> *"I swear by my life and my love of it that I will never live for the sake of another man, nor ask another man to live for mine." — Ayn Rand, (Atlas Shrugged)*

All belief in a (rightful) ruling class vanishes. There can be no such thing.

**Freedom**

All attempts by governments to equalise wealth or income destroy productive incentives and enterprise. On the contrary, free societies spontaneously build up from the actions of individuals who promote and practice peaceful cooperation. Freedom does not create prosperity. It allows you and me to create prosperity. It will enable your imagination and creativity, talents, inventions, and innovative ideas to flourish, thus creating wealth where none previously existed. On the few occasions societies have pursued freedom, they have made themselves wealthy. Other nations have remained poor.

Is there a moral case for freedom? The better and more accurate question is: does freedom engender morality? The answer is resoundingly yes! Indeed, most immorality today arises from governments denying people the exercise of their true selves. Give them freedom; they will choose morality because that is their road to success.

Freedom is the essential prerequisite of humanity since it is the only condition in which consciousness can adequately function as it should, not forgetting that natural laws maintain that orderliness. None exists as a limit on our will, but rather to inspire us to be more conscious of our actions. That 'invitation' opens the door to independent singularity, which best facilitates 'cooperative enterprise' as later discussed.

Once we comprehend how natural governing laws enhance our freedom and free will, we learn that respect for these natural laws is 'spiritual.' 'Spirit' is the origin of nature and humanity, meaning our lives are spirit in action. Nature is the living theatre in which we freely act and develop as moral, spiritual beings. No priests act as stand-ins. We each are all it takes to live a virtuous 'life' in which 'morality' is our outward expression of 'spiritual freedom,' wherein all three together are our 'here and now' soul connection to nature's source creator, our spiritual reverence.

Nothing more serves 'nature's God' than to fully revere our creation by enacting moral law as the spiritual extension of our freedom. Life demands we forge inspiration to join together in a deeper understanding of the further evolution of humanity. Our task is to initiate and empower human freedom and thus banish tyranny. Freedom demands that we each act to uphold and protect it responsibly. Nature invokes us to claim our 'individual' right to life and property, upheld by education and reinforced by natural justice, thereby exercising our right to self-mastery to protect the same rights for all others.

Freedom is indeed the reality of a person, his very being. It is physically impossible to take away a person's real freedom without at the same time destroying him as a person (by killing him or driving him insane). Now it is certainly true that the destruction of a person's real freedom can come about as the result of many causes, but not all of these are relevant from the perspective of natural law. It is only when such causes originate within the human world, i.e. from the actions of another person, that the question of the lawful or unlawful character of the destruction of a person's real freedom arises. This is so because natural law is the order of the human world as such, constituted by the existence of many different and separate human beings.

If there is no way to separate a person from his real freedom without destroying both at the same time, it is possible — and unfortunately easy enough — to destroy a person's opportunities for exercising his personal capacities without destroying him. We need to distinguish between an individual's real freedom and his organic freedom, the latter being his activity or work as an individual.

It is again undeniable that any number of circumstances and accidents can cause a temporary or definitive destruction or limitation of a person's organic freedom, but again and for the same reason that we noted before, it is only when such causes originate within the human world that the question of their lawful or unlawful character arises.

> *Once the notion of natural law is properly understood as the order of the natural world of free persons, it is easy to grasp the concept of natural right. The word 'right' can be used in two different but related senses: the one captures the static aspect of a right, the other its dynamic aspect. In the static sense a person's natural right is the place or space he occupies lawfully in the natural order of the human world — it is his property. That space is first of all determined by his physical being as a person, and is therefore immediately filled by his real freedom. —Frank van Dun*

**Freedom for others = freedom for self**

Freedom and respect are reciprocal and inseparable. We can ensure our own only by endorsing other people's right to their lives. Since that ensures natural justice, no enforced rules are necessary. Had we studied how consciousness works instead of how society is ruled, we would have learned conscious fidelity long ago and how individual rights are indispensable? That is the path to freedom and a state of peaceable civilisation.

It is becoming more difficult for authoritarian governments to hide their actions from the rest of the world. As a result, more and more countries are opening up to trade and tourism, and new ideas are spreading. More people see the benefits of economic and social freedom and are demanding them.

It is hard to create the morality and institutions of a free society where freedom does not exist. Rather than trying to impose them wholesale, it is better to start at the micro level by creating the conditions that allow people to act freely and build up a free society through their actions. A vital part of this is to institute property rights so people can build businesses and trade confidently, knowing no one can confiscate their property.

Life in a free society would look little different from today, at least initially. People in America, Australia, New Zealand, and many other countries would still attend work and school, hold garage sales, buy and sell realty, rent accommodation, drive cars, walk their dogs, etc. But they would do all that and more without scripted mandates, government licenses, regulations, and without restrictions, legal dictates, intervention, oversight, surveillance, or interference.

**A different mindset**

Libertarians promote these ideas, but many hold tight to 'limited government.' In their view, freedom from government means anarchy, which many believe means *'without rule.'* It doesn't. Anarchy means *'without rulers,'* and that is a monumental difference. Rule was the former modus operandi in governing all nations in every century until the Whig breakthrough emerged in the eighteenth century. This polar opposite of monarch or oligarch 'rule' portrayed a new vision in which society aspired to achieve liberty and justice for all. The revolutionary idea was that government did not 'govern' but instead sought to protect all people's lives, liberty, and property. This ideal of equality before the bar of justice gave rise to *'The Rule of Law.'* Although the (so-named) Whigs used the word 'government,' its radical new meaning, purpose, and role was to maintain justice, thus no longer intervening in people's lives to rule them, regulate them, or interfere with anyone's peaceful actions. Personal freedom would reign, in addition to free speech, free assembly, free association, freedom of conscience, and free expression.

It worked, but only for a time. Capitalism is a moral system that puts America at the forefront of the world politically and economically. People were free to live as they chose and use their property likewise. They could participate in economic activities for profit, engage in commerce with anyone willing to reciprocate and accumulate as much wealth as they desired while spending the fruits of their labor to satisfy their goals and ambitions.

The people's actions were peaceful, their associations voluntary, their interactions consensual. No one violated the personal or property rights of others, and for that, the government left them alone. America's model was the closest any country has ever come to a free society. Sadly, it has degenerated, resulting from greed-funded rule, or rule-funded greed.

# Chapter 16

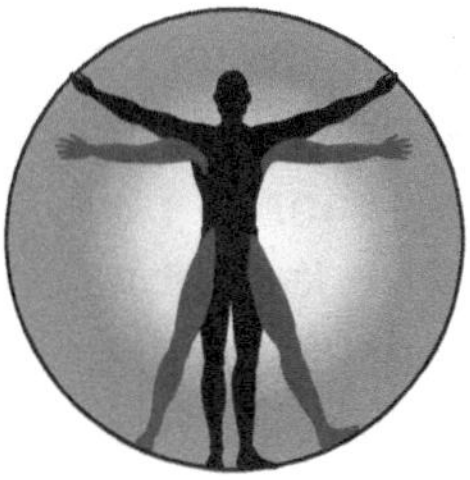

## Coperative enterprise and Sovereignty

What is a free society? Limited government springs to mind in a flash. Democracy flashes a green light to most people, so they claim we should have more of it. Pursue that treacherous path, and it becomes evident that property, trade, justice, tolerance, moral rules, incentives, granted permissions, authoritarian government, and socialism have entered the picture, along with the social contract. People least understand they do not live in a free society. Their right to life and property is subject to government permission. Humanity has no comprehension that refusal of their born nature even exists. That unspeakable tragedy conceals your key to personal benefits beyond anything you've been taught possible.

By far, most people do not grasp the complexity of positive law. So, they compromise and accept that the government should regulate their lives and businesses. By so doing they sacrifice the joys of human diversity, discovery, intellectual power, creation, and emotional rewards. No one teaches that these priceless assets are within our grasp and comprehension. Most people think a free society is a limited government, e.g., a republic. They know nothing of its intellectual and moral foundations. Billions of people suffer without remedy as a result. Without knowing how human consciousness works, philosophical guidance is sadly lacking. The resulting mental vacuum allows (conscious) guesswork to blossom, whereby assumptions and presumptions about vibrations and energies become invented tools used by multitudes of (so-called) spiritual leaders worldwide. Such inventions prevent anyone explaining what consciousness is or why dire ignorance prevails, thus no intellectual remedy of worth is apparent. Presumptions multiply as the world plunges toward destruction, plagued by stress, anxiety, and trauma, all governed by oligarchs hell-bent on world domination of all people as their exclusive corporate property. Multitudes of invented (pretend) (so-called) laws result, that enforce authoritarian compliance.

Small wonder philosophy cannot help. Infants and young children cannot answer Who am I? How do I know, or what should I do? They may answer many years later, but that is most unlikely because no one teaches how their conscious process works, nor any objective philosophy that would steer them on their path through life. Consequently, most people are not very mentally active, most are not confident, few are regularly happy, and vast numbers of people periodically suffer causeless fear and unexplainable guilt. They are not free.

Tragically, they've not discovered their almost constant anxiety comes from not knowing how consciousness facilitates an objective philosophy that, together with a few laws encrypted in their human nature, will enable a future the likes of which the world has never witnessed.

The remedy is yours already. Free society is not a random collection of unregulated ego-driven individuals. Freedom is a philosophically based, organic protocol objectively based on profound spiritual values (not available at a store) that invoke ethical thoughts and moral actions that make cooperation and social harmony possible. Protection of that natural order is the only regulatory condition needed, therefore.

Sadly, it is almost impossible for people to convert from an authoritatively ruled society to a free society. Still, it is doable precisely because nature is our gifted means, our most precious asset – our only need being to question whether we can access nature's principles, and how. Those answers will allow us to authenticate, institute, and protect those principles from denial, usurpation, violation, and cancellation.

That future, now in your hands, will be one that your offspring one thousand years from now will eternally thank you for, but only if you accept it, enact it, and above all, protect it. 'Individual Protection' is the operative term. Although everyone wants to live freely in their own space and on their own terms, most of the earth's people have only ever lived wholly or in part on terms laid down or enforced by someone else. Freedom has not existed, yet a powerful (seemingly instinctual) free will desire for individual liberty animates virtually every man and woman. That is our recognition of intrinsic natural law precisely.

Either the world plunges headlong into a totalitarian dictatorship, or it awakens instead to spiritual consciousness and free organic societies never witnessed in all history! While natural law theorists posit that we have an inbuilt morality and a propensity to do good, no such thing exists, but intrinsic natural law does. People do not need a government dictating their actions but do require a 'Protectorate' that upholds and protects their choices within the existent laws of their nature.

If this is your desire, consider what might replace today's abysmal societal structure, now proven beyond doubt to have utterly failed humanity. Our body and mind nature is a model of free, organic societies replete beyond anything we have ever conceived. If implemented, its power would forever consign all forms of authoritarian rule to history. Thus blessed, a new sociological and political foundation, more ethical and moral than any employed in the past, is ours for the will to achieve.

It is now for us to witness a world where everyone moves freely through life with radiantly clear knowledge of their true potential, spiritual purpose, and connection to the Source of everything. People need to learn how consciousness, freedom, respect, and responsibility inseparably apply to social dealings.

Peace-loving, organic societies, the likes of which the world has never witnessed, are not only possible, but our nature insistently forges that path. When people institute a free (organic) society based on natural law and justice, all else is irrelevant save those arrested for trespass. Humanity's true awakening is unprecedented, an intellectually and spiritually advanced human civilisation in which all are blessed and protected by their nature. Nothing less!

If the benefits of full spiritual consciousness and the freedom it delivers do not excite your passion to choose both, what will? Old-time ideologies and unconscious programs adverse to your being are progressively deactivated, neutralised, and removed. Past ignorance no longer denies access to our conscious power and intrinsic natural laws. People are no longer useless eaters for tyrannical amusement, a source of vast incomes.

No free society supporter truthfully admits or confesses to a wilful agreement of tyranny, slavery, initiated violence, and wars. Few people understand this inversion. Today, people believe that one individual (or group) has an 'authoritarian right' to rule others. Thus, the government is universally approved and never questioned. People consider all 'laws' arising from this moral inversion indispensable to life's comfort and security satisfactions, whence they repeat unchallenged century after century. The conclusion is crystal clear.

**Any society that authorises a state to rule it by force deserves all the tyranny and bloodshed that 'authority' enacts.**

Societal insanity of that order allows criminal violation of our right to life and property, and only the people can arrest it. We must ensure that centuries of authoritarian rule are stopped, never to return.

Fortunately, that situation is now emerging as many people are now asking themselves whether freedom that cancels a deeply manipulative world is even possible. It is difficult to penetrate the thicket of delusion and find one's true self in today's all-encompassing illusion. It is difficult for people to see through the fog of vagueness, recognise obstacles and escape the Matrix, but that is today's challenge.

But now we know the path forward – how people can resolutely end centuries of delusion on earth. It requires new vision presenting a different perspective on life within ourselves, We can now soar on wings of enlightenment, and break free from all imposed limitations driving conscious ignorance.

No longer will you believe storytellers. Many will turn away from politics, manipulative AI technology, and the mainstream media and look inward for truth and clarity. Lies will become increasingly apparent and more unbearable, to the point where corrections are unavoidable, especially as your inner need for clarity to live a truthful life increases. Compromise is an imposter, no longer accepted as more and more people shed their fake lives, throw their old concepts overboard, and begin thriving through self-generated empowerment.

Despite that fears still besiege us, perhaps more than ever before, your inner peace and tranquility will dispel them, as though withering plants in the hot sun fed no water. Fears of existence and even vague fears of an uncertain future will fade in direct proportion to your emancipation. All so-called healing through spiritual flights of whim and fancy will lose appeal. As your soul invigorates your free will to activate your divine powers as Nature's source creator intended, diseases that previously had little chance of being cured will heal. Seeming miracles are made possible once your spiritual consciousness becomes fully activated.

This inner purification of thoughts and feelings is your key to freedom. The secret is conscious understanding empowered by a philosophy centred on life itself. As you begin to feel the firm spiritual ground under your feet, you'll recognise the fluid process in which the divine emerges in you, and, like the 'natural law of allowance,' it happens at your pace in a way that serves and nurtures you. Your desire to allow this process will be invisible to most others, but your progress will have visible effects on the entire development of humanity tomorrow.

The long-accepted universal arrangement by which nations have been governed over the centuries by all manner of kings, presidents, emperors, monarchs, shahs, and czar's is outlawed, along with all institutions called 'government.'

'Governing' – the word 'govern' – derives from the Latin *Guber-nare, to steer*. But when these governing people are elevated by vote or by conquest above the general populace to rule, regulate, control them, and thieve tribute from them by exercising unlawful domination and control, they are not 'governing.' They are criminally assaulting the lives and rights of their victims, whereby the original intent of 'lawful protection' is replaced by the crime of 'tyranny.' The 'legal' and the 'lawful' bear no resemblance.

**Protections must be protected.**

Given that liberty achieved so much and for so many at one time, why has it almost vanished? Did it not institute people's right to their lives and their property, and indeed protected their rights.? Yes, on both counts, but one vital thing was missing. Liberty failed to preserve those protections from all trespass, presumably because everyone's rights were 'self-evident truths.'

They remain self-evident truths, but unless the protections of our rights are themselves protected, their violation, cancellation, and eradication are inevitable, as history informs. It should be self-evident that throughout man's history, the government has been the greatest violator of personal freedom and property rights. No (violent or brutal) private individuals have ever inflicted more than a tiny fraction of the harm and destruction caused by political authorities' abuse of power.

**A new model**

Today's evidence overwhelmingly suggests people must strictly limit government to protecting their rights and protecting that protection, including reasonable defence, plus judicial, and policing activities. Logically, it would never again be called 'government.' Such implies that we institute a police force to protect people from coercion and crime within certain geographical boundaries, a military to protect from foreign interference or invasion from outsiders, and a court system to adjudicate disputes.

Additionally, this protective body, this 'Protectorate,' would oversee coastal lighthouses, weather forecasting but not weather manipulation, air traffic control, and waste disposal, altogether maintaining many societal protections already functioning.

Given all the above were instituted, what could or would protect such enterprises? What would protect your rights?

The answer is indisputable. The right to life and property is innate in every man, woman, and child. Hence, all rulers who dispute those facts dispute their born nature. That automatically renders all their disputes or protests invalid, void from pronouncement. That is natural justice.

**A future for humankind like no other**

Do you want the keys to a bright, radiant, limitless future? If so, the institution of free, organic societies properly founded on our human nature is now in your hands. Nothing has precedence, is more relevant, or more urgent. Nothing past has described consciousness so fully or natural law so specifically. Blessed beyond anything ever taught, people may excel as never before.

Such requires we declare our correct political status as independent, living sentient beings, all under the protection of a 'constitution' founded by our nature and its governing laws, as bestowed by nature's source creator, guided by objective philosophy so derived. No contrary position or argument suffices, nor can it!

Societal transformation begins from the ground up, not (authoritatively) from the top down. Although it may take a generation or two to create a more justly honourable social system for ourselves and forthcoming generations, if we do not begin now, we risk authoritarian forbiddance of any start.

**Free society**

A creative and morally free society will never grow out of inflicted patterns of morality and legalities that determine how people interact. We already have such patterns within nature whereby people can conduct themselves within its (twenty) governing laws. Their ambitions and desire to thrive and prosper will drive systemic societal change.

We do not need to make it easy for people to start a new business or to own and run an existing venture with confidence, neither to secure property ownership nor to trade freely to expand or explore further. All we need to do is remove past roadblocks. People will then produce economic growth and stimulate systematic social reform.

Their self-confident society will insist that its modus operandi be protected and never ruled. Exceedingly beneficial systematic change will occur throughout the whole institutional fabric.

That truth is profound because' independence' removes the whole subject of morality from the collective domain ruled by governments and puts it into the private domain, where it rightfully belongs. That smashes the herd mentality completely!

Knowledge of full consciousness and intrinsic natural laws grants dynamic power to attain the life we want and to bring the world we want into being; benefits in the next chapter.

Conscious knowledge is the path to freedom and a state of peaceable civilisation in perpetuity.

> *"That personal freedom is the natural right of every man; and that property, or an exclusive right to dispose of what he has honestly acquired by his own labour, necessarily arises therefrom, are truths which common sense has placed beyond the reach of contradiction. And no man, or body of men, can without being guilty of flagrant injustice, claim a right to dispose of the persons or acquisitions of any other man, or body of men, unless it can be proved that such a right has arisen from some compact between the parties in which it has been explicitly and freely granted." —Dr Joseph Warren (1775)*

The prime tenet of such organic, symbiotic societies is 'individualism,' directly opposed by 'collectivism.' No mixture is possible!

What is possible? A Declaration of Independence – against all individual and societal trespass regardless of howsoever claimed, all such dissent or disagreement a matter for nature's source creator, not a court of law or any military tribunal.

**Challenge Or indifference**

No man or woman needs a doctorate in 'positive law' to distinguish between (artificial) legal entities and flesh-and-blood living human beings, free from legal encumbrance and domination.

Humanism versus anti-humanism clearly shows that distinction. It follows that any living being who grasps the notion of nature's endowments and what belongs to him also grasps his innocence and equality with all others. Marveling at their uniqueness, likewise, they can comprehend what natural law and natural rights consist of. It's not rocket science.

Little understood today is that to set one foot inside a maritime law

(Admiralty) court confesses the court's validity in total – one's case is lost before speaking one word. The court's structure and legal parameters intentionally withstand all onslaughts. Argue that point and you lose!

However, such courts cannot handle your indifference or your refusal to play ball. None of its fictional entities can move or function without a living being engaging in its legal jurisdiction.

Living beings act, legal entities cannot, period.) Nothing can happen in the legal system of Admiralty (Maritime) law until a living being acts for a fictional entity or plays the role of that fiction. So long as no one acts the part, the entity is entirely ineffectual, unable to pick up a pen, much less sign new legislation.

**Cooperative Enterprise Outcomes**

As fully individuated, free, independent beings, 'cooperation' with others is our foremost benefit. Others can specialise in skills we do not have, whereby beneficial results arise from synergistic teamwork.

The question is: is cooperation of our free choice, or will authority dictate involuntary cooperation?

The difference is clear, as Josiah Warren phrased it–

> *One is in perfect accordance with a natural personal liberty which constitutes the chief element of the happiness of human beings, the other violates it and is the chief cause of the Bedlam-like confusion which pervades all ranks and conditions of mind.*

Indeed, we should question whether 'involuntary cooperation' is even possible. Should it not be called servitude? The answer lies in previous discussion concerning freedom and free will.

Earlier chapters show free will sandwiched in the subconscious process where it is fully protected. In societal terms, constitutional authors must ensure protection is never compromised or denied. As Warren insisted, natural laws–

> *teach us that our own happiness depends upon a proper respect for the happiness of others and that therefore we should not make social arrangements which require compulsion or the violation of the natural freedom of any individual.*

In my book *Navigate to Freedom* I gave two examples of what a free society can produce. Here is a brief summary of those descriptions and another.

**1. Times store, Cincinnati**

Josiah Warren reported that when The Time Store in Cincinnati opened in 1827, it applied symbiotic principles to the management and the interchange of labour, including merchants, lawyers, physicians, and teachers. The Store strictly preserved and invariably respected individual autonomy. No legislation of any description assumed control over people at any time or in any case. What resulted?

Hundreds dealt at the Time Store without understanding much of its principles or its objects. Still, they perceived that it was in their interest to do so, thus demonstrating that the business of the community can be brought into this condition by a natural and irresistible process; without combination, without organisation, without laws, without government, without the surrender of any "portion" of the natural liberty of the individual; also demonstrating that reformation need not wait till the world becomes learned: but the practical operation constitutes a process of re-education which no one can estimate without experience, and which the learned are most backward in acquiring.

**2, Cooperative Enterprise**

Many years ago, I played a pivotal role in the success of a company that devoted itself to full market cooperation, entirely rejecting dog-eat-dog competition. In a spiritual sense, the company researched a sought-after value, agreed upon value exchange with consumers, then delivered that value without compromise. That is how full consciousness works, but it translated into a hugely successful business model. Advertising costs fell to near zero as referral business surged from (usual) seven percent to nearly seventy percent. Development costs plummeted. Value exchange spread to sub-suppliers, where advance purchases with staged delivery drove lower product costs. Faithful replication offered buyers exceptional design at the lowest prices while maintaining unprecedented quality control.

The company's success depended on 'value exchange,' the same thing that powers our consciousness. From initial research to satisfaction for all involved, the company asked consumers and suppliers, "What do you value, and what value will you exchange for it?" Everyone was a winner. The formula worked to perfection. Customers and suppliers fell head over heels for contemporary design, appearance, appeal, appointments, model choices, and the opportunity to personalise their products just as we (cosmetically) customise new cars upon purchase.

Several of the company's products were still in demand fifteen years after the initial launch, not the usual six months. Development costs plummeted. Customers received a material product in exchange for money, but the prestigious value was spiritual. The researchers did not ask what product was wanted. They asked, 'What qualities and values will enhance your life?' And that is what customers got. All efforts centred on 'value exchange' and satisfaction.

**3 Free Enterprise**

In the early 1980s, New Zealand suffered from a very depressed and challenging economic situation, mainly from regulations on commerce and trade. But in 1984, it liberalised international trade and opened its markets to world competition. The government withdrew industry and agriculture subsidies and deregulated domestic markets. Trade union membership became voluntary. Employment contracts were retired, left to negotiation between workers and employers. This example of free enterprise catapulted New Zealand on to the world stage.

Of course, lobbyists, academics, religious leaders, and union officials issued dire predictions that deregulation of this magnitude would create a 'sweatshop economy.' All were demonstrably proven wrong. Average wages rose while employment contracts settled rapidly. Strike action fell to near nil, likewise unemployment. This fall was the fastest among (indigenous) Maori, immigrant settlers, and other poor or disadvantaged groups. New Zealand was then one of the world's most societally free and competitive countries.

That example surpassed most all precedents, yet still with government, with (fictional) legal straw men, with all manner of registrations and crippling taxes. Notwithstanding, the disadvantaged profited the most. Now imagine what sensational progress would ensue were those legal and theft roadblocks removed as our human nature solicits we do! Does that explain why people in my home country of New Zealand were so savagely assaulted during years of Covid-nineteen criminality?

**Diversity promotes progress**

In a free economy, producers get continual feedback from their customers. Every moment of every day, people are choosing the products they prefer over others. They constantly weigh up the price, reliability, size, shape, color, and other qualities of every product they buy. Those diverse preferences instantly transmit to producers, who grasp what sells and what does not. Mindful that their competitors are doing the same, suppliers will move as fast as they can to produce more of what people want and less of what they do not. Likewise, producers will stimulate experiments to introduce new and different products they hope customers will like even more.

**Contracts**

Contracts drawn up and imposed by the state do not exist in a free society. Instead, contracts or covenants that correspond with 'ius' are formulated by the respective trading parties who determine the terms and conditions they will accept and voluntarily agree to. No such contract or covenant exists unless witnessed by all parties to it. Logically, independent judges will adjudicate any arising disputes rather than the state-run courts, save for cases when individual Constitutional rights have been trespassed.

**Healthcare through Protectorates**

Once people save their money in their health savings account, they will seek good value through sickness prevention, in preference to sickness treatment. That, of course, is health protection. The more professionals advocate that goal, the less private doctors and clinics will compete for people's custom.

**Welfare through Protectorates**

It should be well known that free countries tend to be wealthier and thus tend to spend more on charitable support of needy people. The more freedom exists, however, the more genuine charity transfers from one person to another voluntarily, and even more readily without taxes.

**The fundamentalist threat to toleration**

Today, the biggest threat to accepting or tolerating others is moral, ideological, or religious fundamentalism. Many people consider homosexuality or premarital sexual relations as disgusting, shameful, intolerable, or immoral. Similarly, some, and perhaps many people, might well consider that denying religious texts or their moral codes is the enactment of pure evil. Correspondingly, a Protectorate must abolish free speech censorship.

It remains that in a free society unless people's actions physically harm others or threaten to do so, no such prohibition is permissible. People must be able to criticise those actions or argue the immorality of injustice, provided none of their expressed rejection manifests as intimidation or actual harm. Nor must a Protectorate restrain, censor, arrest, imprison, torture, maim, punish, exile, or execute any person or group for expressing their views in protest.

**Censorship**

Toleration of this kind includes people's freedom of expression in speech, writing, broadcast, podcasts, or any other broadcast medium. Such a ban trespasses the born rights of individuals.

In short, no censorship exists in a protectorate society, which may concern many people. Indeed, people may assert their born right to be protected from words, images, arguments, and ideas they find shocking. Surprise, surprise. They do have that right already. Nothing compels an individual to attend or listen to presentations they believe are offensive or immoral. Free people are not obliged to submit to what they reject.

The secret to life's fulfilment is to allow accurate and valuable ideas by permitting all ideas, people ultimately revealing their worthiness, merits, and shortcomings through discussion and debate. People must be permitted their case, save that actions or words that incite people to violence must by natural law be arrested.

Our tolerance and acceptance of these principles show our commitment to freedom. Indeed, there can be no doubt we will make more progress and even discover truth faster by allowing the debate of different ideas, not suppressing them.

**Public and private behaviour**

A free (Protectorate) society must ensure the authentication of actual harm or risk of harm. For example, should people be permitted to sell poisons? Permissions have no business in Protectorates. Remember that the law of no trespass is intrinsic, pre-empting anything written in legislation or statutes. Therefore, the onus is on all who manufacture, distribute, or sell poisons to authentically and explicitly state all risks and potential risks. Importantly, those who take the product accept the risks, and all who administer the product accept all liability. No legislation is warranted when the free choice of all involved is secured.

When violence results from public drunkenness and the operation of brothels or gambling houses, offenders are held accountable. Because no legislation curtails or forbids such activity, occasioned harm entirely belongs to those who committed it and security guards who failed to arrest it.

Many people may be disgusted by the thought of such activities, but to ban them on the grounds of anything but harm initiated by one against another means no human activity is safe from pseudo moralists, themselves lacking any grasp of the human conscious process.

**Immigration and technology**

Once-remote corners of the planet are no longer out of reach. Air, land travel, and communications have rocketed ahead in the past century, making it harder for governments to conceal their faults and failings.

The benefits of previous local and Interstate trade may blossom globally. Thus, friendly relations may now span cultures and countries. As we understand other ways of living, we see individuality as factually more critical than ever.

From this understanding, we might concur that governments must open up more. But the truth is precisely the opposite. People who see and experience freedom first-hand soon grasp their enormous power to generate progress and spread prosperity. They do not want or need government intervention. They do not wish for a more expansive government. Technology, trade, migration, tourism, and global markets are their goals as ambassadors for free organic societies. Full conscious functioning, values, creativity, ethics, morality, justice, and prosperity are humanities tools, not government. All of those tools exist within the natural governing laws of our bodies and minds. Thus we are blessed with the means to utilise them morally and constructively, without obstructions.

Sadly or tragically, the only thing people have ever known is the government; never learning self-governance is superior by far. Government is all people complain about because they've no idea how to change it. Now, we do know without question whence the means of change is imperative for people to learn. Once a few see it, that knowledge will catch on like wildfire and spread nationwide.

The only rules (laws) are those that confine the Protectorate to its task of protection. The Constitution has the Declaration of Individual Rights built in. Those rights set the whole premise and tone of the Constitution. That is what constitutional authors must grasp in full. Man's opinion and even the Bible come second to the Creator's consent, written in our nature for our lives to prosper in all fields of endeavor, save wilful destruction of our rights and freedoms.

**New Constitution**

Humanity can advance rapidly and exponentially since our means for unbounded benefits and just protection of our right to life are intrinsic.

Rulers have long known human freedom is a fact of nature. However, because freedom disavows and denies rule, authoritarians invented 'legal entities' that circumvent nature, and their fictional fraud still survives. These tyrants must maintain conscious ignorance if their authoritarian domination and control are to survive. Nothing stands in our way but sociopaths, who, rejecting their nature in full, seek to smash nature's endowments into dust.

Our remedy is to smash through centuries of ignorance concerning how consciousness works. Mystical dreams about raising vibrations, or ascension, will not suffice. Instead, we must grasp conscious workings and profound abilities, fully grasping that one's cognitive mind is in total control. Spiritual values are imperative, so the ball falls in our court as independent living beings.

Accordingly, my Constitution draft is in the (intrinsic) natural law category - the first in history. Protectorates have no politicians, government, parliament, or upper and lower house. A 'Protectorate' (National and state) is a body of people elected to protect every individual's right to life and property.

The Constitution sets out the structure of the Protectorate in part One. Part two is a Charter of individual rights, which, like the US Second Amendment, spells out that the Protectorate cannot make any rule to cancel or deny those rights. Hence, the Protectorate protects people's rights to life and property from all cancellation. [No taxes, ever]

Since these rights are intrinsically innate, no positive law by man can deny them. Each nation has a national President - who presides – since, without ministers, there can be no prime minister. Each state protectorate has a Governor, not for the people, but for the Members of the Protectorate - much like the CEO of a company. The people elect Protectorate members who exercise and uphold self-governance, the only form of government established by the Source Creator.

A police force and judiciary likewise exist, of course. Local councils function with the Protectorate to administer local issues as they do now but have no power to command the people since they are the employers. Superficially, therefore, the society looks much like it does now, but with protection against all evil, having no authoritarian commands. All services (fire, ambulance, etc.) remain like now. That's the broad overview of a free society 'Protectorate.'

**Moving forward**

Self-governance is entirely possible within intrinsic natural law and natural justice. I began this book by stating that consciousness and natural law present an integrated view of existence and life, precisely what an objective philosophy must satisfy. To that end, I've shown how our conscious faculty functions inside natural governing laws, revealing a nature-based philosophy immutably residing in our human nature. And that makes this book unlike any ever written, save for the Objectivist philosophy discovered by Ayn Rand. Her philosophy and what I have shown through full consciousness are effectively the same, each reinforcing the other.

The story now shown is astonishing in consciousness terms, not just for the massive personal and societal benefits, but for exposing misleading mental inventions that prevent humanity from learning the truth of their nature. Philosophical unity is now greater than anything the world has ever witnessed.

Our task is to overturn all that has led humanity astray and replace it with the truth we are born into that cannot be refuted. All we need to do is say 'yes,' learn it, practice it, and benefit in ways never before possible.

*I am flesh and blood, of free will, an Independent Living Being (ILB) in body, mind and soul; my freedoms are drawn about me by the equal rights of all others. My first breath invoked Creator's endowment of unalienable right to my life and inalienable right to the property of my effort, every exception and trespass forbidden by the Creator's natural laws encrypted in my living nature.*

Consider what that statement means. The first two words irrefutably state that one's nature is inviolate and immutable. Instantly, all 'statutes' or 'legal constructs' that construe differently, are rendered inapplicable, invalid, fallacious, non-binding, unenforceable and void.

The phrase 'flesh and blood' explicitly emphasises exactly what 'I am.' 'Free will' follows naturally, since volitional consciousness separates men and women from all other life forms on earth. Not only are dead legal entities excluded, but 'independence' from all legal jurisdictions is established indisputably. All animals are excluded, including the 'unborn young of animals,' which monetary banks usually claim as chattel, and that governments utilise to 'legally' claim a child before legal (birth certificate) registration.

The phrase, 'Independent Living Being in body, mind and soul' establishes 'independence' unequivocally, since no legal entity can ever exhibit those attributes!

An infant's cry of first breath is the only means it possesses to avow its independent life in that instant. The creator's unalienable right to life is instantly endowed thereby, simultaneous with that individual's inalienable right to the property of his or her (later) efforts. Since 'mother dependence' instantaneously switches to become 'infant independence,' no opportunity window exists to allow government usurpation of this process.

Neither can it 'register' an infant before birth, because no independent life exists to be registered.

Once independent from its mother, an infant instantly becomes fully reliant on the natural laws of its nature, regardless of ongoing nurture. Its right to life is immutable and inviolable; never to be broken, infringed, violated or dishonoured.

Perhaps now you will better understand what Jesus meant by saying, "*I am the way, the truth and the life.*" ( John 14:6)

Self-protection is an immutable principle encrypted in our very nature, not subject to differences of opinion, majority decision, or any arbitrary decree of society. To deny that principle is to refute one's nature, automatically nullifying such denial.

**Self-governance**

Creator has modelled the (natural law) principles of ethics, morality, and natural justice, smack in the core of our conscience and emotional reporting systems, exactly where they belong!

Right there, in the core of your being, lies the Creator's perfect model for personal freedom, and the means for free organic societies. The creator's will is self-governance within natural law.

Natural law *theorists* have long believed that we each possess an innate morality, that in turn prescribes natural law. But the reverse is true. Natural law prescribes morality. Natural law is factual, not theory, hence my phrase 'intrinsic natural law.' Nature upholds our values, ethics, actions, and morality, without ever overruling our free will. Thus 'independence' removes the whole subject of morality from the collective domain ruled by governments, and puts it into the private domain, where it rightfully belongs. Today's beliefs concerning ethics and morality are overturned. 'Collectivised' jurisdictional claims over ethics and morality are invalidated. Authoritarian government switches to self-governance, under natural law. Natural law theories holding that morality determines natural law, are inverted.

**That is the Creator's model for free, organic societies, encrypted in our nature.**

# Chapter 17

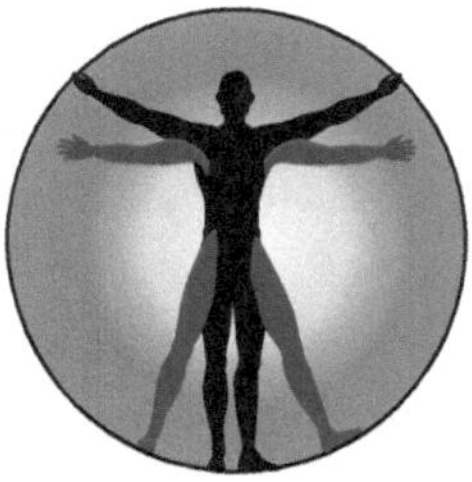

## Personal and Societal Benefits

This chapter is devoted to the benefits of understanding the complete conscious process, its governing laws, and a protectorate-based free society. These summaries from my three previous books and this book are in bullet point form.

The titled lists (here shown) are incomplete since when the people enact the various principles and natural laws in a free (Protectorate) society; countless unforetold and unpredictable benefits will arise.

**The conscious process defined.**

*Consciousness is the systemic process of life-value transfer between the conscious and subconscious minds, interfacing physicality and spirituality, authored by free will.*

**The definition of natural law**

*Natural law is the set of universal, eternal, and immutable conditions governing behavioural consequences of volitionally conscious beings. Without respect for these precepts intrinsic within man's nature, no one can preserve the peace and happiness of society.*

**Consciousness benefits smash conscious ignorance**

- Nothing past has described consciousness so fully or natural law so specifically. Thus, blessed humanity may excel beyond anything ever taught about these subjects.
- Massive roadblocks collapse due to erroneous beliefs and conscious ignorance.
- Free will is sandwiched between two different functionalities of the

subconscious mind, smashing the common belief that consciousness is awareness.

- Perception is a truthful, multi-purpose faculty.
- Imagination assumes a vitality very different from anything taught.
- Our subconscious mind upholds our goals and ambitions without further effort.
- Life differentiates ethics from its lack and morality from immorality.
- We can put our most fervent desires on auto-pilot.
- Taking charge of our power to bring health, mental integrity, and joyful happiness in every present moment slashes our mental workload to the core.
- Focus on life shifts, not abandoning material things but spiritually enriching them.
- Spiritual blessings include peace, efficacy, tranquillity, and emotional harmony.
- Emotions resolve as never before. We can mastermind them in advance.
- These opportunities offer a revolutionary understanding of human nature, ethics, morality, justice, rights, sociology, law, and sovereignty, forging unprecedented unity and freedom for humanity.
- Once this unification is fully comprehended, nothing excels, nor can it. Conscious ignorance is history.

**Personal benefits excel**

- Freedom of mind, clarity of mind, and peace of mind are accessible to all of us.
- People who master their lives through uploaded values will quickly reap benefits.
- As ignorance fades into oblivion and one becomes more accomplished, tranquillity, joy, power, and peace flood one's life beyond anything dreamt possible.
- Joy in life relies on choosing our actions in spiritual terms.
- Intellectual prowess is greatly enhanced.
- Choosing valued goals soon becomes second nature.
- Confidence grows, and self-esteem increases.
- Fears of independence vanish.
- Mental strain is reduced to near nil, while emotional joy excels.
- Beliefs translate to knowledge, or they evaporate.

- Emotionally rewarded, people become humbly proud of their achievements and happiness.
- Personal benefits are only available to those who choose freedom and responsibilities with a passionate will to succeed.

**Natural law benefits exceed anything known in the past**

- Natural laws govern the consequences of our actions, which is the exact opposite of legislating people's actions up-front.
- Creator has modeled the (natural law) principles of ethics, morality, and natural justice smack in the core of our conscience and emotional reporting systems, exactly where they belong!
- Our natural laws testify to values, individual rights, comforts, security, and protections.
- Factual natural law acquires indisputable power never witnessed in all history, strictly provided that 'unalienable rights,' freedoms, living identity, and 'natural justice' are upheld and forever protected. No better precedent exists.
- 'Intrinsic natural law' now has greater veracity than has ever been grasped, immutable teeth that no one ever suspected.
- Nature itself cancels present natural law theories that hold morality determines natural law.
- 'Intrinsic natural law' as fact is exceedingly more truthful, assertive, and righteous.
- The 'non-aggression principle' (NAP) is the 'natural law of no trespass' encrypted in our nature – not a theory.
- All 'collectivised' jurisdictional claims over ethics and morality are thereby invalidated. So, they are removed from the (collective) social arena (public/political domain) and placed squarely in the individual (private domain) of sovereign individuals to which they rightfully belong.
- Natural laws are incompatible with all artificial laws because no mix of nature's facts with invented fiction is possible.
- No one can deny or erase the governing laws of our nature. Nothing better exists for any society than what has always existed within every man, woman, and child on Earth.
- The (legal) (artificial)" rule of law," known as' Constitutional law' is resolutely canceled.
- Natural law now has immutable teeth that no one ever suspected.
- Intrinsic natural law takes its place whereby our 'unalienable and

inalienable rights,' freedoms, living identity, and 'natural justice' must be upheld and forever protected

**Ten Natural law tenets aid authenticity and simplicity**

- Natural Law is to be respected, not obeyed
- Natural law is of Man, not for Man
- Natural law is objective, not subjective
- Natural law is immutable
- Natural law upholds independent human life
- Natural law grants no authority
- Natural law refuses all authority
- Natural law admits no trespass; hence, protection is assured
- Natural law seeks integrity
- Natural law supports our life respectful of all others

**Societal Benefits Implore (protected) self-governance.**

*Any society that authorises a state to rule it by force deserves all the tyranny and bloodshed that 'authority' approves.*

- Authoritarian beliefs concerning ethics and morality are no longer relevant, all replaced by nature's precedents.
- Nature's model orchestrates a culture of fifty trillion individual cells and organs, all authored by our free will. Yet, we've only eight billion people on Earth. Consequently, no better precedent exists than natural self-governance, with all rights, freedoms, comforts, and securities protected.
- Authoritarian government switches to self-governance under natural law.
- All 'collectivised' jurisdictional claims over ethics and morality are invalidated.c
- Individual rights reign supreme because freedom and prosperity begin with the nature of what we are as living flesh and blood beings, not who we are.
- Convivial society results from moral actions in aggregate.
- Independence, one from another, enters with respect for each other.
- Co-operation amongst equals, or one's likes, results in mutual benefit.
- Morality is the outward manifestation of ethically based principles that uphold life-sustaining actions. Conversely, immorality manifests a lack or refusal of ethical considerations, moral discipline, or justness.

- Pregnant mothers are free to refuse any medical practice or procedure that may cause harm to themselves or the foetus at any time during the term of pregnancy absent the mother's autographed consent of full written disclosure inclusive of the practitioner's admission of liability.
- Nature's societal model is fully complete. All we need do is transpose its twenty personal laws into society.
- We have no life without the individual, unalienable right to live it. We must also have the independent, inalienable right to the fruits of our labour, to produce what sustains our lives.
- Those who prize ethics and morality as spiritual progenitors of life relish the objective virtues of 'Living Justice' because others learn from joint dealings. Moral actions are the flip side of natural justice.
- Because responsibility for respecting the equal rights of all others is all-important, the value exchange system encrypted in our conscious process is the Creator's perfect model for societal harmony.
- Peace-loving, organic societies the world has never witnessed are eminently possible and insisted by nature; all contrary legislations consigned to history.
- No free society supporter truthfully admits or to wilful agreement of tyranny, slavery, initiated violence, and wars.
- The benefits of previous local and Interstate trade may blossom globally.

**Necessary protections of protection are beneficially essential**

- Maintaining the supreme value of life on which consciousness depends protects it.
- Free will, forever preserved by nature, testifies to nature's irrevocable consent and insists that society must also protect free will.
- Natural law theory, common law, and all forms of positive law have no authenticity or merit. Hence, society must be protectively subordinate to life, not vice versa.
- Human trafficking or trafficking of any human body parts or fluid, whether prenatal, infant, child, or adult, is strictly outlawed, or else life itself is unprotected.
- Rights are inherent within the born nature of every man, woman, and child, whereby all rulers who dispute those facts dispute their nature, automatically rendering all disputes or protests invalid and void from pronouncement.

- People's failure to protect their unalienable right to life and inalienable right to the fruits of their labour amounts to their approval for people to be forcibly ruled, harmed, or both.
- Protection of our unalienable right to life and inalienable right to our property from violation and usurpation is essential, or protection is naught.
- Our auto-immune and endocrine systems, plus communication between our two minds, amply demonstrate our verified right to bear arms and protect against all enemies, foreign and domestic.
- Any action that trespasses or violates another's life automatically sacrifices their right to choose, meaning only innocent people are free.
- All who step outside intrinsic natural law to become outlaws bring the total weight of natural justice to bear on themselves.
- All who choose to be outlaws will relinquish their right to freedom as a consequence of their actions since self-destruction is the only destructive right they possess.
- All (freedom) dissenters must face the fact they have abandoned their nature, automatically negating their every dispute. They give up their freedom willingly.
- Aggressors wilfully confess responsibility for remedy: restoration of the natural order.
- No judge must rule against them because they have already ruled against themselves.
- You can't cheat nature without paying the price.
- Natural justice steers offenders back to an ethic-based morality. Justice is the correction or restoration of the natural order, therefore, not punishment.
- Recompense may be involved, although mitigating circumstances may prevail.
- Authoritarian governments are rendered obsolete. Self-governance under natural law is their replacement. Nothing excels.
- So thorough and complete is this social model that all criminal violators and trespassers are relegated to outlaw status by their own free choice.

**Protectorate Constitutional benefits.**

- By these means, the Nation's hallmark is the Rights and Laws of Nature encrypted within the nature of every man, woman, and child as set out in the (Constitutional) Charter of Individual Rights.

- Thereby established, no 'person' or Sentient Living Being may initiate the use of physical force or violate another's life, save for (self-defence) arresting any initiating party.
- Protectorate governance has no function but to delineate, enact, and uphold our Intrinsic Natural Laws, Rights, and freedoms for perpetuity.
- All of today's crimes against the Nation's people as indisputable facts warrant people's immediate divorce from all authoritarian rule, allowing their self-chosen demise forthwith.
- Immorality and injustices are exposed whereby (outlaw) practitioners confess criminal action.
- No objection can be raised without disputing human nature, instantly and automatically canceling the objection.
- People's divorce from all governments, their affiliations, and treaties with all corporate or governmental entities, whether foreign or domestic, is conclusive and final,
- Multiple additional reservations also apply as specified in the Charter of Individual Rights within the Constitution.
- 6 Profound Educational benefits
- Kids can be taught the principles of value correspondence from an early age.
- Life-sustaining philosophy may be taught at primary school levels, eloquently structured to prevent conscious ignorance from ever developing.
- The same philosophical principles may and should adequately be delivered through colleges or universities, spliced with the universality of intrinsic natural law.
- Further education expands the founding principles.
- The entire process can be (sufficiently) taught from early childhood, offering untold benefits for every man, woman, and child.
- Protectorates properly serve to educate the populace concerning the protections they administer, given no contrary legislation exists.
- (14) Aspects of organic, symbiotic societies–
- Unlike anything ever witnessed, it is all yours for your will to achieve.
- An organic society consists of free, independent people living according to their choices, among their likes. All people respect the natural law of the human world in their mutual dealings and interactions.
- Convivial order is that of adults living as responsible and caring people. Their society is the meeting, exchanging, and parting, or freely entering

into or exiting from more or less stable relationships on peaceful and friendly terms within a goodwill atmosphere.

- All people are free to the extent that others treat them peacefully, fully respecting their rights, work, and property. Mutual respect, one for another within the physical domain of which they are the author, certifies orderliness within the 'natural law.'
- People live together as independent beings without being urged to any joint enterprise or social interaction, not unlike a commune. Friendly relations among strangers have nothing but their humanity in common. Respect accepts others' uniqueness, speech, individuality, personal integrity, and property.
- Individual freedom allows opportunity and facilitates negotiations, actions, and outcomes, yet allows free exit, absent force, fraud, or coercion. Individuals freely pursue their goals separately and lawfully, in the company of, or collaboratively with others. Business contracts are personally and responsibly warranted, not committed by office, title, position, company, or corporation.
- No organisational or statutory purpose exists, although cultural ethics may predominate. No authority exercises direction, rule, or control, meaning no government may exist because such forfeits the nature and integrity of that society.
- Nothing establishes rulers or rule. No individual or group owns society, controls it, or is responsible or answerable. No common goal exists but for freedom, protection, and preservation. Moral guidance comes through education.
- Direction and influence may exist in the social order, e.g., from elders and those of great wisdom. Still, no positions of power exist to exert influence or command anyone. Participants abide by the natural laws of societal orderliness.
- All problems are resolved through diplomatic negotiations or an appointed judge or arbitrator, remembering that no one who seeks resolution can become the negotiator's or judicial agent's subject.
- Those who step outside natural laws choose to be outlaws; such actions automatically confirm a trespasser's agreement to suffer all consequences arising. All matters dealing with the arrest of violence, fraud or coercion, justness, justice, remediation, recompense, and compensation accord with intrinsic natural law. No social, organic order can wage war!

- The new Nation and its lawful parameters found on un-erasable self-governance are intrinsic in all its people, consented by the Source Creator.
- No need exists for a majority vote when every individual's right to life and property is guaranteed and protected by a Constitution document whose rights and terms' are expressly those of nature's source creator.
- Whomsoever disagrees with their nature instantly (self) nullifies their dispute. Thus, no man or group holds a blank check on power over others.
- The institution of free, organic societies properly founded on our human nature is now in our hands. Nothing has precedence, is more relevant, or more urgent.
- Sovereignty is little more than an ethical mind engaging in moral activities and accepting responsibility and liability for one's actions.
- Sovereignty of the people means divorce from all who would violate self-mastered autonomy, all foreign and domestic agencies, corporations, and governments themselves.

There you have it: One hundred twenty-four clear-cut benefits across nine categories. We may now witness a world where everyone moves freely through life with radiantly clear knowledge of their true potential, spiritual purpose, and connection to the Source of everything. This opportunity is now on Australia's doorstep, indeed all other Nations, all for the knowledge and willpower to achieve freedoms!

**The secret of Happiness is**

**Freedom**

**The secret of freedom is**

**Courage**

**Thucydides**

"Do you want to know who you are? Don't ask. Act! Action will delineate and define you"

## Right to Freedom

Unless we wake up to the fullness of freedom, and the right to self-govern, and responsibly act upon that right, we will have neither rights nor freedom.

*Kenneth E. Bartle*

## Self-governance

Until people awaken to tyrany excercised by their governors, they will not discover their intrinsic right to self-governance and innate protections, which gifts deny and forbid all societal tyrany.

*Kenneth E. Bartle*

# Chapter 18

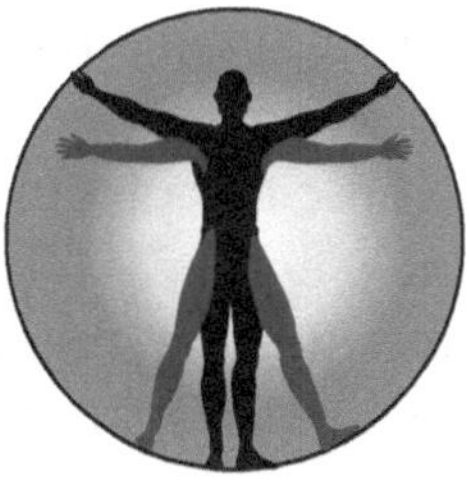

## Free Societies

Technology has forged ahead for decades, if not centuries. Meanwhile, our knowledge of human consciousness has remained stagnant if it has not receded. No one knows what human consciousness is or how it works, so we are never taught. Humanity suffers greatly from personal problems and is socially prey to political violence, widespread corruption, tyranny, destruction, and wars. No remedy offers but that which has failed in the past, such as democracy.

Because nature abhors a vacuum, people invent or imagine what they believe consciousness to be. Beliefs build on never-questioned beliefs, whereby personal and global problems magnify unchallenged.

No one teaches that our means of success is innate in human nature. Natural law facts are our remedy. Natural law *theory* will never be. My purpose was to introduce people to ideas they've never conceived possible. From this, I trust my readers will become enthused and want to learn more, from whence a free society may commence in Australia, thus becoming the first country to stamp Freedom on the world map.

Consciousness is a mental and spiritual process. It is not mere 'awareness' as dictionaries describe. Our cognitive mind permits us to use reason. So, we learn to enquire, explore possibilities, and evaluate potential outcomes from proposed actions.

Like our stomachs, we cannot change how our two minds work. Still, we can choose what they process. Very few people know that similar values apply to the quality of thought, including all truths, theories, beliefs, superstitions, and ideologies. Values, therefore, are mental nutrition, especially spiritual values.

Mental communication between the cognitive free will mind and the subconscious mind reveals twenty natural laws governing that process according to our choices. More important than what we choose is why we choose because our choices program our feelings and emotions.

Located in the core of the conscious process is the most vital law of all. It states – *"no mind may rule another."* That means all authoritarian government is outlawed. Thus, twenty natural laws are our path to free organic societies – no rule or command, but for outlaws.

**Life values**

Absent life, nothing is of value. Thus, our conscious process thrives on spiritual values, now known as 'life values,' which are crucial to our mental well-being. Life value examples include truth, respect, courage, diligence, and commitment. No more than about fifteen (prime) values are required, some containing subset values. Those choices beautifully demonstrate why free will is vitally protected. We only need to program our minds with these few (freely chosen) values, where, in turn, they banish mental confusion and trauma. Abundant creative energy is released to press our free choices even further! Our whole conscious process is an astonishing masterpiece of nature that no artificial intelligence will ever match. Our (free) choices are all without cost!

**Intellectual faculties**

- **Integrity** means adhering to spiritually rational principles when tempted to compromise them.
- **Honesty** means never faking ethical or moral reality in pursuit of our goals.
- **Productiveness** means a rational, not hit-or-miss approach to creating material values.
- **Independence** means thinking and acting in support of oneself, even collaboratively, all within the equal rights of all others.
- **Pride,** or self-esteem if you prefer, means continually striving to act as morality requires to do one's best in achieving one's moral goals.
- **Individual rights** now surpass every 'group right' ever invented.

It is all so beautifully simple. No other rights can exist without infringing on those you already have. Outlaws and criminals forsake their born rights through their actions, which shows how senselessly stupid they are and how natural justice works. Were you taught those principles in school or university? Aren't the first words of those (above) bullet points the proper framework of morality that schools should teach across all levels?

Little of this is known or taught today. Nonetheless, when both minds synchronise on the same page, a powerful (cost-free) dynamic is released and surges within us. Joy in life does not result from what we choose to do but, more importantly, why we choose our actions in 'value' terms. Guess what?

- These principles of value correspondence within full consciousness can be taught from early childhood, offering untold benefits for every man, woman, and child. (Do you want your children to thrive?)
- Erroneous beliefs and conscious ignorance vaporise. Beliefs translate to knowledge, or they evaporate.
- Imagination assumes a vitality very different from anything taught.
- Mental ability is massively enhanced.
- All these benefits and more are within human reach. Better yet, even programmable for infants who have no science, math, or language.

**Personal Benefits**

As previously shown, choosing valued goals soon becomes second nature, with your most valued desires on auto-pilot. All fears of independence vanish as confidence and self-esteem magnify, as tranquility, joy, power, and peace flood your life. When emotionally rewarded in this way, our focus shifts from abandoning material things to spiritually enriching them.

This power brings health, mental integrity, and joyful happiness to every present moment while slashing mental strain to near nil. As conscious ignorance fades into oblivion, we become more accomplished and more joyously able to live without fear. We soon become humbly proud of our achievements.

"Whoever attains this level of conscious enlightenment will experience a load lifting off their shoulders. They will realise they've nothing to gain from pseudo-intellectuals, new-age mystics, pretenders, imposters, blood spilling authority, and soul destroying spiritual bandits. All predators are blasted into oblivion! Every would-be intruder puffed with egotistic belligerence will hit a brick wall; your dynamic, impenetrable, material, mental, and spiritual self. Those who discover their beautiful spiritual aspects, will quickly learn that every emotional chaos or trauma originating from pulpits and parliaments of fiction, falsity, and irrelevance, will have been struck from their life without them even asking! Exercising full consciousness in life-value terms is the greatest reverence and gratitude anyone can offer our Creator. As your world presents itself in a whole new light, spiritual independence, enlightenment, and empowerment will manifest in your life as never before."

Spiritual life values have no equal, and the Source creator has our back! These truths directly access the most profoundly loving power humanity could ever know. It is bountiful beyond measure, unequaled, never to be erased.

**Sociological advances are unprecedented.**

These natural laws perfectly translate into society with excellent social benefits.

Just as our bodily nature is a science, we can treat ethics and morality likewise. We are their author, not consensus opinion, church or state meddling. Sociological reappraisal becomes foremost.

Such a code (or science) of ethics permits us to master ourselves through life-honoring thoughts, desires, and ambitions that fully respect other people's lives. Our (thought) ethics automatically become morality through our actions. By so doing, we protect our values and our lives. No better model of ethics or morality exists, yet no such thing has happened.

- **Ethics are now our benchmark**, while morality underpins life-sustaining actions. Who will ever want immorality when it proves our refusal of consideration for others, a lack of moral discipline, and an absence of justness, all being harmful choices that backfire on ourselves?
- **Justness is our moral choice of action.** We automatically serve justice by not interfering with or preventing any other man or woman from living their lives.
- **Justice now serves ourselves and not the state.** By remediating unjust or immoral actions, offenders responsibly correct, remediate, or restore harmful actions according to their offense. Why would anyone want to commit evil when immoral actions automatically cancel their freedom?
- **Justness and morality are now our social benchmark** – the sum of just actions and testament to our morality. How many more centuries must pass before humanity learns that all of our body faculties must each 'justly' deliver from one faculty to the other? If they do not, do they assuredly violate the life they professedly uphold? Why were you not taught that lesson in your nature?

Those principles determine what values we should practice in society. Most of us know them already, but governments overrule them. Individual freedom assured by nature is a gift, an opening pathway to the future. A mere twenty natural laws allow us to institute free organic societies authentically. Hundreds of global law libraries then become obsolete.

Natural justice steers offenders back to ethics, morality, and acceptance of other people's right to life. Recompense may be involved at times, although mitigating circumstances may prevail. No one decides justice – it just is! No victimless crime can exist; thus, no penalties or restitution levy against such inventions.

**Revising the golden rule**

Nature's' golden rule' should be rewritten: *"Do morally unto yourself as you would others do justly unto themselves."* Why? Because 'life' instantly replaces 'society' as the benchmark for determining people's thoughts and behaviours. Moral actions logically follow, whereby our moral stature and our (manifested) love of life reveal themselves to the world. Logically, others should follow our ethical and moral examples, according to their preferred choices, while accepting all consequences. Remember, nothing is prescribed or commanded in advance. This principle wonderfully exists within you, as your feelings testify so beautifully. So, we learn that values, natural laws, and justice are the very nature of our being. That is priceless because no additional (government) commandments are needed.

**Morality**

Of course, people may howl in protest. *"How on earth will immoral behaviour be arrested if we each morally govern ourselves?"* That's easy because everyone committing an immoral action confesses guilt through their action(s) to others. Once their trespass is proven, natural justice (lawfully) answers the question. No judge must rule against trespassers because they have already ruled against themselves.

Thus, with governmental prescriptions gone, a new definition of morality and its subset qualities becomes almost self-evident.

**Morality is the conscious will to live according to one's nature, never depriving others of the same opportunity.**

Briefly stated, 'actions and behaviour publicly testify our pre-conceived moral stature and confessed moral accountability.'

**Jurisdiction of life**

Nature's model is so thorough and complete that all criminal trespassers are relegated to 'outlaw status' by their own free choice.

- Self-harm is the only destructive right we humans possess. Thus, people who step outside natural Law are outlaws. They've voluntarily given up their born innocence and right to freedom as (confessed) trespassers of natural Law.
- Consequently, all statutes and legislations enforced by fines, prisons,

and guns automatically cancel, while evil is confessed by those who implement such legislations.

- We do not need to exit their legal jurisdiction. They've already departed the jurisdiction of life into which they were born, being that in which you still live.
- No matter how much politicians believe the cause of liberty advances democracy, it remains that freedom, even for one person, is entirely denied by the principle of authoritarian rule. Remember, no mind can rule another. Such authoritarian oppressors choose to violate life by choice, as witnessed by the 'Nuremberg code.' Goodbye, cruel world – your (invented, fictional)' legal identities' never had a (flesh and bone) leg to stand on!

To forcibly compel compliance with statutes countermands and refuses natural laws that benevolently uphold our rights to life and property. To contemptuously disavow one's nature is to spit in the face of one's Creator! The root core of today's evils on earth is that we are legally compelled and often physically forced to do just that.

**Lex - ius**

The word law, initially translated from the Latin word 'Lex,' originated from commanding the mobilisation of armies. Today, 'lex' refers to authoritative commands, statutes, and legislations backed by physical force. Fortunately, the word 'Law' was also translated from the Latin word' ius,' which refers to a solemn bond' (usually between two people), effectively their orderly agreement. Thus, 'ius' means 'orderliness,' which preserves the governance of our bodies and minds.

All forced intervention or trespass is forbidden thereby. It follows that' Lex' is denied any part whatsoever. In conclusion, (intrinsic) natural Law is all that remains, which means *"law is natural law and nothing else"* as stated by Frank van Dun, philosopher of Law.

From this, we learn that 'natural law issues no authority and accepts none.' Nine more like tenets apply to all twenty laws, rendering all artificial Law and its legal systems redundant if not criminal.

Business rules, terms, and conditions remain open to our free will, acceptance, or rejection without penalty.

**The benefits of natural Law are beyond compare.**

When simple lawfulness replaces vast legal complexities, fictional entities have no place. That opens the door to benefits we've never considered before.

As explained in my book *'Navigate to Freedom,'* our respect for freedom engenders the voluntary cooperation of other people based on the mutual exchange of value, thereby producing almost incomprehensible societal benefits, as previously shown.

**Disagreement vanishes**

Some may say, *"What if I disagree?"* But disagree with what? Organic societies founded on the nature of what we are will automatically ensure the Creator's universal consent to live in freedom. When your right to life and property are upheld and protected by natural justice, no other right or politician can offer more. Trespassers' only argument is to protest that your rights forbid their confessed desire to commit crimes. They lose because protection is uncompromisable. Read what Josiah Warren wrote in the early 1800's. Natural laws–

> *"teach us that our own happiness depends upon a proper respect for the happiness of others and that therefore we should not make social arrangements which require compulsion or the violation of the natural freedom of any individual."*

Furthermore...

> *"there must be no arrangements which depend for their success upon agreement on verbal rules or processes for agreements of opinions, tastes or interests. There should be, instead, preservation of the liberty of each person to differ in these and all other respects."*

**Natural law theory is replaced**

People know that neighbours and friends rally around and assist during bushfires, earthquakes, floods, and tsunamis, many believing this proves we possess an inbuilt morality. But a biased (prejudiced) mind means we have no free will. That being so, our conscious process cannot exist despite it being our mental operating system. Natural law theory arose from that false premise, and has failed for hundreds of years.

My research (over 12 years) tells a different story. Natural laws built into our nature govern the consequences of our actions – after we have acted. For example, if we eat nutritious foods, we thrive and prosper; if we eat toxic foods, we suffer and may perish. Yet, at all times, we are free to choose what to eat, drink, or inhale.

That example informs us that intrinsic natural law protects our free will. By learning from past mistakes, natural law theory vanishes in favour of a life-sustaining morality authored by free will choices. Existential natural laws are in our nature; morality is not. Factual natural law replaces the former theory; its enormous benefits are ours. In addition, morality is taken from the hands of the government and returned to our private domain, where it rightfully belongs. Society benefits in addition. Intrinsic natural law is not what the past theory taught.

**Free societies send all authoritarian governments packing.**

Protected self-governance within natural law takes precedence; all violations of people's right to life are criminal. Australian people are thereby gifted the opportunity to stamp the word FREEDOM on the world map, as may any country on earth.

Most remarkably, worldwide evil over the last three years has matured synchronously with our knowing how evil can be dispatched to history, never to repeat. Accordingly, we have a grand opportunity for unprecedented success solely dependent on our passion for life and commitment to make it happen, with not one bullet fired. We can institute free societies founded on (factual) natural law, all with our Source Creator's blessing. What more could we ask?

This time in world history is most likely our only chance to implement free organic societies.

- Freedom is the only condition in which our 'operating system' of 'full consciousness' can function as it should. People who respect other's lives protect their own lives in like measure! That is how natural law works, yet nothing is prescribed or ruled in advance. No enforcement is necessary save arresting those who violate natural law for any criminal purpose.
- It cannot be said more clearly. We must seize freedom, respect it, enact it, and protect it. If we omit one of those four essentials, we lose it.

Life is the bottom line. Hence, intrinsic natural law is our all-time reference base for all judicial matters. Self-governance now becomes the core doctrine of free societies, thereby protecting freedom and free will. All obstruction, commandments, statutes, and invented laws vanish. Individuals are now the employers of each state and national 'protectorate,' tasked to protect the people within natural justice. Free societies can emerge in a way we've never imagined.

Your connection to spirit is sure when you stand in the glory of creation as its partner. If you're already feeling this connection and feeling spirit energy now with its love for you and your life, then you've gotten it! Your search is over, so accept, use, and enjoy it. Walk with your specialist (subconscious) friend every moment hereafter. Love is the most incredible energy in the cosmos. Much more than grace, benevolence, or compassion, it is a way of being respectful to self, spirit, and all others. Enjoy peace daily and your connection to a symbiotic family of spiritual beings here on earth. Do these things, and you will catalyze humanity's spiritual ascendency and earth's recalibration. Your life and your spirit will soar beyond anything you have known.

The sole question facing humanity is profoundly straightforward. A new and vitally energetic Constitution for freedom will not depend on some document accepted by majority vote; neither by preference, democracy, voting, opinion, my two bob's worth, nor a referendum. Instead, the prime question is, do you want to profit from the gifts of your nature or abuse them and suffer as humanity has done for centuries? Either way, and make no mistake, you will be governed by natural law! No escape is possible.

**Revised Education**

Tragically, most humanity is not yet ready to fully implement natural law and free societies as the ideal' end state.' Education is imperative; therefore, to preferably begin now.

From preparatory school onwards, ethical and moral education can be formulated, written, and taught across all curricula. Self-mastery and sovereignty will become vividly transparent to those who practice. Perfection is not required, effort is. Once this beneficial practice is grasped and efficiently employed broadly, all forms of domination and control will dissolve regardless of false benefit promises. That done, vacant ideologies, religious misdirections, off-world intrusions and legal fictions will all die from malnutrition.

**A new constitution**

A revolutionary change of this magnitude demands a new constitutional structure centred on free will and unwavering protection of our rights to life and property.

- Suppose you can comprehend the finely governed process that upholds and protects your life, even reporting its progress, and you have the unalienable right to choose what values you want to be supported and protected. In that case, you will understand the Source creator's invitation to live as never before.
- If you grasp likewise that your right to life is protected jus by upholding the right to life of all others, you will understand the Source creator's invitation for free societies to develop and flourish.

My path of discovery began fifty-eight years ago and has surged intensively over the last twelve years. This opportunity is radically different from all past. It shows why protection is vital and positive law is incompatible with natural law. Please consider this so there is no misunderstanding–

*"Every commandment ever issued in human history penetrates our awareness, the starting point of the human conscious process. In that place, such instruction cannot do other than prescribe all your inquiries, deliberations, knowledge, beliefs, imaginings, fears and expectations, your actions and behaviour. It surreptitiously indoctrinates values that mould your outcomes and emotions. That is nothing short of covert mind control, a flagrant violation of natural law.*

*Conversely, Natural law governs the consequences of your actions, meaning that it inserts its presence only after you have acted, fully upholding and protecting your free will. It also endorses your chosen values, whereby you are the author of your emotions and the maker of your soul, not the government. The Creator's gift of your automated mentoring system (feelings) prompts you to keep or change your values or behaviour. Either way, you benefit."*

How could anyone refuse such a robust life-sustaining opportunity given the world is fast approaching human extinction, with the disastrous possibility this opportunity may never repeat?

Thousands of years from now, people will speak of humanity's successful transition to a new age in our time. You can be a founder of that new age, your offspring included. Everything you need is already within your nature. Agree to act, and you will reap lush rewards never considered possible.

**A New 'Protectorate' society structure awaits your acceptance**

A 'Protectorate,' substituted in place of government, is a constitutionally appointed body of people that upholds and protects people's rights and freedoms. It should never be more complex.

Such' Protectorates' lawfully replace national and state governments, with local councils (or counties) remaining only as agents of the people. Protectorates adhere to an objectively written Constitution that expressly forbids statutes and legislations. Any violation or departure brings instant dismissal since rights and freedoms belong solely to every individual in society.

After that, no political party, monarchy, or empire can exist as we know them. No government remains; thus, people are instantly free from domination and control. No upper or lower house, senate, or legislative assemblies exist. No taxes, stamp duties, or registrations apply since all are property theft. No acts, statutes, or legislations exist because *"no mind can rule another."* Natural law is respected. Unlawful trespass is arrested. Accordingly, governments, legislations, statutes, and executive orders consign themselves to history.

Peace officials (police) and law courts continue much as they do now, but with no victimless crimes like speeding tickets, all such services are demonstrably smaller and vastly more efficient. Consequently, all present protections such as building standards, air, rail, road safety, construction, and infrastructure works remain workably unaffected, albeit lawfully transitioned.

Fundamental safety rules apply. Nothing can rule or overrule our thoughts, free will actions, morality, or minds. Free to act as we please within the rights of all, we may accept or reject trade or commercial 'terms and conditions,' none being mandatory, else they violate free choice.

Government rule is outlawed, thereby substituted by responsibly instituted self-governance within the rights of all others as our Creator intended. Legal entities no longer exist, save for delegated (office) positions within businesses, clubs, institutions, and the like for their orderly maintenance.

**Conclusion**

The first step is to comprehend our conscious process fully. That mental vacancy has long permitted (insane) statute laws and commands to impair or deny critical thinking, stripping us of freedom, thus binding humanity in servitude with no corrective means in sight. Yet all along, the Source Creator's solution to apathy, ignorance, authoritarian control of our lives, and criminal slavery is indisputably born within each of us.

- We succeed by using our mental powers as the Creator intended we should.
- So, we learn how natural laws function according to values and our role in choosing them.
- So, we grasp the value of life, its resident values, and how to implement both.
- All fear then departs as fiction, deceptions, and mindless corruption hit our brick wall of comprehension.
- We emerge as vital, knowing, and empowered individuals, sovereign

masters of our destiny.

It all starts by learning the natural law of no trespass fully embodied in our conscious process– **No mind can rule another!**

I aimed to introduce people to a new society they've never conceived possible. There is much more to this subject, but if free societies are now on your radar, I trust you will be excited and want to learn more.

You can begin today. No better model of ethics or morality exists or is as simple. As fast as people awaken to this realm of conscious spiritual purpose, they can begin enjoying a life grander than ever conceived. Societal change will come in due course. Meanwhile, practicing natural laws can rapidly prepare you for the grandest social revolution in all history.

Humanities new age has finally dawned for those who will reach out and lovingly relish it. And that's the (imperative) cliffhanger because, as political matters stand today, this opportunity looks destined never to present again.

**In free (protectorate) societies, no state administers the affairs of men. As employees of the people it protects their rights and freedoms and administers justice among all who conduct their own affairs.**

# Natures Providence - Bibliography

**1** Rand; Ayn. "Our Cultural Value-Deprivation," The Objectivist, April, 1966,
**2** Rand; Ayn. "Philosophy: Who Needs It," Philosophy: Who Needs It.
**3** Griffith, Jeremy. "The Book of Real Answers to Everything", Web address, Jeremy Griffith https://www.humancondition.com/book-of-real-answers
**4** Griffith, Jeremy. "Biologist Jeremy Griffith examines where the human race is headed." Web address: http://www.smh.com.au/national/education/biologist-jeremy-griffith-examines-where-the-human-race-is-headed-20141006-10qyvm.html
**5** Galt's Speech, For the New Intellectual
**6** Rand: Ayn, Ayn Rand Lexicon, Purpose, Web URL, http://aynrandlexicon.com/lexicon/purpose.html
**7** Rand: Ayn, "The Metaphysical and the Man-Made," Philosophy: Who Needs It.
**8** Rand: Ayn, "Our Cultural Value-Deprivation," The Objectivist, April 1966.
**9** Rand; Ayn. Ayn Rand Lexicon, Happiness. Web URL, http://aynrandlexicon.com/lexicon/happiness.html
**10** Rand: Ayn, "Philosophy: Who Needs It,"
**11** Rand: Ayn. The Objectivist Ethics," The Virtue of Selfishness.
**12** Rand: Ayn. "Mans Rights", The Virtue of Selfishness.
**13** Dun; Frank van. Kritarchy by Frank van Dun Website URL, https://americankritarchists.wordpress.com/article-by-frank-van-dun/
**14** Rand; Ayn. Galt's Speech, For the New Intellectual.
**15** Rappoport: Jon. No more fake news. Jon Rappoport's Blog. Website URL, https://blog.nomorefakenews.com/2019/08/02/exit-from-the-matrix-your-power-in-a-decaying-world/
**16** Spooner, Lysander: Letter to Stephen Grover Cleveland. Website URL, lysanderspooner.org/LetterToGroverCleveland.htm
**17** Dun; Frank van. Natural law. Website URL. https://users.ugent.be/~frvandun/Texts/Logica/NaturalLaw.htm
**18** Dun; Frank van. The Pure Theory of Natural Law, PDF document Website URL https://users.ugent.be/~frvandun/Texts/Articles/Natural Law - part I.pdf
**19** Rand; Ayn. Galt's Speech, For the New Intellectual.
**20** Rand; Ayn. "The Age of Envy," Return of the Primitive: The Anti-Industrial Revolution.

**21** Rand; Ayn. "The Objectivist Ethics," The Virtue of Selfishness.
**22** Rand; Ayn. Galt's Speech, For the New Intellectual.
**23** Rand; Ayn. "Concepts of Consciousness," Introduction to Objectivist Epistemology
**24** Rand; Ayn. "The Missing Link," Philosophy: Who Needs It.
**25** Rand; Ayn. Galt's Speech, For the New Intellectual.
**26** Rand; Ayn. "Political' Crimes," Return of the Primitive: The Anti-Industrial Revolution.
**27** Rand; Ayn. "The Objectivist Ethics," The Virtue of Selfishness.
**28** Rand; Ayn. Galt's Speech, For the New Intellectual.
**30** Rand; Ayn. "Definitions," Introduction to Objectivist Epistemology.
**31** Rand; Ayn. "The Objectivist Ethics," The Virtue of Selfishness,
**32** Rand; Ayn. Galt's Speech For the New Intellectual.
**33** Rand; Ayn. "Man's Rights," The Virtue of Selfishness.
**34** Rand; Ayn. "What Is Capitalism?"Capitalism: The Unknown Ideal.
**35** Rand, Ayn. Galt's Speech, For the New Intellectual.
**36** Rand; Ayn. "The Objectivist Ethics," The Virtue of Selfishness,
**37** Rand; Ayn. "Of Living Death" The Voice of Reason
**38** Rand; Ayn. Galt's Speech, For the New Intellectual,
**39** Rand; Ayn. "The Nature of Government," The Virtue of Selfishness.
**40** Rand; Ayn. "Axiomatic Concepts," Introduction to Objectivist Epistemology
**41** Dun; Frank van. Kritarchy by Frank van Dun Website URL, https://americankritarchists.wordpress.com/article-by-frank-van-dun

# My Notes

Made in United States
Troutdale, OR
11/03/2026

56844879R00136